Success on Our Own Terms

Success on Our Own Terms

Tales of Extraordinary, Ordinary Business Women

VIRGINIA O'BRIEN

JOHN WILEY & SONS, INC.
New York · Chichester · Weinheim · Brisbane · Singapore · Toronto

Library of Congress Cataloging-in-Publication Data:
O'Brien, Virginia, 1946–
    Success on our own terms : tales of extraordinary, ordinary
business women / by Virginia O'Brien.
            p.   cm.
    Includes bibliographical references and index.
    ISBN 0-471-17871-3 (cloth : alk. paper)
    1. Businesswomen—United States—Case Studies.
2. Entrepreneurship—United States—Case studies. 3. Women
executives—United States—Case studies. 4. Success in
business—United States—Case studies. I. Title.
HD6095.D27   1998
658.4'09'082—dc21   97-43845
                                                          CIP

Printed in the United States of America

10 9 8 7 6 5 4 3 2 1

for Seana

Acknowledgments

I am thankful to all the people I spoke to during the course of writing this book, but I am most deeply grateful to the corporate women who were willing to share their stories with me. Without their openness and without their success, this book would not have been possible. I was extremely moved by my conversations with them, so a heartfelt thanks to Sunni Acoli-Squire, Becky Allen, Erin Andre, Joyce Bailey, Judy Beaubouef, Diana Bell, Lucy Berroteran, Monica Boyles, Jean Brennan, Cynthia Cannady, Sari Chapman, Joyce Cofield, Lynn Crump, Cynthia Danaher, Margo Davis, Ann Delvin, Beth Dudley, Donna Eidson, Teresa Elder, Julie England, Meredith Fischer, Ellen Gabriel, Gail Gaumer, Ann Ginn, Kim Hains, Beth Kaplan, Kwok Lau, Sue Manix, Vela McClam Mitchell, Diann Monroe-Jones, Carmen Monserrate, Karen Moreno, Marlene O'Toole, Gloria Santona, Charlotte Schutzman, Jacqueline Sinclair-Parker, Beth Rader, Darlene Solomon, Shaunna Sowell, Cathy Spotts, Jan Tomlinson, Carol Tuthill, Connie Van Zandt, Teresa Wahlert, and Florence Williams.

As I began to put my acknowledgments on paper I realized how many people contributed in one way or another and I appreciate the time and help everyone gave me. Special thanks go to corporate staff, who provided background information and linked me with the women, and to researchers and consultants, who shared their findings and knowledge. Without the help of Dorian Burden, who was the managing editor at *Executive Female* magazine, I would not have been able to conduct the national survey. I truly appreciate her willingness to work with me and publish the survey.

I am also grateful to Janet Coleman, my original editor, who believed in my ideas and advocated for them on my behalf, and I appreciate the faith Jim Childs, my publisher, demonstrated in me. This book would not have become a reality without Renana Meyers, who became my editor in January 1997. Renana helped me to reshape and restructure my manuscript, and I am truly thankful for her direction and guidance. I also want to extend sincere gratitude to Marcia Yudkin, Ph.D., for her encouragement and keen editorial assistance.

My women friends provided support and nurturing. Without listing all of them I want to give special thanks to Diane Driscoll and Mary Morrison, former English teachers who provided guidance on my original manuscript. Deep and heartfelt gratitude to my dear friend Diane Smith, who read the entire manuscript for me and whose support and belief in me are a cherished part of my life. I am also grateful to Louise Antoniolli and Dana Britt, who brainstormed with me at the very beginning of this project. Louise gave me Marlene O'Toole's name and set my interview process in motion. And, throughout, Barbara Day bolstered me, listening to my struggles and triumphs.

Finally, like the women in this book, I must acknowledge and thank my husband, Buzz Jenney, my biggest supporter. He developed the database program and tabulated the findings from the national survey, and he served, as he always does, as an attentive editor. Without his effort and help, I'm not sure I could have met my goals.

CONTENTS

FOREWORD

The American workplace is changing for the better each day. Demographics and technology, in tandem, are among the forces creating a more productive and more flexible workplace. The traditional workday and the traditional workplace are both giving way to alternative arrangements. More and more workers perform their jobs away from the office. And more and more workers are finding that their work and nonwork responsibilities can complement rather than have to compete with each other.

American women, as they participate more fully in the workforce, both benefit from today's changes and accelerate the need for business to adopt new approaches to the workplace. Twenty years ago a company that had flexible work arrangements, family-friendly policies, and career development systems focused on women was called "progressive." Today that company is called "smart."

This gets me to why I value greatly this book's publication. As I travel the country, working directly with a number of companies, speaking to groups large and small, women approach me with two themes most common to their situation in the workforce.

One is that the burden of mentoring the next generation of successful women falls disproportionately on the current generation of successful women. This is because, as this book well documents, the pipelines are full of well-educated, talented women ready to move ahead in corporate America. While there is no shortage of women role models, there is a shortage of women at the top who can interact directly with the next generation of women who need this assistance to realize their career goals.

The second theme is that many women, in companies of all sizes, believe they are isolated from the support systems necessary for their careers to be effectively developed. Aggregate statistics showing women in increasing numbers in leadership positions mask the reality that not all progress is distributed evenly throughout a company or throughout the country. Countless women are still the only women professionals in an office, or on a job, or in a community. The issue for these women is not the overburdened women at the top. Unlike many of their male colleagues, whose careers are often assisted formally or informally by their male superiors, these women do not have any mentors or any colleagues who are women.

These voids must be filled by something or these women, their companies, and our country will pay a steep price. And that is what Virginia O'Brien has done with this book. Its premise is that women are making real progress in the workforce and are doing this on their own terms. I agree. I just don't think the change is happening fast enough.

What will speed things up? Obviously a more committed, smarter corporate leadership will help. So will having more women in more leadership positions within companies. But until these things happen, until women are less isolated as gender role models, women need some practical help.

This book fits the bill. It is a how-to manual for women in the pipelines, for women at midcareer, and for women struggling with choices and issues they believe are unique to them. The fad in management today is to identify, adapt, and apply the best practices from other companies to help improve their own company. The examples of the successful women in this book are more than the stories of successful women. They are the best practices, the lessons that each of us can adapt and apply to help us all realize "Success on Our Own Terms."

—Lynn Martin
Former U.S. Secretary of Labor
and first Chair of the Glass Ceiling Commission

Success on Our Own Terms

INTRODUCTION

My Irish temper and stubbornness account in part for this book. I was compelled to write it because I got extraordinarily aggravated reading negative reports about women's progress in corporate America. Yes, I know that the old boys still rule at the top and there are less than a handful of female Fortune 500 chief executive officers. And, yes, I know that many women have left the corporate arena because they grew tired of dealing with a value system based on a male, hierarchical model and a culture they often found wanting. My instincts, however, told me that corporate America had to be laced with the stories of women's success—stories that we didn't hear about because they didn't take place on the CEO level or because they weren't about women on the verge of breaking through or dropping out, but stories that, nevertheless, would reveal how far women have come in business and how much feminine energy has infused the organizational system. My logical mind told me that there were holes in prevalent claims of a glass ceiling. I didn't think we were getting the whole story.

The Glass Ceiling Commission and groups like Catalyst, a New York–based nonprofit organization, have conducted valuable research that has kept us aware of organizational cultural issues with regard to the advancement of women in management. However, the data from these studies generally get presented with an emphasis on the negative. Press coverage tends to focus on the small number of females in corporate CEO and senior management posts, rather than on the programs and initiatives that have moved women forward.

Highlighting bad news isn't unique to women's issues—it's a common complaint heard in reference to the media—but with the

1

manipulation of statistics and the burying of good news, the picture of women's progress gets distorted. In 1996, Catalyst studies drew negative headlines across the country from "Women at the Top Still Are Distant from CEO Jobs" in the *Wall Street Journal*[1] to "Glass Ceiling over Women Still Intact in Workplace" in the *Los Angeles Times*.[2] Similarly, an article in the *Boston Globe* started with this negative lead: "Nearly a fifth of Fortune 500 companies don't have women directors."[3] Well, that's true, but the flip side is that four out of five companies do have female representation. And female numbers *are* growing: Between 1993 and 1995 the number of female board members increased by 12 percent.[4]

Headlines finally started changing a little in 1997. The *Wall Street Journal* ran a front-page article: "Broken Glass: Watershed Generation of Women Executives Is Rising to the Top." But the paper couldn't leave this positive header alone; it had to tag on the subhead: "But Ranks Are Still Lopsided." The article ended, as many articles do, with an often-heard line, "But it's painfully slow."[5]

My argument is that too much focus is placed on counting the number of corporate CEOs. With that focus we tend to see only the negative side of the story. Moreover, these numbers alone are not an accurate indicator of progress. They need to be scrutinized more carefully and not accepted at face value as proof of lack of progress. Using this sole measurement skews perceptions of women's advancement in business. This statistic misleads us: It doesn't give us room to understand the broad spectrum of women's success or how the combined impact of organizational culture, societal values, and market changes contributes to these numbers.

We are, in fact, beginning to see changes in corporate America and we need to herald those changes. Between 1982 and 1992, the number of female executive vice presidents at Fortune 1000 companies more than doubled and almost a quarter of senior vice presidents are now female.[6] By 1994, 48.1 percent of the managerial/executive positions in U.S. organizations were held by women,[7] and by 1995, 417 Fortune 500 companies had one or more women on their boards.[8] The companies represented in this book show how women's numbers in senior management are growing. At Bell Atlantic 10 percent of the top officers and 21 percent of the company's senior executives are women. At US WEST, over 20 percent of the corporate officers are women, including the CEO of MediaOne, the third largest cable company in the country. There are three women on the board of directors, and, in 1995, the first woman of color was made an officer of the company. And at Gannett, women represent 33 percent of the board of directors, 23 percent of operating unit heads, and 40 percent of all department heads.

In the first chapter of this book, I show how the numbers of females at the top of major corporations couldn't have added up to be much more than they are today. Corporate leadership requires mentoring, training, and experience acquired over time. When today's male CEOs began their grooming process 30 years ago, there were few women being trained alongside them. At that time, women didn't think about being, nor were they educated to become, CEOs in the 1990s.

Another factor of great significance—and one that often gets lost when the lack of senior female executives is discussed—is that many women are achieving according to their own definitions of success. And these definitions don't necessarily include climbing to the highest rung on the corporate ladder. Studies show that more men than women aspire to these top jobs.[9] If we can turn our focus away from these numbers, we gain a better view of the progress women have made in the corporate world.

When I look back 33 years to the time I first started working, I see an enormous difference in women's position in business. Women now have options and choices that didn't exist when I entered the workforce. My feeling of hope and sense of opportunity stem in part from my own story, which is atypical in some ways, and yet in other ways serves as a metaphor for all the challenges women have faced.

Graduating from high school in the early 1960s, my ethnicity and socioeconomic class shaped and limited my options. Mine was an Irish-Catholic household in which education money was set aside for the three male children. If a young woman didn't want to become a teacher or a nurse, which I didn't, money spent on education was considered wasted. My sister and I were expected to get married and produce children, and how we occupied ourselves in the meantime was of little significance. After high school I worked as a clerk in the Bell system, where my first job was taping nickels and dimes onto postcards to send back to customers who were owed change from public telephones. Needless to say, after counting and taping coins for a while, I realized I needed to take some kind of action and I signed up for evening courses at the local university. But because of my meager wages (I made about $40 a week and paid my parents room and board), I couldn't afford more than a course or two a semester. After several years, with the road ahead seeming endlessly long, I left home and joined a major airline. This was considered a bold and daring move in my neighborhood, where young women didn't leave home before marriage. Today, the job of flight attendant is not viewed as it was when I was young. At that time, being a "stewardess" had an aura of glamour to it. Years later I saw the sexist nature of that glamour, but back then I thought it was a grand adventure—it gave me an escape, a way to be independent and to travel.

While I was flying I met my first husband and I eventually turned from a stewardess into a corporate wife, which actually didn't require much of a transformation. Unfortunately, those stories about corporate wives of the past are true—we were expected to be corporate cheerleaders. It was a recognized fact that a successful man had a wife at home to take care of all the details and to provide the moral support that was needed. In fact, before my husband was hired by a major pharmaceutical company I had to go through an interview process as well. The company needed to make sure that I would be a team player. I was still working for the airlines at the time, and the interview contained a string of questions about my willingness to quit working and follow my husband wherever his career path led. I had to convince his future employer that I wouldn't be a snag in his upward progression. And I wasn't. I did what I was supposed to until divorce caught me by surprise. Then, at 34, I found myself with a young daughter, no husband, and no education.

By the time I was 41 I had a master's degree under my belt and I had started writing and working in the field of communication, both in a small business environment and as a freelance writer. In some ways I fit into a category of women that Joline Godfrey calls "late bloomers"—those women whose strength comes from reflecting on past experience and confidence gained from age and survival.[10] I definitely consider myself a survivor. This book is a means to expand my reflection beyond myself—to reflect on the positive experiences of women across a span of age ranges, so that we can share an understanding of our progress.

Perhaps because of the fact that I have come from one end of the spectrum, I find the growth women have experienced to be exciting and uplifting. But I know I'm not alone in my feelings. When I spoke to the women whose stories shape this book, each one of them got excited. It buoyed us both to talk about their progress, their professional accomplishments, and the support they have received from their organizations as well as from their husbands and families. Story after story revealed how they used their intelligence, their ability to form relationships, and their management and communication skills to move themselves into positions of their choice and to join with other women in making change within their organizations.

When women join together, their merged energy makes its way through the organizational system. Female managers at Texas Instruments told me about the Women's Initiatives they helped to create. The Initiatives opened the way for the advancement of more females into senior management positions and drew attention to the need to create better work/life policies. At Deloitte & Touche, women joined with senior management to improve the retention rate of female partners by creating more flexible environments and greater understanding of gender differences. At Hewlett-Packard, women described how female engineers banded together to create a professional network that enabled them to highlight their work, gain recognition, and share knowledge. The women's enthusiasm and power drove these efforts. Margo Davis, a 54-year-old ex-teacher who is now a corporate education program manager at Hewlett-Packard, cochaired HP's 1995 Technical Women's Conference. After 2,700 women spent three days learning together, Margo says the atmosphere was incredible: "It was like the roof was coming off. The energy level was so high it was terrific. Lew Platt, our CEO, just stood there and he could feel it. He said, 'If we could harness this energy, there isn't a company on earth that could top us.'" Women came away from the conference profoundly moved. A woman on the verge of quitting HP called Margo to tell her she had changed her mind because the conference gave her hope.

When women visibly come together in support of themselves, it makes the struggle that women have endured worthwhile. That's part of what has motivated me to undertake this project: to give recognition to women's successes and to pay attention to how far women have come, in order to support further movement. Corporate America has made changes in the last decade. I believe we are going to feel women's energy in the corporation even more as the twenty-first century unfolds.

My goal in writing this book was to find out how women across a wide management spectrum gauge their own success and to provide a forum for them to share their success strategies. So, I set out to track the business journey women had undertaken over a quarter century ago and to answer some key questions. Could women get where they wanted to go? How did they feel about the level of management they had attained? What motivates them? What are their visions and goals? What strategies helped them achieve their objectives?

In search of the answers to these questions, I interviewed 45 women at various management levels in 23 major companies and their subsidiaries. I asked the women to tell me about their careers, to define success, and to explain how they balanced their lives. In conjunction with *Executive Female* magazine, I also conducted a national survey that reached beyond this corporate sample in order to ensure that I heard from a broad range of women in management. Almost 700 women responded, describing their viewpoints of success and their feelings of satisfaction with their own advancement. Over and over, whether the women in this survey worked in corporations or whether they worked in smaller enterprises, they described success in terms of being happy, meeting goals, and having passion about their work and their lives. Their feelings are reflected by one woman who wrote, "Success is not a destination; it's a journey," and another who wrote, "It's not all about advancement; it's about enjoying your life."

These findings encouraged me and spurred me on to write this book honoring not only the women who have climbed corporate ladders, but also those women in management who seek career satisfaction in a multitude of other ways. The 45 women I interviewed aren't superwomen, but they are extraordinary, ordinary women. They represent the woman next door and the woman down the street. Their stories demonstrate how far we have come. Several of the women I interviewed are CEOs and presidents of banks and subsidiaries, and some are vice presidents in a range of functional areas. But half of the women are managers and directors at middle management levels with a range of professional goals.

I purposely chose to interview women working in major corporations that have been identified as progressive with regard to women's issues because I wanted to acknowledge the corporations that have developed programs and initiatives in support of women. Policies and programs in these companies provide useful benchmarks, and women who work in less-than-supportive companies can see the possibilities that exist when corporate cultures are changed. My focus on the corporation as opposed to small businesses or female entrepreneurs stems from the fact that corporate America has tremendous influence in shaping society; therefore, women's success and influence inside corporate walls is extremely important for determining the course of our future.

The women in this book represent the best of all of us—they helped establish initiatives for women in their companies; they participated in new accelerated development programs and used the programs their companies offered to help themselves advance. When some of the women realized they couldn't find the balance they wanted working full-time, they broke new ground and created job shares, flextime, and part-time arrangements in their companies. They have been true pioneers. These managers learned how to make the corporation work to their benefit and they found ways to achieve their goals. They built their careers with their own determination, quest for excellence, and balance, yet they acknowledged they could not have found success without the help of their mentors, husbands, and families. And they pay tribute to the role that enlightened senior management played in helping them to get where they wanted to go and allowing them to work in the way they wanted to work.

These women planned career strategies, held onto their values and their management styles, and articulated their needs to their bosses. They worked on developing significant relationships and learned how to use the system to improve their expertise and skills. Through their stories I hope you will be able to learn lessons you can apply to your own career. And through their voices I think the true story and the full scope of women's success emerge. I cling to my belief that progress has been made and the wind is at our backs.

THE FACTS ARE IN: WOMEN ARE SUCCEEDING

*I was always very focused on making a contribution and moving ahead.
I got a lot of encouragement early in my career. I knew there weren't any
limits on what I could do. I always felt if I made a real difference to our
business and organizational results, there was nothing standing in my
way of becoming an officer of the company. It was a personal objective.*
BETH KAPLAN, Executive Vice President
Rite Aid Corporation

It generally takes 25 to 30 years to "grow" a CEO—equivalent to
the time it takes to grow a tree. Picture, if you will, the visible potential of a young oak, with a slender trunk, supple yet strong. As you
pick out a tree from the nursery you imagine it in your front yard.
You can envision how it will serve you and benefit your home, providing hope and promise in the spring, an umbrella of shade in the
summer, vibrancy in the fall, and protection in the winter by breaking the cold blasts of freezing winds. But in order to ensure your
tree will reach maturity, you have to prepare the ground before you
even plant it, digging up the earth and blending the soil with the
right mixture of fertilizer and humus. And through the years, you
will continually need to nurture its growth, watering it, feeding it,
providing stakes for early support, pruning branches when they
begin to grow in the wrong directions. The same kind of process is
required to develop corporate leaders. The people who look like they
offer the greatest potential to serve the organization throughout its
own seasons are the ones selected for planting and the ones who
are groomed throughout the stages of their development.

Time and experience shape an executive's ability to serve the
corporation. But in the discussion of women's growth in business,

the concepts of time and experience seem to get short shrift. Twenty-five to thirty years ago, there were few women waiting to be chosen, and the culture couldn't envision a woman having the strength and resiliency to weather corporate storms and to provide the protection and leadership an organization needs.

We have witnessed tremendous change in organizational life over the last quarter of a century. Now it is no longer difficult to imagine women growing into CEO positions, because we have seen a few women do it. Now there are many more women waiting to be chosen in the years ahead. In fact, now there are almost as many women in the pipeline as men. Younger female managers are being trained and positioned to step up the highest rungs of the corporate ladder. A quarter of a century ago, that wasn't true—there simply weren't that many women to choose, and the supports and development they needed weren't available to them because their potential wasn't recognized.

Over the years some of women's progress has been easy to see: The pipeline *is* blossoming with women. The resiliency and strength of women in their 40s and 50s, who broke through hard ground during the 1960s and 1970s without much fertilizer or nurturing, have kept possibilities open for female managers in their 20s and 30s. Now at the end of the 1990s, handfuls of ripened female executives are waiting to be picked for corporate CEO positions. But rather than understanding how successful their growth has been, we often hear the question: Why aren't there more women?

The answer, I believe, lies in understanding the past. It is difficult to understand how women's growth process was affected by the culture that surrounded those first female managers because it is buried deep in the root system of society. Because we can't see the roots, we tend to forget how they affect the growth of the forest.

In the first half of this century, women pursued jobs in teaching and nursing, which were socially acceptable because they reverberated with the nurturing values of home life. When women now in their 40s and 50s first went to work they were still influenced by those cultural norms and values. I find it extremely interesting to note that almost half of the women I interviewed in this age range started out as teachers, social workers, or homemakers. To me, it isn't surprising that they started out in those fields; it's more surprising that they came as far as they did in the corporate world after having traditional beginnings.

As I listened to the stories of the women over 50, it was apparent to me that each woman arrived at her present level of business success in her own unique fashion. Not one of the women started out thinking she was going to climb a corporate ladder and end up on the top rung. At 17, Marlene O'Toole left high school to get a job and through diligence, rugged determination, and hard work climbed to a position as a regional manager of customer support services at IBM. Joyce Cofield, a biochemist, worked in Polaroid's lab environment before becoming assistant to the president overseeing diversity issues. Margo Davis, who was a teacher, is now a corporate education program manager at Hewlett-Packard. Becky Allen, president of Barnett Private Client Services, dropped out of college to get married and was a stay-at-home mom until divorce drove her to the workplace. Judy Beaubouef made it into the innermost sanctum of her corporation as chief legal counsel, yet Judy started out as a social worker.

The culture of the United States in the 1960s and 1970s affected these women and their perspectives on work. The corporation itself is only one part of the larger social system. Nothing happens in isolation. Each part of a system both influences and is influenced by the overall system. Equating lack of progress with absence of women at the corporate CEO level discounts important social factors and ignores the interconnectedness between the corporation and society. Companies alone are not responsible for women's position, or lack of position, in the corporate hierarchy. Nor have men been the evil villains; without men opening corporate doors, women could not have entered the organization or gained access to any executive suite. The women's movement wasn't totally responsible for women's progress, or lack of progress, either. But it did give a voice to the changes that were occurring below the surface of the larger social system and it became a vehicle for bringing those changes into full view. The masculine culture of organizations, societal norms, values and beliefs, technological changes, and market reactions all combined to set the pace for women's advancement in management.

TRICKS OF FATE AND CHANGING ROLES

Thirty years ago the concept of a glass ceiling didn't exist—women didn't even think about invisible barriers preventing them from getting to the executive suite. They just wanted to be welcome inside the corporation's front doors. The 1960s marked the beginning of cultural changes, but those changes didn't necessarily position women to be future CEOs, they simply made allowances for equality. Harvard Business School said okay to women in 1963 and allowed them to enter its hallowed halls and expand their education.[1] The Equal Pay Act of 1963 said okay to women and allowed them equal pay for equal work. And the Civil Rights Act of 1964 said okay to women, assuring them that companies with more than 15 employees couldn't discriminate against them. But the Civil Rights Act wasn't a nurturing gesture meant to guarantee women a spot at the top. In fact, women almost didn't make it into the bill. Rather than being a deliberate attempt to provide the equality that would begin to position women as future corporate leaders, it was the arrogance of one male that unwittingly created a greater opening for women. "Senator Howard Smith threw the word *sex* into Title VII of the act as a joke," because he didn't think the bill would ever be approved. When the act started gaining acceptance and passage seemed surprisingly probable, a committee tried to get the reference to sex removed, but Senator Margaret Chase Smith and Representative Martha Griffiths threatened to stall passage if the word was taken out.[2] Thus, without Congress really intending it to happen, it put a law on the books that women could use to their advantage. So an opening was created. But the idea that women shouldn't be discriminated against and the idea that women could head major corporations are not necessarily the same.

Meanwhile, in the cities, in the suburbs, and in rural areas, deep cultural beliefs and attitudes continued to link women's roles to the home. In 1962 a Gallup poll indicated that "few people are as happy as a housewife."[3] Women's apron strings were definitely still tied to their kitchen cabinets. They could go only so far outside their houses without getting pulled back in. Women themselves questioned their own abilities; married women then, as now, were concerned they wouldn't be able to manage working both inside and outside their homes. Even more frightening was the idea that an economically free woman might also be a sexually free woman, and this freedom was terribly threatening to the social system. Both men and women had fears about changing their long-held roles and identities. On the cusp of this transitional time, there simply wasn't enough support inside or outside the organization for women to be seen as future business leaders. There simply weren't enough properly trained women, who had entered the system in the 1960s, to become CEOs in the 1990s. Women in the 1960s and 1970s held less than 5 percent of the graduate degrees, and 80 percent of the women who worked held jobs categorized as "female," meaning they were clerical, not managerial.[4] Women did not have the supports they needed early enough in their careers to sustain their growth and development equal to the growth and development of their male colleagues. If a large number of women weren't well positioned, identified early enough, or educated well enough, how could they compete for top positions in equal proportion to men?

TERESA WAHLERT: A WOMAN OF HER TIME

In the early 1970s, as the women's movement gained momentum, women sought to loosen the restraints that biology had on them. The idea that women are more than their bodies was a key theme. However, the older I get, the more I know that biology might not be destiny, but hormones and DNA have a lot to do with who we are. As women, our psyches are tied to the deep biological truth that we can bear children and men cannot. The biological urge to have children and the cultural norm to marry have always influenced the way women work. Even as attitudes began to change, the cultural assumption that women would quit working when they married remained. When Teresa Wahlert, a vice president at US WEST, first entered the workforce her attitude was similar to that of most other women of her time.

> *I was just trying to get to the next level. In our company, at that time, you worked, you got married, you had kids, and then you stayed at home. Of the women who were hired with me during the early '70s, most of them followed that pattern.*

Teresa didn't think about climbing as high as she has. Northwestern Bell hired her out of college in 1970 and trained her in computer languages and data processing. For four years she worked as a programmer. Who knows what would have happened to her career if AT&T (the largest private employer in the United States at the time) and its operating companies hadn't been charged with discrimination and mandated by the U.S. Department of Labor and the Equal Employment Opportunity Commission (EEOC) to establish goals and timetables for hiring and promoting women and minorities into management ranks. Companies in the Bell system agreed to assess the potential of women with college degrees and consider them for middle management positions. Teresa was among the ten women at Northwestern Bell who were identified as management candidates; thus, she was one of a small number who had the opportunity to participate in her company's accelerated development program.

Teresa told me the 1970s were a "critical time" and she credits the male leadership for going through a "learning process" with regard to women and minorities. However, even though career development programs were opening up for women like Teresa, corporate cultures were only beginning to change. The idea of equality had really just been introduced—actually mandated. Without government intervention, the question remains whether millions of women would have had the opportunities that became available to them. And even with management doors opening, many women themselves still viewed work as a job rather than a career.

It was only after the birth of her first child that Teresa had what she calls "an awakening." Just as she became pregnant in 1976, she was given a "great line opportunity." After staying home for four weeks when her baby was born she realized that she "really wanted to work." As she describes it, "I love small children, but I found that what I could get done on a Saturday when I was working, I couldn't get done all week long." Being at home just didn't give her the fulfillment that she found in her corporate job. However, as Teresa recalls those early days as a working mother, she says it wasn't always easy maintaining her career.

> *Back then, I had to deal with the corporate perceptions of what a mother with small children is supposed to do, and it was certainly not to come back to the office. I had a supervisor sit me down and tell me that my first job was my family and my children, and that if I caused a divorce, it was because I selected to come back to work too soon. That's a little tough when the person is your direct supervisor, with power over the perception of your job performance. You have to find a way to handle that advice and put it in a constructive framework; otherwise, it could destroy you. The person who said those things to me had a concern about me personally making the right choices, but as my boss he was getting a fair amount of grief from those above him.*

I also had feelings of guilt coming from a traditional family and doing some nontraditional things that I thought were right for me personally.

As Teresa reflected on the beginnings of her career, she reminded me to set her story in the "context of the time," saying, "We're all a product of where we've been." Teresa is one of those first, groundbreaking women. Throughout her career, she has held positions in finance and accounting and was made a vice president in 1990. She is now in charge of public policy in Iowa. At 47, she is still younger than the average CEO and fits into the category of women who have the ability to climb to the uppermost level in the next decade. Whether she wants to is something she is still assessing, but whatever she decides, she will find success on her own terms.

I still have a lot to give that hasn't been tapped yet, and I am looking for ways to do that. I always try to keep my options open.

When Betty Lehan Harragan wrote *Games Mother Never Taught You* in 1977 she advised women to aim for CEO positions no later than their early 50s and to calculate their career advancement by recognizing that it takes ten promotional steps over a 30-year period to reach the top.[5] The average age of today's chief executive officer is 56; therefore, he probably started being groomed around the age of 26. So, although Teresa still has some time, for most women in their 50s, Harragan's advice came 10 years too late. When today's 56-year-old woman started out in business in 1967 there simply wasn't a place to position herself. At that time, the idea of a woman heading a major corporation was a thought outside the realm of possibility.

In 1975, two years before Harragan's book was published, women made up 40 percent of the workforce. Yet the deck was heavily stacked against them making it to the top. At that time "only 11,000 women managers earned more than $25,000 in comparison to 449,000 men."[6] Those are pretty tough odds. Let's assume for a moment that these 11,000 women, because of their salaries, were the high-potential candidates—they would have required either an extraordinary amount of luck to beat the mathematical odds or a historical record-breaking change in organizational cultures to outdistance the vast number of men who surrounded them. Why is it startling that, less than 25 years later, those female managers didn't surpass that huge field of male competitors to become CEOs of the Fortune 500?

PERCEPTIONS OF PROGRESS: BELONGING TO THE GROUP

One of my most intriguing discoveries is the difference between how a woman views her own progress and how she sees women as a group advancing. For example, think how you would answer the following question: Are you satisfied with the level of management you have attained in your career? If you are feeling pretty good about your own accomplishments and feel satisfied, you answered like a large majority of women: All the women I interviewed had high levels of satisfaction, and over three-quarters of nearly 700 women in the national survey I conducted said they were satisfied with their own career advancement.

Now ask yourself if you are satisfied with the overall progress of women in management. If your answer tends to be negative, once again you are in the majority: Only one-third of the women in the national survey were satisfied with women's advancement, and many of the women I interviewed voiced concerns, not about themselves, but about women as a group. Yet, if a majority are satisfied—if almost eight out of ten women are satisfied with the management level they have achieved—why does such disparity exist between individual levels of satisfaction and perception of women's progress? Why aren't women reveling more in both their individual *and* collective accomplishments? Why is there such a disconnect between how women feel on a personal level and how they feel about the progress of women as a group?

One possible answer might come from the fact that we are constantly hammered with the sound bite that there are only a few female corporate CEOs, so the deeper systemic issues never get fully explored. As Caryl Rivers, a journalism professor at Boston University and author of several books on working women, writes, "The American press greatly exaggerates the problems of women—especially working women."[7] Women, bombarded with the negative, begin to believe what they read and hear. A woman might think that her own good story is somehow an anomaly; therefore, she remains concerned for her female colleagues and for the well-being of women as a whole.

Another reason might stem from women's desires to relate to their peer group. If a woman questions what she perceives to be the prevailing consensus, she consciously puts herself outside the group. And as linguist Deborah Tannen points out, "Both women and men pay a price when they do not behave in ways expected of their gender." Women expect women to stick together. After struggling to break barriers, if a woman proclaims that she has succeeded when the numbers seem to indicate that others haven't, she sets herself apart. Tannen's research indicates that women's conversational strategies are often ways to maintain an appearance of equality and a means to avoid appearing boastful.[8] If women acknowledge they are personally satisfied, but they join in lamenting with others about the perceived predicament of the group, they demonstrate their concern for, allegiance to, and equity with the group.

I personally struggled with the issue of setting myself apart even as I wrote this book. As a raging feminist in the early 1970s, I picketed and marched along with my sisters. I have encountered male bias in the workplace and even sexual harassment. But my belief, as is obvious by now, is that we have made great progress. However, when I found that my feelings of satisfaction about the overall advancement of women in management put me in the minority, I hesitated, questioning whether I was doing a disservice to others. I was not without apprehension in publicly disagreeing with the general consensus. So I have personally grappled with that strong tug to conform.

However, I think we need to talk more openly and proudly about the success we have achieved. Looking at ourselves more closely helps us understand how our personal success is a small reflection of the success of women as a whole. If a majority of women across a wide sample declare they have feelings of satisfaction about what they have personally accomplished—regardless of the barriers they might have encountered—there is definitely something positive happening. We shouldn't try to mimic men, but, sometimes, it wouldn't hurt us to adopt at least a smidgen of their braggadocio. In *Fire with Fire* Naomi Wolf discusses the difficulties we encounter as women when we don't allow ourselves to engage in "victory talk." She writes: "If 'victory talk' is taboo, women have no comfortable framework for presenting their resources or skills to one another in a way that leads to consolidating political or economic power."[9] I believe we need to acknowledge our individual and collective success and talk about how good it feels to know we have hung in there, found our voice, and succeeded on our own terms. In less than a century, we have progressed from winning the right to vote to earning a seat at the corporate table. So that's what this book is about: unabashedly reveling in our success.

The stories of Judy Beaubouef and Becky Allen illustrate the advances that have been made. Both women are in their 50s and hold senior management positions in the Barnett Banks corporate family. Judy is chief legal executive of the corporation and Becky is president and CEO of Barnett's Private Client Services. Both women were 30 when they began their careers. Yet they still managed to rise—not to a Fortune 500 CEO position, but high enough to show that cultural change is taking place and women are progressing. Neither one of them envisioned that their professional lives would unfold the way they did. They represent the possibilities that exist today for women.

But how did they do it? How did these women, who could be your next-door neighbors, climb so high? What made them different from so many other women? Beyond acknowledging the obvious characteristics needed for success—intelligence, determination, courage, and communication skills—their timing was right. They were both fortunate to hook up with a progressive company, in a female-friendly industry that was attempting to improve itself with regard to women. Time and place played a role in their success.

JUDY BEAUBOUEF: FROM SOCIAL WORK TO CORPORATE COUNSEL

Judy Beaubouef certainly didn't envision herself in business. She followed a typical pattern for women her age: She majored in English, graduated from college in June, married in October, became a social worker, had her first child, and eventually quit working. But after a couple of years at home, she was "intellectually bored" and started going to law school at night. At this point, the story she tells departs from a traditional path: After graduation from law school she specialized in commercial litigation and eventually ended up working for a big law firm where the atmosphere was intensely competitive and 80-hour workweeks were the norm. Although she described herself as a "very competitive" person, she began to question whether the constant battle of litigation and its drain on her time and energy were really worth it. One of her good friends in the firm left to join Barnett Banks and encouraged Judy to make the switch too. But, at the time, moving from private practice to the corporate world translated into a sizable cut in pay for Judy, so she thought carefully about the move. When she did make her decision, she told me she had a "gut feeling" that it was the right thing to do. Now, as the most senior female executive in her corporation, she is one of the highest-paid women in this book.

After two years at Barnett, Judy undertook a six-month project surveying and analyzing how the bank handled its legal affairs. Without a law department of its own, Barnett was spending large sums of money outsourcing its legal work. Judy wrote a white paper, recommending the creation of a legal department. Her ideas were well received and, subsequently, she was assigned the role of developing and running the department. In this turn of events, her boss, whom she considers a great friend and teacher, ended up reporting to her. And, in 1994, Judy became the first woman to join Barnett's Management Executive Committee, which is composed of the six highest-ranking people in the corporation.

Yet when Judy gained entry to the top, she experienced some of the pressures that women of her age have faced as they move upward in their careers. Along with learning the nuances of operating within a male-dominated environment, women have had to develop a new mental model for themselves as they make the transition into their roles. And role transitions require support. Judy found that, even though she earned her elite position, she wasn't always completely comfortable with it. She had to deal with feelings of insecurity about not having the same background as her male colleagues.

> *One thing I still struggle with is the fact that I didn't grow up in a business setting, so questions about whether I belong still pop up for me. My undergraduate degree is far from business and even as a lawyer who has dealt with financial statements, I just don't have the business background that the rest of the team has. The Management Executive Committee is a very business-focused group and the men on it have a 30-year head start on me. During my first year on the team, there were times when I really struggled with that because I felt like I wasn't able to contribute as much as they did.*

Judy's concerns demonstrate how women of her age group almost had to teach themselves new ways to think. In order to integrate themselves successfully into male-dominated groups, women were told to be aggressive and to act like men. They had to have tremendous faith in their own abilities while learning to speak a new language. Not only did women have to wear rigid business attire in the 1970s, but it was as if these new business suits were too tight, constricting their movements and speech. Women had to be careful of what they said or did lest any emotional words or feelings escape from their breast pockets. Locked in a managerial style that didn't fit, many women breaking into an organization did everything to prevent the feminine from breaking out. But when Judy entered the male domain at the top of her corporation, she had the courage to expose her feelings of discomfort to her male peers.

> *I realized I needed to talk to some of the other managers about my concerns and their response was very affirming and supportive. They acknowledged my strengths, telling me I had great ideas, good common sense, legal knowledge, and the ability to develop and run a new department. They hadn't appointed me expecting me to contribute the same level of business expertise they had; they just wanted me to give them my best thinking. That was very affirming and made me feel a lot better. And it freed me up to be more open about my ideas for the company.*
>
> *This experience has been a lesson to me and fortifies my belief that it is far better to be open about insecurities. I don't know if exposing insecurities works in other companies, but I knew I needed to do it. I also knew that I had done a good job and they were impressed with the way I saved the company a lot of money when we created the legal department.*
>
> *Now I realize how I contribute in a different way. Sometimes I'm even a little bit of their conscience. I look at issues in a different way than they do.*

Part of the reason Judy was able to speak with such honesty has to do with the fact that the consciousness of the men in her company had already been raised. Had she tried talking so openly even ten years earlier, I suspect that she would have been shut down because neither men nor women then were as knowledgeable about—or skilled in overcoming—gender differences. But Barnett's training classes in executive leadership enabled senior managers to learn how to work together more effectively.

Working with my peers in the training setting, I began to recog-
nize individuals' areas of strength, and as a group we had an
opportunity to talk about both our strengths and weaknesses.
It gave me the opportunity to talk about my concerns regarding
my ability to contribute and it gave others a chance to acknowl-
edge and value my contributions. It was also helpful for me to
listen to the men talk about their own insecurities and the areas
they wanted to work on in terms of their management styles
and personal development.

Learning together enabled the group to relate on more human
terms with each other. Her group was supportive of her and listened to her views. And by trusting her own instincts and allowing
herself to voice the concerns she had about her position, Judy
enhanced the men's ability not only to comprehend more fully
what it is like for someone with a different set of skills, but also to
understand a woman's perspective on a deeper level.

BECKY ALLEN: FROM HOUSEWIFE TO CEO

Becky Allen also hooked up with Barnett on the recommendation
of a friend, but her path differs dramatically from Judy's. Becky
was forced into the workplace as the result of a divorce. She had
dropped out of college to get married and followed a traditional
track, staying home to take care of her children. She kept active
in volunteer work and helped out in her husband's store. But
when divorce hit in 1971, it carried a financial wallop. She and
her three children had to move out of their three-bedroom home
to live in a trailer park. Faced with single parenthood and the
need to keep food on the table, she went to work at a Florida
bank, making $400 a month, and launched her career. Banking
was an industry that provided more opportunities for women, and
Becky found that the organizational skills she had developed
through volunteer work and running her house easily transferred
into the work setting. Within four years she had advanced to the
point at which she could become an officer, but, as she tells it,
cultural norms got in the way of her advancement. Her status as
a divorced woman tainted her image: The bank president recognized her talents, but didn't believe it was proper to have a divor-
cée as an officer. In some ways, her second marriage saved her
career.

> *To this day, my husband still teases me. He says he is really responsible for my success because I would never have been promoted if he hadn't married me. It was funny. We married in November and they promoted me in January.*

Becky stayed with that bank for 11 years and worked with one other organization outside of banking, before taking a position in 1984 as the director of marketing at one of Barnett's banks. Her career at Barnett progressed rapidly, and she was appointed president of a small bank in 1986.

> *After I had worked for Barnett in Gainesville for a year and a half, my boss asked me if I had ever thought about being a CEO. I said that I had to develop my financial, accounting, and commercial lending skills; my strengths were in marketing and community building. He agreed that we would work on them, but then a short three months later the CEO position at Vero Beach opened. I was afraid I wasn't ready. But he assured me that the CFO and the management team would keep me out of trouble and the man I was going to report to assured me that no one comes as a complete package.*

As the first female CEO at the bank, Becky admits that she probably was a token female, but with the support that she was offered, she accepted the stretch.

> *Women, at that time, were just starting to break through and I know I got the job because I was a woman. I didn't get the rest of my jobs because I was a woman, but I got that job because they needed a woman. And I'm really thankful they gave me that opportunity.*

Since that first promotion she has been promoted two more times, and each time she was given larger and more complex organizations to lead. According to Becky, Barnett Banks helps both its male and female managers to succeed because the company understands that good managers can't be experts in every area. Senior management identifies people with capabilities and the desire to learn and helps them stretch by surrounding them with people whose complementary skills fill in the gaps. When Becky was given the chance to run the Vero Beach bank she realized it was a great opportunity to learn in a safe environment—the bank was small enough that she felt she could make mistakes without jeopardizing the organization.

> *I was not afraid to say that I didn't know something or didn't understand. When I worked with the team members individually, I told each one what he needed to teach me. The expert in corporate lending, who had also been a contender for the CEO position, taught me a lot about corporate lending, and I had a terrific CFO—we are still big buddies today. They knew I needed them and that we were all part of a team. They made me feel very welcome. I think they went out of their way to be supportive of me. I think they realized the importance of having women be successful in these roles. They were genuinely pleased for me; at least, that's the way I've always looked at it. I still look back at that bank with the fondest of memories because they were a wonderful group of people.*

The culture in which Becky and Judy grew up influenced their earlier choices. They began their adult lives following traditional paths for women—motherhood and social work—and later turned to banking and law. Opportunities that advanced their positions within the corporate world were provided later on in their professional development when a progressive-thinking company in an industry filled with women shifted enough to offer them a chance to move into senior management slots. Barnett was consciously trying to increase the number of women in senior management positions and the bank provided the women with support—management wanted them to succeed. Judy and Becky were in the right place at the right time. Their skills and abilities were valued and supported because Barnett Banks recognized it needed to make changes in its organizational system.

Culture inside and outside of Barnett Banks shaped both the women's professional development and their organization's readiness. In order for a woman to climb to the top, she and her organization have to be in sync with each other. As Judy and Becky were developing professionally, Barnett Banks was maturing in its acceptance of women in senior management. Systems adapt in response to their environments, to keep themselves thriving and alive. Introducing women into the workplace shook organizational systems, but it didn't threaten them. Legislation in the 1960s and 1970s prompted some superficial changes, but the deep cultural transformation that alters values and beliefs occurs only when the system itself recognizes the need to adapt. Women alone could not alter the system. Greater cultural change was triggered in organizations in the 1980s as technology, global markets, and shifting demographics altered the way work was carried out. The organizational system was further spurred to change as bottom lines reflected negative numbers caused by the exodus of women. Corporations started to get the message and understand on a deeper level that they needed to transform themselves. The organizational system is like a living system that responds to its environment. It has to have a reason to evolve; then deep change comes from within the system itself.

Another factor that might have influenced Becky's and Judy's success and set them apart from other women their age is somewhat more intriguing. Both Judy and Becky were driven partially by the reality of divorce and the recognition that they needed to be the major providers for their families. They admitted to me that divorce drove them harder. It provided additional fuel. Women in their age group didn't expect to be business leaders and they didn't anticipate divorce. They started out believing they would be happily married wives and mothers. Unless a woman of that age was truly unique, she didn't strive as hard to achieve in the professional area of her life. Women now in their 50s and their late 40s experienced tremendous role confusion—torn between the old role model their mothers presented and a new model of the modern working mother. They felt conflicted about where to put their energies. Divorce removed that confusion.

In *The Managerial Woman,* the classic study on women in management, Margaret Hennig and Anne Jardim discuss how psychological development and role expectations influence the career development of men and women differently.[10] Historically, men, not women, were expected to provide financial support for their families; therefore, men were more driven to succeed in their careers. But when a woman is faced with the reality and the fear that she alone must provide financial support for herself and her children, it changes the way she approaches work. Without that additional fuel, many women of that age group simply didn't identify or envision the top of the corporate ladder as a professional goal. Since women didn't start out in the 1960s with the same professional expectations as men, and since the number of female managers was far fewer, it is not surprising that there is still a difference between the number of males and females in senior management ranks.

MEREDITH FISCHER: CREATIVITY AT WORK

Pitney Bowes provides an example of another evolved corporate culture that has opened itself up to allow women in senior management. Meredith Fischer, a 43-year-old, free-spirited vice president of communications, marketing, and future strategy, says her company is experiencing "generational and male/female shifts." According to Meredith, the environment at Pitney Bowes is more casual and inclusive, and corporate leaders are younger. She told me, "The culture of executive row has changed: 20 percent of our senior management is female."

In this open environment, Meredith gives her creativity free rein and manages according to her own style. She also dresses according to her own dictates and doesn't allow herself to be hampered by her title or her position. She admits to using her looks to be disarming and describes her clothing as "colorful and bizarre," acknowledging that she wears "too much jewelry." Sometimes she has cut her hair so short that her scalp is visible and other times she has dyed it "virtually every color under the sun." Meredith feels her appearance "adds lightness" to her relationships and conveys a sense of self-confidence and creativity that suits her marketing job. She also admits she's not above laughing at herself and treats her appearance as a toy to play with. Imagine how different Meredith's life at work is from that of a 40-year-old female executive of the 1970s. Think about what would have happened to a female director or vice president walking into an office with a close-cropped coiffure or a mane of burnt sienna in 1975. If she made it in the door at all, she would have been assigned a cubicle buried in a back hallway. And she might just as well have worn a sign that said "Discount me," for she would have swiftly lost credibility.

Yet, even with the cultural changes that have taken place in progressive companies like Pitney Bowes, it is unlikely that Meredith will become a corporate chief executive, because her education and functional expertise aren't considered broad enough for a CEO position. Her story illustrates how the career paths of women—even women in their early 40s—have been influenced by their backgrounds. Like Becky Allen and Judy Beaubouef, Meredith never envisioned going into business. Growing up in Texas, she always knew that work was going to be an important part of her self-identity, but her original vision of her career differed from her later reality. Her mother was a commercial artist, and the arts were a big part of Meredith's life. She studied music in college and voice in graduate school. Realizing, however, that she might continue to be "poverty stricken" if she stayed in music, she took a job as a manager of promotion and public service at a local broadcasting station. For most of Meredith's career she has been in public relations or marketing communications, which are staff functions. Historically, CEOs of major corporations have climbed through line assignments that are directly accountable for profit and loss. Women interested in making it to the top of corporate ladders are advised to hold these positions. The underlying principle here is that CEOs need to understand the business side of their business.

However, Meredith hadn't planned on a business career; she hadn't envisioned herself sitting in a chief executive's chair. When Meredith married, she followed her husband and his career to Florida, where her promotional experience at the broadcast station enabled her to get a public relations job with Exxon. During the time she worked there, her business unit experienced fairly constant upheaval and Meredith says she had a new boss every six months, which helped her to build skills.

> *I have the kind of personality that thrives in chaos. Working in an environment in which you can't clearly see six months down the road has never particularly filled me with anxiety. Because of the upheaval, there were always things that no one was really doing, which gave me opportunities. I had achieved a certain level of credibility with senior management and when I saw something that I thought needed to be done, nine times out of ten they let me do it. This enabled me to broaden my experience across a span of marketing activities. I did everything from writing collateral literature to sales support to creating corporate slide presentations.*

In this somewhat chaotic environment, Meredith was never worried if she didn't know how to do something; "admitting ignorance" was never a problem for her. She trusted her creative instincts and took on new challenges without stressing herself.

> *We worked with a big New York ad agency, but I didn't feel threatened about managing a $17 million advertising budget and telling this established advertising firm that I had never done this type of work before.*

Although Meredith took advantage of the opportunities her environment provided to expand her skills during these early stages of her career at Exxon, she hadn't yet developed a long-range view of her career possibilities. It was the president of her business unit who recognized her abilities and tuned her in to the need to create bigger goals for herself.

> *One of the most astonishing conversations I ever had was with the president of the Exxon business unit in which I worked. We were on a flight together talking about the imminent transitions in the business. I had a great relationship with him and I spent a great deal of time with him because I was writing speeches for him and doing press relations. He asked me what I would like to do. Of course, because I didn't have any better sense, I told him I wanted to be the director of media relations. He told me I wasn't setting my sights high enough and that I ought to be vice president of marketing for a big corporation. I had never thought about that. After he said that to me, I started developing a longer range perspective about how far I could climb.*

That nudge and encouragement from the president enabled Meredith to change her perspective and look at her career with new vision. Meredith's skills earned her a great job opportunity in Connecticut, which she realized could enhance the future direction of her career. However, she faced a personal snag in her career development plans: Although her new position was going to pay significantly more than her husband was making, and although the couple had come to an agreement about following the career that was showing promise, her husband "was not happy about relocating." As she described it to me, what once had seemed like a simple decision became much more complex. One problem she and her husband experienced was the conflicting demands of their separate careers. Her husband's field was broadcasting and he needed to jump markets every 18 months to get his career moving, while Meredith needed to stay in one place to succeed. After the pair had been in Connecticut for about a year and a half, they once again faced relocation and career decisions. Meredith's husband accepted a position in Phoenix, but Meredith decided not to follow him. Although they remained friends, the couple ended up divorcing.

As changes continued to take place at Exxon, Meredith realized it was time to move on. She could have accepted a position in the public relations department of Exxon's main business, but the job would have limited, rather than expanded, her responsibilities and expertise.

> *I would have been slotted into a particular task within the function, either writing press releases all day or writing sales literature for one particular product or market segment. After having managed advertising, public relations, collateral, sales presentations and incentive programs, the thought of going into a very narrowly defined environment was not enticing.*

An old friend from Exxon, who was doing well at Pitney Bowes, gave Meredith a contact name and suggested that she call for an interview. Within a week of her initial phone call, Meredith was hired as the director of marketing for the facsimile division and within three years was promoted to vice president.

Over the course of her career Meredith has focused primarily on marketing communications and public relations because she "loves" that kind of work and says it motivates her. More recently she has taken on additional responsibility for future strategy and she is one of four senior planners working on a cross-functional business development team that is examining new partnership and market opportunities. Yet, given her career track, and with an advanced degree in music rather than in business, Meredith is realistic about future possibilities and acknowledged to me that a CEO position in a large corporation is most likely out of her reach. She does think that she could become the CEO or the COO of a smaller company. However, as a corporate officer she already puts in over 70 hours a week and believes a CEO position would require an even greater time commitment that she's not sure she wants to make. But, she says, "Who knows what I'll be thinking when I am 53? I might have a very different view."

Women who are over 40 were raised in a highly transitional time. They got all kinds of mixed messages, so it is understandable that many were unable to form a clear vision of their careers as they looked to the future. Many women had late starts and lacked business backgrounds. And many, like Meredith, developed career tracks without thought of becoming a CEO, yet by their 40s they reached vice presidential levels working in corporate areas they enjoyed. They chose to work in functions that brought them feelings of satisfaction—that's progress.

EXPECTATIONS OF
THIRTY-SOMETHING WOMEN

The younger women I interviewed—the thirty-something group—have experiences that differ from those of women in their 40s and 50s. These younger women have far more opportunity to be in sync with their companies. The culture in society and in their organizations had altered by the time they set out on their careers. The barriers they faced were fewer and smaller. In fact, most of these women told me they haven't experienced a glass ceiling at all. Because of their age, they see a far greater range of possibilities in front of them—their expectations are loftier. They have had female mentors and role models. Female networks are now in place, and using them strategically is far more natural to them. The clearing created by the female managers who preceded them enabled these thirty-something women to look ahead and see that a CEO spot as a distinct possibility. Teresa Elder, a dynamic 34-year-old general manager for AirTouch Cellular and a mother of two, says she has never had constraints on her vision.

> *I don't feel like there has ever been a glass ceiling for me. My boss is a woman and my boss' boss is a woman. We have high ranking women at US WEST. I have role models, whom I highly respect, who have small children at home. So, I have people to talk to and I feel supported.*

The women in Teresa Elder's family were teachers, but when she went to college she majored in chemistry because her original intention was to become a doctor. After one semester, however, she switched to sociology, and a year later she switched again. She ended up graduating with a degree in business, a minor in computer science, and a 3.9 average. When she started working right after college, Northwest Bell immediately put her on a fast-track program for high-potential candidates and she is now the youngest and the only female general manager in the cellular group. Teresa says she "loves running an organization and working with a large group of people." She sees herself in some ways as more like the men in her age group than like women 15 years older than she. Older women, she claims "had to claw their way into a man's world."

*I've never felt like I had to be a different person to be success-
ful. It sounds trite but I'm more successful the truer I am to who
I am. You can't pretend to be something you're not—you just
can't. And on a long-term basis, you will never be able to sustain something you're not.*

It is only because of the changes in the organizational environment that Teresa has this freedom to be herself. She can make
decisions based on her own value system and can set her goals and
assess her potential jobs by continually questioning herself.

*I've never thought there was any job that was out of my reach.
The criteria that I always use are: Am I challenged? Am I having fun? Am I having a positive impact? Can I keep my life in
balance?*

Kwok Lau, another young female executive and a mother of two,
is a 38-year-old vice president of business and operations management for AppleSoft. She echoes Teresa's sentiments about
changes in the workforce.

*At Apple, being a woman and being Asian hasn't made that
much difference. I've had plenty of good role models and peers.
In all fairness, because I'm Asian and have a name that sticks
out [Kwok is pronounced "Coke"], I tend to get a little more
recognition, which has both an upside and a downside: I'm
more visible, so I can be criticized more easily, but I'm always
well prepared for my jobs. I've never felt like a token. Never. I
just can't say I've experienced a glass ceiling.*

Kwok has spent all her career in manufacturing operations, an
area that has historically been identified as being less than welcoming to women, but Kwok told me manufacturing operations
offers a wide variety of challenges. She has been involved in high-
tech operations such as surface-mount technology and board
manufacturing, and has opened and shut down plants. She has a
breadth of experience that includes production, materials, and
procurement, and she has interfaced with engineering, marketing,
sales, and distribution. Until Apple's restructuring in 1996, Kwok
was the vice president for Pacific operations and "loved working in
the Asia Pacific region." In fact, if the reorganization hadn't happened, she said, "No one could have torn me away from it." But

when her division relocated to Singapore she didn't want to transplant her husband, children, and parents. As the company restructured, she moved into her new position with AppleSoft. Even though her company is presently in chaos, Kwok looks to the future with a sense of confidence, saying, "I know that if I continue to work hard and focus I can do whatever I want. I've proven to myself what I'm capable of doing."

Twenty years ago, it was unheard of for a woman to open or shut a plant or to have control over an international division. Then, a woman the same age as Kwok, particularly a woman from a minority group, would never have had the confidence that she could do whatever she wanted in a manufacturing environment, especially in the midst of upheaval and change—nor would she have been given any of those opportunities.

At 38, Beth Kaplan has also had a range of experiences in significant line assignments and a rapid corporate climb. Beth joined Procter & Gamble (P&G) in 1981, became a brand manager within two and a half years, and was then given a strategically significant position managing Always, which at the time was a new feminine hygiene product. She stayed with Always for seven years, which was unusual by P&G standards, and ended up knowing more about the brand than anyone else in the company.

Working in a women's business as a female gave me a big advantage and being there for that long gave me a tremendous amount of credibility. Those factors leveraged my career.

The fact that the business succeeded also helped, and Always went on to become a top global brand for P&G. By her tenth year, Beth was promoted to a general manager's position in the food division, and three years later she became a vice president and officer, heading the Cosmetics and Fragrances USA division.

Beth was first introduced to P&G when she was a campus tour guide at the University of Pennsylvania's Wharton School of Business. Unbeknownst to her, she took one of P&G's advertising vice presidents and his family on a tour of the university. Two weeks later, she received a letter from P&G inviting her to lunch with the corporate recruiters, which led to a summer internship with the company. After receiving her MBA and getting offers from numerous companies, Beth told me she decided on P&G because the summer internship had given her a good sense of the ethics and values of the organization and of the caliber of people with whom she would be working. She saw great opportunities, and the company's strong cultural values fit her "hand and glove." P&G's focus on internal development also appealed to her, and she says, "People were only limited by their own potential."

Recently, in a major career move, she accepted a position as an executive vice president at Rite Aid Corporation, a major P&G customer, and has the corporate pinnacle in clear sight. She had turned down Rite Aid's offer twice and told me her decision to leave P&G was harder than deciding to marry her husband. But because of her experience at P&G and because of the opportunity presented by her new, top-level position at Rite Aid, she says she is optimistic about the future of women in management.

> *The number of women at senior posts in Fortune 500 companies has increased substantially. The number of women on boards has also increased. When I look around and see women in senior jobs today, I'm very hopeful. In small and privately owned businesses, women are clearly the key drivers. So, there are reasons to feel very good and optimistic.*

These thirty-something women see the future in terms of its possibilities, not its limitations. Gender doesn't seem to be an issue for them. Their biggest concerns are meeting their goals and balancing their lives.

FUTURE PERCEPTIONS: CATCHING UP WITH FACTS

As the twenty-first century approaches, technology, changing markets, and new organizational structures are opening corporate doors and influencing women's roles, just as these issues did at the turn of the twentieth century. Dramatic changes in markets and machinery create bigger openings for women than do smaller, incremental changes that occur with time. Cross-functional teams and flattened structures are creating working environments that benefit from women's egalitarian nature and collaborative skills. Companies expanding into global markets gain from female managers' abilities to build relationships and to understand the minds of female customers. Technology is introducing new flexibility, opening possibilities for women to work in new ways. The system is changing. The process of cultural change, which has seemed to many to be torturously slow, has picked up speed. Over the past decade, there has been a shift as major companies have consciously attempted to increase the number of female executives at the tops of their corporations.

Changes in organizational and societal cultures have affected women's visions and their career plans. Looking back over the century, we tend to view progress through the lenses of our personal experiences. Each woman's corporate culture, her age, her individual personality, her personal experiences, and the time at which she entered corporate life combined to shape her achievements and her perceptions of success. Understanding the experiences of women who have been in the system longer, and the choices they have made, is critical for more fully comprehending all the reasons there are not more women at the uppermost level of the corporation. And understanding that thirty-something female executives don't feel they have bumped against glass ceilings and don't see impediments blocking their visions helps us to realize that more female executives will occupy senior management positions in the future. Hearing the full saga of women's experiences and listening to women of all ages give us a more complete story and a better vantage point from which to view the full scope of women's progress and achievements. The pipeline now has a sufficient number of well-prepared and educated women to compete equally with men. The road *is* rising to meet us. But the paths we take depend on our own definitions of success.

SUCCESS, STYLE, AND VALUES: WOMEN'S WAYS OF WORKING

The key is understanding what works for you—what you want out of life, from a career and from a family. And don't let others define it for you. Your company will try to define it. Your husband will try to define it. Your boss will try to define it. You've got to figure out what drives you and what will make you happy. It's really important that you have your soul-searching done so that you can carve out your own path and work towards your own goals.

ELLEN GABRIEL, Partner
Deloitte & Touche, LLP

Donna Karan peers from a glossy ad page celebrating 20 years of *Working Woman* magazine. Her caption reads, "As women, we used to think we had to act like men to succeed. We came to work on their terms, dressed in power suits, armed with shoulder pads. No more. As we have gained confidence through our accomplishments, we've learned to access our femininity—because it is our very womanliness that gives us strength and makes us leaders."

That's what makes women different today and what gives us so much hope—women in corporate America have begun to be themselves. They are leading and succeeding on their own terms. The women I interviewed and the women in the national survey described success in multidimensional terms, reflecting their need to fulfill their multifaceted roles. They designed their career strategies and set goals based on *all* the important areas in their lives. Their value systems influenced their decisions and guided them in choosing which companies to work for, what functions to work in, and how far they wanted to climb. Their hearts led them to professional activities they enjoyed and to environments in which they felt valued and could build relationships. The more these women acted according to their own feminine instincts and values, the more they used management styles that came naturally to them, and the more they sought careers that allowed them to fulfill their own definitions of success, the happier they seemed to be.

MULTIDIMENSIONAL WOMEN, MULTIDIMENSIONAL SUCCESS

Career opportunities for women have notably expanded, but women's definitions of success haven't changed significantly in 20 years. The successful female executives that Margaret Hennig and Anne Jardim interviewed for their classic study on women in management saw their careers as providing them with personal growth, self-fulfillment, and satisfaction, as well as a way to do what they wanted while making a contribution to others.[1] Today that same viewpoint prevails as women overwhelmingly echo similar sentiments. Success for contemporary women means: liking, loving, and having fun at their jobs; achieving professional and personal goals; finding harmony and balance in life; having rewarding relationships; being fulfilled; giving their personal best; making a difference; and making life better for others. As women wrote and spoke about success, three main themes emerged:

1. *Achieving goals.*   Women are goal-oriented. They care about results and the bottom line and want to meet the organization's goals as well as their own personal goals and objectives. They want to do their personal best—to perform at optimum levels. And they also want to enjoy the work they do—if women can't be happy and fulfilled by working, then what great freedom have they won?
2. *Balancing work and family.*   Women want to meet the needs of their families *and* their organizations. What good is success at work without personal happiness? Women work hard to balance their lives. They strive for balance consciously and continuously, yet they understand that perfection doesn't exist. Many women feel they have achieved balance, but they don't expect it all the time.
3. *Contributing something of value.*   Women want to make a difference. They want their work to have a positive impact on their families, their organizations, and their communi-

ties. Success involves making a difference in others' lives and is seen in relationship to how a woman's actions help others.

The women I interviewed stressed the importance of finding fulfillment both in the office and at home—they want to be happy in everything they do. And whether they are twenty-something or thirty-something or forty-something, whether they are black or white, they defined success similarly. For example, Sunni Acoli-Squire is a 27-year-old, single, African-American field-operating supervisor at Consolidated Edison of New York. Sunni has worked for Con Ed since 1992 and has completed her company's three-year management training program. She has a master's degree in electrical engineering and is now studying for a second master's in financial engineering. As the utilities industry deregulates, she hopes to position herself as an expert in its new financial products. When Sunni described her vision of success to me, she said that happiness ranked near the top of her list.

If I am happy with my personal relationships, my family, and my career, if I feel fulfilled and feel that I am making an important contribution to society and if I am financially comfortable and feel in control of my life—then I am successful.

Although 15 years older, Caucasian, married, and the mother of two young boys, Elizabeth (Beth) Rader gave me a definition that is not unlike Sunni's. Success has several elements for Beth. On the professional side, it means having a challenging career that provides her with a feeling of "making a contribution" and using her "abilities to their fullest." And on the personal side, it means creating a family life that gives her happiness and satisfaction.

Beth has worked for Deloitte & Touche LLP since 1983, and in 1993 she became the firm's first part-time partner. She helped pave the way in her firm for working toward business success in a balanced way. Her reduced-hours position reflects both her efforts to control the balance in her life and her firm's efforts to keep her career on track. Deloitte & Touche's new policies, initiated in 1992 under the umbrella of the firm's Women's Initiative, allow women and men to work part-time without interrupting the progression of their careers. These new policies were devised in an attempt to retain talented females by helping them meet all the demands in their lives. Initiatives like those of Deloitte & Touche exemplify the changes taking place in leading-edge companies that are striving to change their cultures and increase female numbers in senior management while enabling executives to meet both their professional and personal goals.

As an executive vice president at Rite Aid Corporation, Beth Kaplan is a thirty-something woman who truly relishes her work and always thought it was possible to become a corporate officer. Striving for success in both the professional and personal areas of her life has always been part of her plan. A short time before I interviewed Beth she told me she had cleaned out one of her drawers and found a description of success she had written back in high school in 1975. And what she found made her chuckle.

> *I was nearly hysterical laughing when I read it because my definition hasn't changed much. At 16, I said success was having my own identity, having a career that made me feel good about myself, contributing something of value, and at the same time having a very good family life.*
>
> *And I would say the same now. Success is finding the right balance and I've been lucky. Some women get up in the morning and feel guilty and torn, but I don't feel any of that. I really don't. If I stayed home, I would not be a happy person. I have to have a life apart from my child and husband; yet, I have to have them too. Both are very important to me and I've been blessed because I've been able to have both.*

Beth has the top spot in close sight. However, she willingly acknowledged to me that she would not be happy and balanced, nor be as successful as she is, without the help of her husband, who takes over responsibility for the domestic side of their lives.

> *I am confident that I could not be doing this without the arrangement we have. If I had a husband who was in a similar corporate job or had similar demands without the flexibility, I don't know what would happen with our son or our personal life, and I don't know how we could be happy.*

Both work and children enrich women's lives. Studies show that most women prefer to work.[2] Contrary to the conventional wisdom that portrays women as wracked with guilt and confusion, a 1995 survey conducted by *Working Mother* magazine found that nine out of ten working mothers are happy. Like Beth, three-quarters of the happiest working mothers said their husbands supported their career ambitions, and the majority of them had husbands who pitched in and pulled their weight at home.[3]

Since success for women includes the achievement of both personal and professional goals, what happens in one sphere can influence the success of the other. Cynthia Danaher, a 37-year-old mother of three young children, is the first female and the youngest general manager of Hewlett-Packard's Medical Products Group and is responsible for 5,000 people—5,000 people with whom she personally wants to connect. Relating to her employees and her team is a critical element of success for Cynthia. But so is taking care of her family.

> *Business success is bringing in the numbers, growing, getting new products, and having people at HP say, "Wow, the Medical Products Group is really well run." But if that means that I don't see my children as much, and my friendships aren't kept up, and I don't feel strong ties with my team, then I'm not going to be happy. I just want to be happy. If I can't shape a job into something I like, then I don't want to do it. I'm not willing to compromise my personal success to get business success. And unless I achieve my definition of personal success, I don't think I'll be successful in business either.*

Cynthia seeks jobs based on her own value system, a system that honors her need to give her family the right amount of attention and respects her desire to lead her team with her own personalized style of management. Cynthia told me she enjoys her job because of the people at Hewlett-Packard. Success for her includes working in relationships that improve her life, her employees' lives, and the life of her organization.

> *The thing that really motivates me is liking what I'm doing. I come to work because I love working with people with whom I feel personal ties and making people's lives better. So the title, the prestige, the money, and the stock options don't motivate me. I like them; they're attractive, but I want to be happy each day doing my job.*

Her approach to work—asking for what she needs and setting boundaries on her activities and time—epitomizes the changes that are taking place in leading-edge companies and demonstrates how far women have indeed come.

Each woman has her own method for combining the personal and the professional: There is no perfect method or perfect mix. But being able to make and manage that mix is crucial. Jean Brennan, a 42-year-old director of succession planning at Pacific Gas & Electric and mother of two children, creatively combined work and family by instituting a groundbreaking job share in 1990.

Jean works in human resources and says she loves HR because it fulfills her need to be of service to others. She told me she is committed to people and society, but she also admitted to having workaholic tendencies. When her first child was due she realized that a full-time job and full-time motherhood would stretch her too far and she had to make some serious career decisions. The job share she designed with her partner Erin Andre enables her to maintain the balance that makes her feel happy.

> *Success to me doesn't mean getting to the CEO position; it doesn't mean getting to the vice president of HR position. It means how much change I can make in an organization or in society. And to me I'm a happy person if I lead a really balanced life where I'm contributing. I want to make a difference.*

Success at anything, however, comes with a price. Jean admits that saying no to higher-level jobs hasn't always been easy. Women like Jean recognize the alternatives facing them and make conscious choices about how they wish their lives to unfold. As they seek to achieve their goals, they recognize there are trade-offs and compromises, and they are willing to make them.

THE FEMALE VERSION OF HOW TO SUCCEED IN BUSINESS

There is more than one way to succeed in business. According to author Betty Lehan Harragan's premise in *Games Mother Never Taught You*, if a woman wanted to succeed in a man's world, she had to do it by mimicking men. "For seriously ambitious women," she wrote, "there is only one logical objective: to become the chief executive officer." Attitudes and beliefs have changed during the last 20 years. As the volume of businesswomen's voices has increased, female leaders no longer feel they have to give up their female styles. Many women view themselves as seriously ambitious, but they don't necessarily want to be Fortune 500 CEOs, especially if it means forfeiting their happiness and the other important parts of their lives.

Connie Van Zandt is a reformed workaholic who decided she no longer wanted to give up pieces of her personal life. Her present goal is to achieve balance, not upward movement. At 37, Connie is the director of planning and fulfillment services at Gannett Company and she was quite emphatic when she told me, "I don't want to be the CEO, the CFO, the C or the O of anything in the company." Connie likes her job and is well compensated. Her goals, she says, "are to have balance in my life, to be fulfilled with what I'm doing, and to do a good job and be productive for the company."

Even in the upper ranks of senior management that top layer isn't always tempting. Gail Gaumer, 44, is a lick away from the top, but says she isn't enticed. Gail's family factors heavily into her decision-making process. When she became the president of Baxter's Renal Division in Europe, the company assisted her husband in finding a position in Europe and agreed that Gail could relocate wherever her husband landed a job. She and her husband ended up living in Zurich for three years, during which time they had their first child. Running the European operation required Gail to travel virtually all the time and she often brought her new baby and nanny along with her. But as her son got older, Gail says, "It was time to make a change." In 1996, Gail became an executive vice president of Allegiance Healthcare Corporation, a new $5 billion Baxter Healthcare Corporation spin-off.

As executive vice president of Allegiance, Gail will have a chance to be a "pioneer in a new area of cost management," with the added benefit that there will be relatively little travel. Yet, as close as she is to the top, she told me she is "not driven to be CEO of Baxter or Allegiance." She wants "to be able to contribute and make a nice income and do a lot of fun things." Gail works "more for the stimulation of the job than anything else," and credits her professional success in part to her ability to take action. Success at work depends, she says, "on being willing to stand up and present your ideas, and then to step forward and make things happen." With a young son and in a good financial position, Gail can even envision herself retiring within a few years, although she chuckled when she told me, "The people I work with would laugh if they heard me say that."

Women gauge success in a variety of ways; therefore, women need to be clear about whose value system they use to judge progress. In their study, Hennig and Jardim pointed out that if women found a way to balance work and family, career paths would "*not need to be vertical to be seen as successful.*"[5] It may be a 20-year-old message, but it demands renewed attention. There are lots of different ways to succeed. We need to ask what matters more: getting to the top or how we get there? Women's focus on goals, contribution, *and* balance can have greater impact on the organizational system and make a difference in the way work is viewed.

Actually, there is evidence that a shift in career planning from a vertical to a horizontal orientation is taking place on a larger scale. When I spoke with Margo Davis, a corporate education program manager at Hewlett-Packard, she described new career paths to me. As companies are flattening, Margo says they are developing a "lattice" rather than a "ladder" approach to career construction. Rather than looking up, managers like Margo can look around the new webbed structure of the corporation to find other settings in which to apply their skills. For instance, an HR trainer might develop specialized training programs for salespeople out in the field; by working directly with the sales force, the manager can expand her skills while repositioning herself outside of a traditional corporate track. Margo, who was previously a teacher, said she decided on a horizontal path after carefully thinking about her abilities and options.

> *I made a conscious decision to be an individual contributor by looking in the mirror, really looking at myself and asking how I could best optimize my skills, my talents and my energies. That can be hard to do. I had to ask how many hours I really wanted to be at work and how many hours I wanted to be doing something else. And then I had to decide what the best path for me was because I don't want to be frustrated. I want to enjoy myself. I decided I didn't want to get to the point where I was battling so fiercely to become vice president or general manager that I blocked out other enjoyments.*

With her career structured the way she wants it to be—free from management responsibilities that would require more time—Margo says she can go shopping on the spur of the moment with her daughter on a Saturday morning without having to worry about work. To her, there is great value in that spontaneity, and that sense of freedom adds to her feelings of success.

THE POWER TO MAKE A DIFFERENCE: SELF-WORTH AND MONEY

If a woman doesn't want the top spot, it doesn't mean she shirks authority and power. Back in 1976, Jean Miller Baker wrote, "Power is almost a dirty word"—an "unmentionable subject"—among women. In pointing out the reasons for this phenomenon, Miller claimed that the concept of power had become skewed and was generally associated with the idea of advancing oneself while simultaneously controlling others. Power is different for women, she wrote, and "may be defined as the capacity to implement."[6] Twenty years later, *power* still wasn't a word frequently used by the women I interviewed, but the concept of implementing change and making a difference was repeated over and over. Beth Kaplan, executive vice president of Rite Aid Corporation, says, "The ability to influence is power and is very important to senior women—it's what we sought to achieve and what we've earned." Being able to influence the organization and to feel connected with others is part of modern women's definitions of success. The intrinsic value of work, the ability to have an impact and operate in relationship with others, seems to motivate women more than anything else—more than climbing to the top, more than financial reward, more than power for power's sake.

Rather than emphasizing *power,* the women I spoke to emphasized *wanting to make a difference.* Cynthia Cannady, vice president of law, manufacturing, and development at Apple Computer, told me she was originally drawn to law because both her father and grandmother are lawyers and because law seemed to be a way for her to make a contribution toward changing the world. At 45, she still has a desire to make an impact: In describing her present ambitions, she said, "I'm already positioned high institutionally, so I don't feel I have to get further promotions. My goal is to use my skills in an interesting job where I have responsibility and can affect things." Beth Dudley, a 46-year-old vice president of quality management and regulatory affairs at Baxter Healthcare Corporation, also has no desire to climb higher on the corporate ladder, but making change and having a broad impact on her organization is extremely important to her. Beth says she "loves" the function in which she works and the responsibility she has: "If you don't have wide responsibility, you don't make a big impact, and it's tough to see change. I have a desire to make a difference, to have an impact, and to make change for the better." In presenting the arguments I am giving in this book, I am not denying the legitimacy of the need to have women in positions of formal authority and power. As US WEST Vice President Teresa Wahlert says, "If we really didn't want to have power, we would never have the jobs we do. We wielded our power our way in order to be where we are." My point is to encourage taking a broader, more feminine, view of success—one that adds all of life's dimensions into the equation.

Another characteristic the successful female executives I spoke with share is their desire for excellence in everything they do. They are driven to meet their organizations' bottom-line goals. They want to make their presence felt and to demonstrate their effectiveness. Julie England, a 38-year-old vice president at Texas Instruments, told me she feels successful when she is "pushing the envelope" and "fully utilizing" her capabilities. She cares about her title and her compensation, but they don't completely define her success. She wants to "keep growing and learning," and she says that when she begins to feel as though she is no longer contributing competitively, then she'll do something different. Learning every day is also important to Cynthia Cannady. She says that when she isn't using all her skills and talents in a meaningful way, she feels like she's "rusting." "Success," Cynthia believes, "is feeling that you are at the height of your powers, doing everything you can to grow and get better." Karen Moreno, a vice president at Gannett Supply Company, defines success as "achieving a reputation for competence and integrity and for valuing profits and people equally," and Erin Andre, who job-shares with Jean Brennan at Pacific Gas & Electric, says, "Success is a feeling that I'm accomplishing my goals, that I have an expertise that's valuable, and that I'm contributing to the organization."

I was surprised at the similarity of themes in women's definitions of success. Becoming a CEO, gaining power, and making money were not dominant themes; meeting goals, achieving balance, and making a difference were. In the national survey only 2 women out of nearly 700 listed becoming a CEO as a marker of success. Less than a quarter of the women included any description of financial compensation in their definitions, and one woman even wrote that "salary is not part of the equation." The absence of focus on earnings tends to support Naomi Wolf's claim that women "lack a culture . . . that casts the pursuit of money as a legitimate feminine drive."[7] Money does seem to be a catch-22 for many women—I know it is for me. And my feelings were reflected in the women's statements and comments. The dilemma for me gets posed something like this: I do want to make a good amount of money, but it's not really what motivates me. ("Good" gets translated into "a reasonable and substantial amount" so that I don't end up a bag lady in my old age.) I also want money because I need to take care of my daughter and to finish paying for her college education without having to remortgage my house. But, essentially, I'm not driven to amass a stack of money; therefore, I'm not wealthy. Because I'm not wealthy, I confess to having fantasies about becoming a millionaire; however, my fantasies always include how I will give the money away!

Money even causes consternation for female executives who make above-average salaries. One woman asked me not to disclose her salary because she was concerned her friends and family would view her differently if they found out how much she made. Another, who was among the highest paid, admitted that her large salary caused her quite a bit of angst.

> *I make a lot of money, but I find it uncomfortable and embarrassing from a variety of standpoints. Many people question whether it's right to pay executives such high salaries. Yet, the other women I work with remind me that my salary sends a signal to the rest of the women in the company and gives them hope that they too can make a lot of money—that it's meaningful to them. But for me, making this much money is causing anxiety, which I ought to be managing better. Money comes with a whole host of issues attached. You think it would be wonderful, but it can be a burden. And it's so weird to say that. It does, however, relieve a lot of concerns. It gives me much more flexibility and I can help other people—from that standpoint it's absolutely wonderful. But it's not a driver—it really isn't.*

On the other hand, I did speak to women who are free of conflict. They like making money, don't have qualms about it, and use it to help gauge their success. But regardless of where women find themselves on the issue, they don't use their compensation as a sole measurement of success. For most women, compensation is just one of many success factors, and how it's viewed depends on each woman's experience. The financial stress that Becky Allen (the plucky housewife who turned into a CEO) faced at the time of her divorce influenced her perspective on money. She describes success the same way most women do, but when I questioned her about the role money played in motivating her, she was extremely forthright in admitting how much she loves earning big bucks.

> *Success is being happy with yourself and being able to look yourself in the mirror every morning and like what you see. It's being able to have things in life that make you comfortable. It's having a loving family. If you are successful at work, but you are not successful at home, then I'm not sure you've been suc-cessful. . . . But I am motivated by money—to me that's the measuring stick. Money says "This is what you are worth in the marketplace." I love making money and I don't know what that says about me. Maybe it goes back to when I got divorced and I didn't have any money. I was determined to prove I could do it. I've often wondered if that might be a reason it motivates me. Maybe I have a Scarlett O'Hara—"I'll never be hungry again"—syndrome.*

Vela McClam Mitchell also admits using money as a measure-ment. We met at her spacious home in a suburb outside of Atlanta and spent a couple of hours talking and laughing over pizza and beer. Even though she is almost a decade younger than I am, we had some things in common, since we were both divorced from our first husbands and remarried to older men.

Vela is an African-American director of sales and marketing at Worldspan, a high-tech information services company. She is a vibrant dynamo of a woman who loves to tell stories, and we hit on a wide range of topics. I tracked her down after seeing her picture in an article on affirmative action in *Working Woman* magazine. Her outspokenness in the article attracted me and she was the same in person. She attributes part of her success to her ability to go for what she really wants, and she struck me as a woman who is not easily daunted.

> *Whenever I want something I never leave it to chance. So what if someone says no. Who cares. I'm not going to die. But, at least, I know I tried. And if I am told "no," the next question I ask is "Why?" If I want a position and the immediate answer is not "yes," I ask, "What do I need to do differently, what do you want to see me do that will prepare me for the position I'm inter-ested in?"*

Vela is driven by "winning the game," and told me, "If I have any advice for women, it's love the game that you're in. You've got to love winning the game." Her career includes positions at Honeywell, Hughes Aircraft, and Northwest Airlines, and she is continually called by recruiters. She likes being challenged and being in charge, and describes herself as "fiercely competitive" and "a natural leader." Vela is convinced that one part of her success comes from building good relationships with her customers and the other part comes from "having guts." Not at all shy, she boldly assured me how good she was by saying, "I am one of the best marketing people you will ever find."

> *I actually get to know customers. I understand them. I know what motivates them. And I deliver. If I tell customers they are going to get a product this week, they get it. I will beat up on the world until I get it to them. I will stay up all night if I have to do it myself. If I say I am going to deliver, I deliver. If I see a problem coming, I'll let my customers know that we've got a problem, and I'll be honest and tell them what the problem is. I tell my customers what is going on. And they value that honesty and commitment.*

When I asked her if money also plays a role in driving her, she unhesitatingly and unabashedly said it does, but it's not the only factor she considers. Vela loves her home and the lifestyle and climate in Atlanta. She has turned down offers for double the money she presently makes because the positions would have entailed moving to cities that are not favorites on her list.

> *I count the numbers when I calculate success. I am paid an excellent salary at my company because I asked for my salary coming in—and I recommend overestimating your worth when asking. But before I do ask for a particular salary, I do my homework. I don't just pull a number out of the sky. You've got to do your research. Find out what they are paying people in similar positions in your industry and geographical location. Call the chamber of commerce. Check with other people in the industry. For example, before taking this job, I checked with headhunters to find out what they were paying marketing directors in Atlanta in technology companies. Then, go in high and let them talk you down.*

*I think I have something to contribute to whatever I'm doing;
therefore, I go for goals full gun. I enjoy the responsibility. I
know who I am. I know what I know and what I don't know. At
41, I'm now choosing the battles I wish to fight. I'm at the stage
in my career where I can make choices. Right now I'm motivated by living here; if I wasn't I would be out of here. However,
if the money stops counting up right, I would consider living in
another state I liked. For example, I would move back to California in a minute. I want to become a vice president. I realize I
can run a company, but whatever I do, it will be on my terms.*

"Doing it on our own terms" is what really counts for us as
women—being able to set our own goals and use our own measurements. Being constantly told what we should be or shouldn't
be strips us of exalting in our achievements. Each woman I spoke
with lives and works by her own standards.

CYNTHIA DANAHER: DOING IT HER WAY

When Cynthia Danaher, general manager of Hewlett-Packard's
Medical Products Group, approached me in the cavernous lobby of
HP's facilities in Andover, Massachusetts, I was immediately taken
by her personal attentiveness. She didn't send someone else down
to the lobby to fetch me, but came down herself to greet me and
escort me back to a conference room where we could talk uninter-
rupted. And as we walked through the halls, she behaved exactly
as she later described herself—she greeted people along the way,
making time to say a few personal words to the employees we met
as we walked along.

Cynthia's family and her relationships are at the top of the list of
things she values. And she boldly puts those personal values on
the professional table so they are clearly visible for everyone.

*You've got to do your work on your own terms. I pick my super-
visors well. I like to make sure they have a sense of family. If I
interview for a job and get bad signals around family issues, I
won't take the job. When I am asked what my weaknesses are,
I say I'm a mother of three. I tell whoever is interviewing me
that I cannot do what the previous person in the position did.
And then I sit there. And I listen. And I can tell in a second if it's
going to be okay or not. I can tell by the interviewer's response.*

I have come to the conclusion that there are two ways of doing a job: Either you do it the way the previous person did it, or you do it your own way. I prefer to do it my way and I ask my managers to measure me on my results and leave the methods to me. I ask potential bosses right up front if they are comfortable with that approach. And I tell them that if the arrangement doesn't work out for them or it's not working out for me, it's okay. I'll go do another job. I can do a lot of things. But being a mother is really, really important to me and I have to balance my job with my family. So I've always worked it that way.

Cynthia stays actively involved in her children's lives even during working hours. The week before I interviewed her, she helped out at her son's nursery school and spent an hour at her daughter's elementary school teaching the class a lesson on the heart. She says her job is "a marathon," not "a 50-yard dash," and she wants the time to fit everything she values into her schedule.

Part of Cynthia's ability to stick to her values so determinedly comes from knowing that she can do other jobs—both because she has the skills and because there are other opportunities for her. Twenty years ago women never would have mentioned motherhood as a weakness. Fortunately, progressive-thinking corporate leaders are adapting their companies to meet the needs of working women and of female senior managers like Cynthia.

When Cynthia interviewed for her present job as general manager of 5,000 people, the hiring manager gave her a calendar that indicated the activities that were absolutely necessary. He told her "Go home and look at this and make sure this is manageable for you. Anything else is up to you." After Cynthia reviewed the job's requirements, she knew she would be able to handle it, and she felt reassured by having the freedom to say no. Shortly after accepting the position, she felt confident turning down a request to speak at one of HP's women's conferences. Using technology and creativity, she sent a videotape instead.

Women like Cynthia, who are candid about what they need, stimulate the efforts of progressive companies. Over time, their actions can infuse the system with women's values. When women first came into the marketplace, they were more or less forced to define success using male definitions. But as Cynthia and the other women point out over and over, to be successful, women must operate according to their own value systems.

You cannot define your success through the eyes of the people judging you. You've got to do it internally. And if you don't do that, you're going to be all over the map. You're just going to be miserable, and you'll fail anyway.

Having known tragedy, Cynthia makes her decisions with so much clarity because she simply wants to be happy. Her sister's death from brain cancer, which left two small children without a mother, had a profound impact on her.

There are enough things in life that are thrust upon you that you have no choice in dealing with. When you make a choice, you should use your choices not to be miserable.

Although work takes up an enormous amount of time in our lives, organizations are finally responding to the need for people to give time and attention to the personal aspect of their lives, and organizational cultures are finally beginning to open up to women's ways of working. This new openness springs from corporate leadership. Cynthia credits Lew Platt, HP's CEO, for his insight and understanding. During the interview process, he acknowledged her autonomy and ability to make good judgments by telling her, "You prioritize. You only go where you need to go." Leadership like Platt's engenders a supportive culture that creates affiliation and draws managers like Cynthia closer to their companies.

This place suits me; it fits me like a glove. Lew Platt became a single parent of two children when his wife died and I think that experience made a difference in this company. Other CEOs, and most men, are clueless about what women battle, getting home, getting things under control. But Lew Platt knows. So he doesn't just say these things—he means them. And that has made such a difference for me. What makes me so loyal to this company isn't the pay or the title or the stock options. Nothing could make me more loyal to this company than letting me help at nursery school, letting me get home when I need to get home, and letting me say "no" to business trips. Those things are far more important.

However, if women want flexibility, they need to be able to produce the results the corporation wants. They need to prove their value system enhances the corporate system. Cynthia says she brings in the results "time after time after time" and cautions women about making sure they are ready to add that value.

> *You have to get yourself in jobs, especially early on, that you are incredibly good at. You have to know what you're doing. You have to put credibility dollars in the bank so that when you need to make a withdrawal, they're there.*

Another way in which Cynthia adheres to her own value system is through her style of management. From her perspective, there are two keys to being a good manager.

> *You have to be secure to the point where you can say this is what we are and this is what we're not. And people have to understand by your actions and your words that they come before you. You have to do those two things. Then, you can make a lot of mistakes and it's okay.*
>
> *Employees can be motivated when they know where they are going, why they are going in a certain direction, and how they are going to get there. So I tell them what things we need to get done. And then all I have to do is keep motivating them to get them done, which is something that comes very naturally to me.*

Intuitively, Cynthia knows employees want to feel "valued, important and cared for." She operates on a system of behavioral values, which she communicates to her employees, asking them to support and believe in one another. In turn, she motivates them by giving them the support they need. Cynthia pulls people together using a practice she says, "might not be great, but I draw a circle around us, and tell them other people aren't sure we can do this, but I think we can." And as a true servant leader, she openly acknowledges that her employees, not she, do the hard work of making the business successful. "Managing," Cynthia said to me, "is the easiest job in the world."

Modeling the behaviors she expects in her managers, Cynthia stays so involved in people's work that when she walks down the hall she can comment on the jobs people are doing. In her last position, Cynthia managed 500 people and yet she knew whose father was going into a nursing home and which employees were battling illness in their families. Losing her sister has heightened her ability to deal empathically with her employees. She asks supervisors to keep her informed of difficult times in employees' lives, and she personally calls employees in crisis to find out how they can be helped through their stressful periods. Her personal style and value system reach beyond her to benefit her employees, who in turn produce results that benefit the organization.

> *I'm clear. I'm focused. I know myself well. I know what I'm good at and what I'm not good at. I listen to smart people around me and choose the few things we should do and focus and encourage people in that direction. I honestly don't think that I'm smarter than anybody else, but I have high emotional intelligence. I can read people and understand what motivates them. I can get people to rally behind me. I'm a very strong leader. People really want to do things for me.*

Cynthia has high standards and says she is tougher on people than most of the male managers she knows. She described herself as honest and direct, and when employees aren't performing the way they should she sits down with them to find out why.

However, traditional male styles of management that aren't as open and inclusive as Cynthia's still influence corporate life—even in progressive companies. And with each of her promotions, as Cynthia was given larger groups to manage, she told me she was warned that her management style wouldn't work.

> *People told me my style works with four people, but it might not work with eight. It works with eight, but it might not work with 40. Then they told me they didn't think it would work with 100, but it did. They told me I would have to change my style working with 500 people, but I didn't and it worked. Now, I have 5,000 people and I'm going to keep using my style. They tell me I can't possibly connect with that many people. But after the first "All-Hands" meeting, I must have gotten 160 letters from people telling me how good they felt and how happy they were to hear what I said. Those people felt connected enough to sit down at the terminal and write me an e-mail note. So, I'm glad I never listened when they told me to change my management style.*

Cynthia's transition, however, has not been without its challenges. She hasn't blindly assumed that her desire to relate on a personal level to ten times more people and to work closely with a staff that she didn't personally select will be a snap. She knows it takes time to build relationships, but she has developed a philo-sophical approach throughout the course of her career and has discovered that "things appear to be bigger than they are."

> *I was a great marketing manager and I loved the job. I was really happy. I had only been a marketing manager for three years when my supervisor was promoted and I was offered his job. When I first took that promotion, as general manager of the Imaging Systems Division, it was a stretch, but everything around me was familiar—I knew all the customers. I knew all the people. I knew the product line. It was like going from sixth grade into junior high. This promotion is a different kind of stretch. It feels like I'm going from eighth grade to college. The transition is a hard one. And it's tough in ways you might not think of—I felt very connected to 500 people and they felt con-nected to me. I loved working with that group of people for whom I felt affection and who felt affection for me.*
>
> *And my staff is also very important to me. Now my staff is already in place and they are mostly all men. I need their knowledge, their expertise and their guidance. In the past, choosing my staff was close to choosing my spouse and now I'm working with a group of men whom I haven't chosen. I need to develop good ties with them and that takes time.*

When I asked her how she handles such enormous transitions, and if she could give any advice to others who are confronted with such daunting challenges, she confidently replied, "Be brave, stare them down, and make them your own. A little anxiety is a good thing; a lot of anxiety just freezes you."

DOING IT THEIR OWN WAY AND DOING IT RIGHT

When women first entered the business world, they were not free to allow their own instincts to surface. Instead, they were told to mimic men and stifle the very characteristics that today are being recognized for the value they add to the workplace. Now that female executives occupy more upper-level management positions, wo-men's leadership skills—the ability to empower employees, build relationships, facilitate change, empathize, communicate, plan, and make decisions—are becoming more evident and respected. In fact, styles of leadership identified as "female" seem to be blossoming in a marketplace that emphasizes relationships and teamwork. Today's leaders are being recognized as having feminine traits, even if they are not being called feminine, and executives attending leadership workshops are being taught behaviors that come naturally to many female managers: how to ask questions, listen empathically, coach others, and motivate through understanding. Margaret Wheatley, author of *Leadership and the New Science*, is one of many writers addressing the emergence of feminine characteristics in leadership.

> *Intuition, sensitivity and timing are key attributes of leaders who know how to nurture rather than dictate. Leadership that relies on such characteristics as relationship building, trust, nurturance, intuition and letting go is the leadership of the future. These traits have often been associated with our feminine side, whether we are female or male, but mainstream organizations have never encouraged women leaders to develop these qualities, and many women neither have nor want to be identified with such attributes. The need for new leaders, however, is inevitable, and it will change—indeed, broaden— our definition of who is effective.[8]*

I find the topic of management styles particularly compelling: Do these feminine characteristics mean that women manage better than men? Women themselves don't agree on the answer to this question. Some of the women I interviewed wisely cautioned about generalizing styles to one sex or the other. After all, we all know terrible female managers who rival the most unenlightened males. As Florence Williams, who climbed through the manufacturing ranks at Xerox, says, "Some men and women are bears and you wouldn't want to work for any of them." But there are many women who have management abilities that seem to be intuitive and enable them to motivate and lead people with a natural ease. In Florence's experience, she says she has found women are inclined "to be more human."

> *Women tend to recognize priorities in life and try to work a balance helping their employees become comfortable with their personal lives so that they can give their all while they are at work. Men tend to be focused on deliverables and don't want to hear the rest. I've watched women managers try to create*

such a comfortable environment in letting people be them-
selves and trying to manage their personal life that people will
run miles and leap tall buildings to deliver their objectives for
them.

I was drawn to this question of management styles several years
ago when I was first introduced to the concept of transformational
leadership. As I observed workshops led by men who were working
with top corporate managers, I was somewhat taken aback that
corporate executives would need to learn what seemed to me to be
commonsense management concepts: how to ask questions, how to
share information, how to listen actively, how to understand what
employees and customers need. I had been working in a small
business environment and I had assumed that managers in large
corporations understood these concepts. Questioning my own reac-
tion, I reasoned that my understanding came from my study of psychology in college and communication in graduate school. Then I
thought back to the days when I was working in the airlines in the
late 1960s and early 1970s—before I got my degrees—and realized
I always intuitively understood these concepts. I had instinctively
wanted to respond to customers' needs and had been confused
when management made different rules. For example, if we were
delayed due to a mechanical problem, which was the fault of the
airline and not the gods who control the weather, then I thought we
should tell the customers the truth and do everything possible to
get them where they needed to go—even if that meant taking them
off of our plane and putting them on a competitor's. Management
didn't see it that way and we always stalled as long as we could.

Not only did management tune out what the customer was saying, but frontline employees weren't listened to either. This made
absolutely no sense to me, since those of us in the front lines spent
the most time with customers and knew what they wanted and
needed. Moreover, if we weren't treated well and felt disempowered,
our frustrations could be reflected in our performance, which in
turn could negatively affect the customer. It seemed to me that the
company should care about our well-being by virtue of the fact that
we were closest to the customer, and I didn't understand why the
company didn't grasp that logic. At the time, I thought I must have
been missing some deep theoretical management concept that was
just too esoteric for my young mind to understand. Now, I realize my female instincts were right on target. And 25 years later,
these ideas became leading-edge. When I read an article by Joline

Godfrey in the course of researching this book, her words jumped off the page at me.

> *The very basic notions of what women defined as success seemed to make their businesses different. The more I heard (and experienced) about women's businesses, the more I felt that what female business owners called "normal" was now being tagged the "new paradigm" by business gurus world-wide. And the national effort to "reengineer" everything was an attempt to get to where women already were. What the new gurus were advocating as a radical change for America's com-panies was standard operating procedure for many women. The very qualities that had been devalued because they were female were now claimed by many male writers as integral to a new and radical approach to the business of management.[9]*

SHAUNNA SOWELL: TEACHING TEAMWORK

These instinctive tendencies to manage well showed up in many of the women I interviewed. Like the women's businesses to which Joline Godfrey referred, women in corporate America were also succeeding at work using their own natural styles long before these styles were touted as "in."

Part of Shaunna Sowell's success is her innate ability to build effective teams that meet customers' needs. Shaunna is a vice president at Texas Instruments, where teamwork is highly valued. Early in her career as a project manager, her organization was able to turn a dissatisfied customer into a supporter of the company by altering the way the group handled work. Shaunna, who led the team through its transformation, emphasizes that she could never succeed without the help of others and modestly told me, "I changed the structure of how we operated simply because it made sense to me."

At the time, TI was building a manufacturing facility in Dallas, and Shaunna had a team of approximately 45 people reporting to her. The group was traditionally organized: Engineers created the designs, material people ordered parts, and mechanics built facili-ties. But the process didn't work very efficiently. Part of the prob-lem, as Shaunna saw it, arose because the mechanics—who spent the most time talking to customers and who knew what designs worked—were at the end of the process, rather than providing input at the beginning. There was no system in place to provide feedback to designers as problems arose. Instead, mechanics frequently fixed problems in the field. This approach cost more, took more time, and often produced poorer-quality products. Shaunna knew the group had to learn to work more effectively as a team.

> *The answer was to bring the team members to the table together to agree to the design plans. At first, there was an emotional reaction to the plan. Yet over time, everyone understood how we all won when we satisfied the customer. Everyone was willing to give up whatever control they perceived they formerly had to be part of the team's success.*

By the end of the project, the customer's views changed dramatically—Texas Instruments was proclaimed to be the best supplier the customer had worked with in 25 years. Shaunna's natural tendencies to lead by empowering others and her skill at building teams contributed to her swift rise at TI. Shaunna says working in the flattened, inclusive web structure of a team provides "a higher probability of success because more ideas and solutions are shared, communication is enhanced and team members feel personally committed."

CAROL TUTHILL: EARLY INNOVATIONS IN MANAGEMENT PRACTICES

Carol Tuthill provides another example of a woman who used cutting-edge management techniques long before they were popular. Carol is a 44-year-old worldwide vice president of human resources and organizational excellence at Procter & Gamble. Like Shaunna, Carol started out as a teacher before switching gears and joining the business world. And like many women of her era, she didn't have specific career goals, but was driven more by a desire "to make a difference."

Before joining P&G, Carol worked in the grocery trade for six years, but wasn't feeling fulfilled. In the process of looking for other employment, Carol sought out advice from career counselors at her alma mater. While speaking with them, a P&G recruiter overheard part of her conversation and invited her to interview for a brand manager position. Without really understanding what brand management was or recognizing that she was interviewing for a highly

competitive position, Carol found herself in the marketing department of P&G's soap and detergent division.

In 1982, after climbing through advertising and marketing in her
brand area, Carol was given a position in personnel, which at the
time was dominated by men.

> *I was invited to come into personnel because I had made a rep-*
> *utation for myself on the line improving systems and managing*
> *in ways that were not typical of my peers in terms of develop-*
> *ing people. As a manager, I defined training plans more tailored*
> *to the individual people who worked in my brand area. P&G*
> *has always offered individualized training, but I added more*
> *definition and structure.*

Carol's group was the first to do any multifunctional training in
a culture where functional structures were very strong and brand
managers (one of the fastest tracks to becoming general manager)
didn't have experience in other functional roles.

> *We combined training for our brand people with engineering*
> *and manufacturing people to accelerate the progress of our pro-*
> *jects. We received a lot of notoriety for doing that. I also had my*
> *subordinates give me feedback on my management style. I*
> *wanted to learn how I could tailor myself to meet their needs*
> *more effectively. I wanted to know what they would like to see*
> *from me as a boss. That was considered a radical thought then,*
> *but now everybody does it.*

P&G recognized the value of the approach Carol was using in her
brand area and how it could enhance the company's approach to
developing workers.

> *P&G is a company that promotes from within and recruiting is*
> *important, but the company wanted to focus more attention on*
> *employee development work. I was brought in to develop sys-*
> *tems for linking organizational capability to the business.*
> *Rather than keeping HR in the policy keeper role, my mandate*
> *was to create systems that would make HR partners with the*
> *business managers. When HR leadership started moving in the*
> *direction of strategically linking HR to the bottom line, it was*
> *obvious that the work that I had done fit in well with that*
> *vision.*

Carol's work was a precursor to the changes that are now being experienced in human resource departments in most major companies. In fact, Carol told me she was not the only female manager trying new management techniques in the early 1980s. Independent of each other, a number of female managers at P&G were innovatively managing in ways that were natural to them. They intuitively knew how to manage to get effective results and they were given enough autonomy within P&G, even back then, to allow themselves to follow their instincts, which ended up benefiting the organization.

Scientific evidence is, in fact, piling up, proving that women do manage and lead differently—and, yes, even better—than men. In the national survey, an overwhelming 94 percent of the women said they perceived a difference in the way men and women manage and they listed women's most effective management skills as their ability to understand, listen, empathize, and build teams and consensus. Although some of the women I interviewed insisted that particular skills and styles can't be generalized to women, the women described their own styles in similar ways, repeatedly mentioning the same characteristics: They tend to manage participatively, but they don't hesitate to be final decision makers; they demand bottom-line results while caring about people; they understand and listen to employees; they motivate through commitment, trust, and flexibility; and they openly share information.

TERESA ELDER: GOOD, OPEN, HONEST BUSINESS SENSE

Thirty-four-year-old Teresa Elder, a general manager at AirTouch Cellular, described herself as candid and direct, and said she has a reputation for honesty. When I asked her if she attributed those characteristics to being a woman, she replied in her practical way, "I call it like I see it. I don't think that's being female, I think it's just good business."

> *My decision-making style is based on collaboration, not consensus. If it's my role to make the decisions, I get input, but then I make the decision. Once I make a decision, I make sure people are clear about it. I believe in having an open environment. If I make a mistake, I'm not afraid to admit it, which I think adds credibility. Nobody's perfect. If I admit a mistake,*

then it creates a culture where people feel they can be open and honest with me. I model the behavior I'm seeking in them.

Most of the time, I don't think you can overcommunicate. So I try to make sure that people get the information they need. There is more power in sharing information and in having more people understand the big picture. The model we are looking for in leaders in the '90s is sharing versus withholding information. So I'm big on making sure people understand the larger strategy, because they are going to be more successful that way.

Teresa's honesty permeates her actions and her perceptions of how people should work. She firmly believes people shouldn't pretend they know answers when they don't, and her forthright approach has helped her solve problems as well as build relationships. As an example, she described to me "a pivotal experience" she had as a sales manager.

One of my reps was called to the office of an executive who was upset about an account and I went with the rep. The executive was irate, asking questions we didn't have the answers to. Finally, he said, "You don't know a darn thing about this account do you?" And I told him he was exactly right. We had problems getting in to the right people and we couldn't get to ask the questions we needed to ask. And I asked him if he could help us. His behavior immediately changed and he asked us who we wanted him to call. I've had a good relationship with that person ever since.

In the middle of her career, Teresa faced a dilemma that tested her to the extreme and once again put her ethics on the line. But true to form, her honesty, her ability to communicate with her superiors, and her dedication to living by her value system saved her from what could have been a nasty situation.

I had a very uncomfortable situation with a vendor. I was so frustrated I almost left the company. I was very concerned that I could possibly become a scapegoat. Things didn't smell right; they didn't feel right. And my husband, who is a lawyer, was uncomfortable.

Two years later I was deposed in a lawsuit and fortunately some of the records that I had kept helped to save the company money. My instincts were right. I wasn't pleased with the per-

son I was reporting to and I wasn't happy with her ethical busi-
ness judgments. Fortunately, I had a mentor I trusted. He lis-
tened to me and he believed me, and he happened to be over
her. I had gone to her first, but she was not responsive to me. It
was uncomfortable going around her, but I had a lot of history
with my mentor. I knew I could confide in him and it wasn't
going to come back at me. I was lucky I had that history.

I knew when I went to him that I might have to leave the com-
pany. If he had reacted differently, I would have left. Fortu-
nately, he helped me move into another position, but it was
extremely stressful. That was a crossroads. I wasn't going to
stay in that situation. But I did want to give the company a
chance because I knew this was very different from the values
I had seen elsewhere in the company. I can't work someplace
where I don't believe in the value system.

The effectiveness of women's management styles in the workplace
are being validated in studies across the country. Dr. Lawrence
Pfaff, a human resources consultant, conducted two separate studies on management and leadership, in 1994 and 1996. His findings
clearly indicate that men and women manage differently. Women
in his studies were rated as better managers by their employees
and bosses, and in their own self-ratings. Pfaff was surprised at the
findings and told me, "The statistical significance of this data is dramatic." Women outranked men in planning, goal setting, and deci-
siveness as well as in expected areas such as communication skills.
Moreover, the areas in which women ranked as much as ten percentage points higher than men are areas that are extremely important in today's changing business environment: the ability to
facilitate change, to set high standards, to evaluate performance, to
be decisive, and to coach and empower employees.[10]
A Houston-based consulting firm came up with similar findings
in 1994 when it conducted a national survey on leadership styles
and effectiveness in managing diversity. When analyzing survey
results, the researchers wrote, "Someone apparently forgot to tell
women that business is a man's world." Female managers were
rated more favorably than male managers in almost every area.
They were regarded as more effective leaders who "go to bat" for
employees and make employees feel they are working *with* managers, rather than *for* them, and who ask for input, involving
employees in decisions that affect their jobs.[11] In 1996, yet another
study, conducted by the Foundation for Future Leadership, found

that women, on average, scored higher than men, outperforming them in problem solving, communication, and performance. Men scored higher in only one area: managing their own frustrations.[12]

VALUES AND THE "VOICE OF THE SOUL"

Reams have been written in the last decade about the significance of living according to a system of values, of listening to what Thomas Moore calls "the voice of the soul."[13] The women I interviewed stressed the importance of paying attention to values. Over the course of a woman's career, she will face myriad decisions that will call for her to assess her values in relation to her advancement. If a woman doesn't have her own value system clearly established and if she doesn't know what she wants or who she is, she will find it ever more difficult to steer her career and make the right choices.

When 44-year-old Diana Bell, operations manager for Hewlett-Packard's Worldwide Remarketing Group, started her career in 1975, her technical background guided her job search and she focused on looking for jobs in the information systems area. Diana, a woman with strong personal values, explained to me how she pays close attention to her instincts. Diana had become familiar with HP's cultural values when she worked for the company during a summer internship. After finishing her MBA and interviewing with a number of companies, she allowed her intuitions to guide her toward HP because she says, "I always go with my gut."

> You have to be tuned in to what is important to you. I interviewed three times with one of our major competitors: out of undergraduate school, out of graduate school, and once when I was considering leaving HP. And every time it just didn't feel right. It just wasn't me.
>
> At 21 and 23, I wasn't able to articulate whether a company's values were or weren't aligned with mine, but I knew what felt right and what didn't. Years later, I still knew the competitor's environment was not for me. When you have feelings, honor them. Don't think you should work for a company just because it has a great reputation. Make sure it fits you personally. Otherwise, it's like saying "I'm going to be an engineer because they make a lot of money, but I hate math."

Get in touch with what makes you comfortable and then get in touch with your skills. If you put yourself in an environment where your values and cultures are aligned and in an environment that needs your skills, you're 80 percent of the way there. Once inside, the next step is figuring out how to get the incremental support you need.

Diana is a tall, willowy African-American woman who loves to talk. She has a deep, soft openness about her, and a compelling honesty and frankness. She admitted to me that, once or twice during her career, the question of whether her values continued to match HP's surfaced for her as the company downsized and her business unit lost its champions of diversity. Each time she had to "soul-search" to determine whether the match was still a good one for her.

Since I have been at HP, there has never been any kind of overt racism or sexism. In the past, however, there has been benign neglect and there has been lack of focused support to change things. When I came into the business in the computer group in the '70s there was a real focus on developing and grooming women and minorities. Many of the women in this company, who are now at senior levels, came through that computer side of the business, which has many more women, many more blacks than the instrument side. And that's because there was a focus on diversity. Now that layer is gone. We should have had a black vice president by now. But all those people left, so we're off by ten years. The same with women.

But things have begun shifting in terms of making a conscious effort since Lew Platt has been CEO. His actions have been consistent with his word. Since he's come, we've had two female vice presidents. There have been numbers of changes in the last several years as he has begun to free up our energy.

So, there have been times at HP when I have experienced what seemed to be a conflict in values, when things didn't feel right, and I considered leaving. Then something would happen in the environment, either because of HP managers or because of the people I was working with, that reaffirmed my belief in the company. I would see the company stand behind its values as opposed to talking one way and walking another way. So, I decided to stay because I was impressed with their commitment to their basic beliefs, which were in sync with mine.

Diana's experience demonstrates how companies with strong cultural values can provide necessary support even in times of change. Diana started out with HP because it felt comfortable. And she chose to stay even when her business unit experienced chaos, because the underlying corporate values remained intact and aligned with hers. Besides revealing how tuned in she was to her own value system, her story also shows how important corporate leadership is in making sure corporate values are upheld. HP's strong cultural values and beliefs stem from Bill Hewlett and Dave Packard, the company's founders. When the company experienced problems in the 1980s, those values and beliefs served as the anchor that helped to keep the company grounded while it set itself on a new course. In recent years, Lew Platt's helmsmanship has continued to steer the company successfully forward.

Periodically reassessing values is highly recommended by US WEST vice president Teresa Wahlert. After working for several companies in the Bell system over the course of her 26-year career, Teresa has experienced numerous changes and transitions, and when I asked her for one piece of advice to pass on, she zeroed in on soul and values.

> *Continuously soul-search as to what your own value set is and what your own personal feelings are—what you are willing to do and not do to attain the big picture. And do not let yourself get out of balance. Unhappiness and drastic changes in life-styles and careers tend to force themselves on you when you don't have yourself in good alignment. Keep two or three values that you won't compromise no matter what. Be very mindful of what they are and how your career and your choices in life impact them.*
>
> *Always be mindful of the next step as well as the big picture. Sometimes the big picture will develop very differently through each of the transition steps. So don't allow yourself to get frustrated by looking at your present position in relation to the big picture; instead, simply be very conscientious about each step along the way. Careers and personal lives ebb and flow and they impact how you think. It's okay to change your mind. Allow yourself the flexibility to make choices. Continual career evaluation is so important. I have not always done that, and although I have been fortunate, and have not had a tremendous amount of conflict that I couldn't deal with, I have treaded*

dangerously close to compromising, which would have made
me very unhappy.

Although each woman's "soul work" is unique to herself, the themes found in women's definitions of success—goals, balance, relationship, and contribution—emerged as women talked about the values that guided their career choices. And their stories, describing how their values shaped their careers, hold both unique and universal elements.

MISMATCHED VALUES, OUT-OF-SYNC STYLES

It's not always easy to adhere to your own personal style. Jan Tomlinson, who believes people are more willing to follow directions and support the corporate vision when they are kept well informed, uses an open method of management. But when she took over as president of Chubb Insurance of Canada, people weren't used to her consensus style of leading.

> *I like people working on things together. We actually had to sit down and talk about my management style because they said they wanted to be told what to do. I explained to them that it's not that I don't like to make decisions, it's just that I think people buy into decisions more if they are part of the decision-making process. We have spent time working through this process and I think we've come a long way. I just received some feedback from one of the men who told me at first it was hard for him, but when he realized that I was really interested in what he had to say, he was able to use some of the creative ability that he hadn't used for awhile.*
>
> *As a leader, you have to be comfortable in what you're doing, and if you're constantly trying to step out of your natural style into another one, you won't be as effective. One of the advantages organizations have today is the increased understanding of the differences in management styles, and I think that is going to help women be that much more successful.*

As Jan indicates, if you aren't comfortable, if you don't like your organization, if you can't work according to your own values and style, you are not going to be happy. And, therefore, you probably aren't going to do a good job. If you don't do a good job, then you aren't going to succeed. But working according to your own value system and listening to the voice of your soul means that sometimes you will have to make moves that are difficult and even risky.

Twice during the course of her career, Becky Allen experienced a breakdown between her participatory style of management and her organization's. And each time, she decided the best solution was to leave the organization.

After Becky first started working in banking, she progressed fairly quickly and in less than five years was made a bank officer. But as the banking industry underwent enormous changes, Becky says the values and culture at her bank began to change.

> *Our bank was owned by a bank in another part of the state. As branch banking made headway in Florida, the owning bank began to exert more control. The banking industry was changing and the owning bank formed a holding company and started centralizing functions. It was not a very thoughtful process in terms of how they were impacting customers. We were not empowered to get things corrected and it was frustrating. I was in a leadership position at that time, but because I couldn't support what they were doing, I felt like I was getting squeezed.*

When her inclusive and empowering style no longer meshed with the corporate model, her leadership was affected. Faced with this strong conflict in value systems, she told me how discouraged and uncomfortable she became and she finally decided it would be best for her to resign. She left the bank and took a job with a commercial real estate developer only to discover that she was still mismatched. Becky was the developer's representative in the community and at that time, she was highly visible because she had held a number of prominent positions in the community.

> *I worked with him for a year and a half, and everything was fine until he decided to move to Florida. His management style and mine were direct opposites. He was very authoritarian; I am very participatory and team oriented. It just wasn't fun. It was okay when he would come down for a week, stir things up, and then leave, but dealing with him day in and day out was too much. From this experience, I learned that I am really a very independent worker. I like to be in charge. I like to be the person*

making the decisions. It was difficult because it was his busi-
ness and he was paying me, and he didn't like my style and I
didn't like his.

Becky, who was now 40, faced another job switch and was hesitant to go back to banking, saying it left a bad taste in her mouth.
Then, a friend, who was on the board of one of Barnett's banks,
told her Barnett was different and suggested she talk to the bank's
president.

I went to talk with him and found out Barnett really was differ-
ent. I learned not all banks are alike and, certainly, not all com-
panies are alike. I joined Barnett in May of 1984 as the director
of marketing on the senior management team and six months
later I took on their largest office. And in 1986, I became presi-
dent of a small bank in Vero Beach.

By not settling for working in companies that didn't match her
values and finding a company that did, Becky was able to obtain
the kind of support that truly helped her succeed. She has since
held two other CEO positions within the Barnett corporate family.

A key to success is to find a culture that matches your values.
Don't try to force a square peg in a round hole. If it doesn't feel
good and it doesn't fit, there are zillions of companies out there.
I got very uncomfortable with the first bank and I left and I got
very uncomfortable in the second job and I left, and here I am
in the third job and I love it. It's a great fit. It's a company that
values the same kinds of things that I value. So keep trying.

Mismatched values become evident when women can't find comfort and support in the culture or when they can't develop alliances
or meaningful relationships. Because good relationships are
important to a woman's sense of well-being as well as to her career
advancement, when she can't find harmony working with others,
she has much greater difficulty fulfilling the varied aspects of herself and finding success as she defines it.

Early in their careers, Florence Williams and Kwok Lau found
themselves working in environments that left them feeling isolated.
By taking control of their careers at an early stage and leaving to
find more supportive corporate cultures, both women put their
careers on fast tracks.

Florence received her technical training in engineering from a top U.S. auto manufacturer and started out working at one of the organization's manufacturing plants. But as she became familiar with the plant's technical environment, she said she was aghast when she looked around and realized how much she didn't fit—even on a surface level.

> *Not only was I the only black female, but I was also the only black face in the whole technical environment. I suddenly felt all alone as a full-time hire. I knew I needed to get into an environment that was more friendly and supportive. I feared sitting at a drafting board alone until I was 60.*

On the advice of a college friend who worked for Xerox, Florence sent in her resume and was accepted into Xerox's Asset Management Program, specifically designed to help women of color advance in manufacturing. As she proceeded through training, she was given the supports she needed and wanted: People related to her and cared about her personal well-being and professional growth. Florence told me there was nothing bad she could say about her experience at Xerox and the more she learned, the more her self-assurance in the manufacturing environment grew.

> *When you have confidence and work hard, you can do anything. Xerox has been a supportive company in terms of opportunities. Every company has its warts, but I never imagined when I was working for that first company that I could be this happy.*

Xerox not only provided hands-on training that helped her develop skills, but the company demonstrated it valued her by having people in place who were able to watch out for her. Thus, from the beginning of her career at Xerox, Florence benefited from the assistance of strong mentors who recognized the importance of connection and relationship. With the support that the company provided, Florence was able to direct her energies toward excelling at her work. She climbed fairly quickly and by her tenth anniversary at Xerox she achieved a career goal when she was offered a position as a plant manager.

Thirty-eight-year-old Kwok Lau also received her engineering degree from the same auto manufacturer's institute and started working at co-op jobs offered through the company's program.

Kwok is now a vice president of business and operations management at AppleSoft, and has been with Apple Computer for 13 years. She, too, realized how much she didn't fit in the automotive environment and how uncomfortable it made her feel. Although she found her work experiences to be valuable and varied (she even took a rotation in Europe), she told me how isolated she felt and actually described the environment as "hostile." Kwok, too, decided to leave the auto manufacturer. But rather than looking for another job, she recognized she would have more options in the future if she went back to school. Kwok headed east to Cambridge and Harvard, and after she had an MBA degree tucked under one arm and a husband on the other, she approached the job market again and targeted the San Francisco Bay and Silicon Valley areas. Once again drawn to manufacturing, she interviewed with Apple and was happy to discover how much it suited her working style.

> *I saw what a different environment it was. Apple's plants are clean and quiet, almost like laboratories, as compared with the dirty, noisy environment of the automotive assembly plant—at the end of a day there, my clothes were filthy. And the people at Apple were young and dynamic. It was really two extremes. Apple manufacturing also presented technical and process challenges because of the technology of the Apple products themselves.*
>
> *Working in a young company in a young industry without a lot of set rules and set ways to do things was wonderful. People were empowered to try new things as opposed to my past experience where people were more likely to say things like, "You've never done this before," or "You haven't been around here long enough: You don't know how to do that." It was a much more knowledge-based, energy-based type of environment.*

Kwok and Florence experienced dissonance and feelings of isolation that came from a lack of support and relationship. When they found the automotive manufacturing environment too uncomfortable, they left to advance their careers elsewhere. Working within companies where they felt free to be themselves and where they could build supportive relationships enabled both women to climb quickly and find the success they were seeking.

The reason women aren't found in greater numbers in some industrial sectors has more to do with the nature of the environment and the culture that dominates the environment rather than with any overt discrimination. In reflecting on her earlier experience at the auto manufacturer, Kwok realized that many of her feelings of isolation derived, not from race, but more from the fact that she was young, female, and college-educated in a blue-collar, unionized assembly plant. Kwok found success at Apple, a company that was young and entrepreneurial and matched her own energetic style.

Florence thrived at Xerox, a company that values diversity, but she acknowledges that the manufacturing environment can be problematic for women who "want a break" from the "old school" methods where "the manager tells you what to do and you do it. You don't think. You just build machines day after day." She recommends changing plant management staff and putting in people "who are more open and flexible." Then, she says, "You would see a lot more women staying in manufacturing."

When 27-year-old Carmen Monserrate participated in Xerox's Asset Management Program, her rotations on the manufacturing floor enabled her to gain an understanding early in her career about the kinds of environments that meshed, or didn't mesh, with her style of working.

> *My experience in manufacturing, while not necessarily enjoyable, has been valuable. It forced me to learn a lot about myself and what my limits are. It helped me see the way I interact with people and the way I react on the spot. It's an environment that calls for quick thinking and quick reactions. Manufacturing is very dynamic. I enjoy having something different every day; it's not monotonous at all. But it's also very stressful. Manufacturing is so fast-paced; it moves very quickly, and timely delivery is very important. Every minute is thousands of dollars. The stress affects the people and creates conflicts. I haven't ruled out manufacturing; however, the manufacturing floor is not the place for me. I enjoy managing and have some good managing skills. I would like to become a vice president, but I don't think I want to manage industrial workers on the factory floor; I'd rather be a product manager.*

Management training programs with job rotations, like those offered at Xerox, are particularly beneficial: Not only do they provide career development, but they also allow a woman to assess the areas that fit her best in a collapsed amount of time. Thus, like

Carmen, a woman can find out what she likes and doesn't like and get herself on the right track more quickly.

FINDING THE BEST FIT

As industries continue to undergo enormous change, opportunities for women are expanding. Now, more than any other time, women have a chance to be themselves, to work according to their own value system and their own game plans. Women who understand marketplace changes and know how to align themselves with the right company will find greater success in moving their careers forward on the right path at the right pace.

Fast-growing and changing markets tend to develop greater gender blindness and generally become more receptive to women. High-growth areas in female-friendly industries include health care and public relations. And hot career opportunities for women are occurring in the male-dominated, but changing, fields of pharmaceuticals, bioengineering, psychopharmacology, and chemical engineering. Computer software engineering, information systems, and multimedia/entertainment are also sizzling.[14] Male bulwarks of the past are beginning to cave in to women as industries change: In the decade between 1983 and 1993 the number of female managers in male-dominated industries such as computers, automobiles, pharmaceuticals, and steel grew dramatically.[15] But even when there are only small numbers of women in an industry, it doesn't necessarily mean that women are at a disadvantage. When Vela McClam Mitchell worked for Hughes Aircraft, she said, she was the only woman in the country selling guided missiles to the military. She said there was an advantage to being the singular woman in a such a male-dominated, high-tech environment, and with her engaging personality, she never felt isolated.

Monica Boyles, an assistant vice president at McDonald's, claims the restaurant industry is ideal for women and female franchise ownership has grown tremendously over the last 30 years. When McDonald's restaurants first opened in 1955, Monica says that it was unusual for women to own businesses. But, by the 1970s, McDonald's had discovered that wives often took charge of the day-to-day restaurant operations for their husbands; therefore, the company started franchising in earnest to women. Monica also says the franchise environment at McDonald's is like a buddy system that provides "a strong network of support for women who might not have had the same amount of business exposure as men."

The people and culture of an organization can be a make-or-break factor. When the culture fits a woman, it enhances her potential for success. The nurturing environment at Gannett helped Joyce Bailey, director of labor relations and labor counsel, to develop professionally.

> *One of the things Gannett did to nurture me was to provide an environment in which I always felt I could ask questions. Regardless of the setting, whether it was in group meetings or sitting around a huge conference table, no question was off-limits. If you can ask questions, you can grow. I did not feel intimidated or put off because I did not understand something. I was not afraid to ask.*
>
> *That type of environment nurtures you in the sense that once you feel free to ask basic questions without fear of reprisal, you will continue to feel confident about asking other kinds of questions. If you are made to feel stupid, it stymies your growth. Once someone feels they have asked a dumb question, they will not ask any more questions; they will not risk the ridicule. This cuts off knowledge and potential leaders.*
>
> *Another thing Gannett did was to give me a lot of latitude so that I could develop my own schedules, make my own decisions, and, quite frankly, have an opportunity to fail. My boss has given me the opportunity to come up with solutions and defend them. I think that is nurturing because it gives me the opportunity to grow. He did not breathe down my neck, telling me to do it this way or that way. He gave me a chance to develop my own style, my own technique, and my own approach to problem solving.*

Organizational cultures steeped in hierarchical, command-and-control models can present barriers that take too much energy to surmount, while open, supportive cultures provide women with the backing and assistance they need to grow as leaders.

SPEAKING FROM THE SOUL

The more that women understand what is important to them and let the voices of their souls guide them, the greater chance they have for growth and development. With 48 percent of the pipeline full of women, there is enough power and force to support and push women's values into organizational cultures. Over and over, women told me they wanted to know their efforts added value— that others benefited from their presence. Because women have a multifaceted approach to success that includes others, when women succeed, everyone succeeds—employees, customers, and organizations.

Women have been in the system long enough to inject it with feminine values. The influence of corporate women is beginning to be felt, and the more that feminine values permeate the corporation, the better the organizational system will be. In her book, *The Chalice and the Blade*, scholar and futurist Riane Eisler claims that throughout the course of history, whenever women have publicly injected their "female ethos," they have "impacted society for the better."[16] As more women inject their female values and more collaborative and open management styles into their companies, they, too, will have a beneficial impact on their organizational cultures. As women continue to talk about success that includes balance and benefits to others as well as bottom-line goals, the potential for reshaping organizational roles and structures grows. The more that individual women, like the women in this chapter, make decisions based on their own personal, feminine value systems, and the more they give voice to their own perspectives of what work means to them, the more they will find satisfaction and success—and the more the company itself will be stimulated to change, seduced by the power of female leadership at all levels of the organization.

NAVIGATING CORPORATE CORRIDORS

Take control and take charge of your career. You have to take your career seriously. It's a huge part of your life. You're at work more than you are home, but people often don't give it enough thought. People plan vacations for months, but how many hours do you think people devote to planning their careers?

BETH DUDLEY, Vice President
Baxter Healthcare Corporation

Career management is like sailing. To get from Point A to Point B on a sailboat, you must not only have good charts to plot your course, but you must also be aware of the vagaries of Mother Nature and carry with you a great deal of respect for her changing temperament. This respect makes you aware of the need for skill—you must know what you are doing and you must do it well. And you must also be flexible—the winds can suddenly shift, calling for quick responses. Mother Nature also demands that you choose your crew carefully. In the worst of times, they can determine your life or death. In the best of times, they provide the skill and guidance that enable you to reach your destination, and, along the way, they offer companionship and camaraderie. While navigating, it is also essential to keep checking your course and to make the adjustments that are required to keep your boat headed in the right direction. It is also wise to check your chart for safe harbors: Sometimes it might be necessary to pull in and fix broken riggings or pick up new equipment and supplies. On a sailboat it's also important to know how to handle a number of functions. If you encounter rough seas, or if crew members become incapacitated, you might need to do a variety of tasks yourself, and having learned only one function can put you in jeopardy.

In a similar fashion, women need to respect the vagaries of the Corporate Father. How well a woman navigates the corridors of her corporation depends on the way she plans her career, the positions that she takes, the mentors with whom she aligns, and the corporate supports she uses. Career strategies, of course, ultimately depend on career goals. For some female executives, the goal is to go as high in the corporation as possible; for others, the goal is to rise within a particular staff function. Each goal requires different strategic positioning and the development of different technical skills, but all goals require forging significant alliances and the development of leadership abilities. And all require excellence. In today's changed business world, women who succeed continually develop their skills in order to enhance their levels of performance. Women with high-level performance skills can steer the course of their careers just as effectively as men can.

In this chapter, we'll hear from women who are corporate climbers in both line and staff positions. Their strategies demonstrate the value of proper positioning—figuring out how to get on the right rung of the corporate ladder and knowing how to expand a web of influence. Their stories illustrate specific strategies and techniques for proactively planning careers, rotating functional assignments, linking with mentors, and increasing knowledge and management skills.

CATHY SPOTTS: ASSESSING THE ODDS IN CAREER STRATEGIES

Maybe the precision required in the mathematical background of Cathy Spotts accounts for the precision in her approach to career development, but, whatever the cause, this vice president at Baxter Healthcare Corporation is an ardent planner who has carefully plotted the course of her career. Only 35 years old, Cathy is already a vice president and general manager of the IV Therapy group at Baxter. Cathy didn't start out directing her career—she was given five different promotions and two relocations before she realized that if she took charge she would be able to select the jobs she wanted. She told me it is critical to be proactive, to know what you want, and to plan a time line for how you want your career to unfold. Through the use of a checklist and job-rating ratio she devised, Cathy has been able to assess the value of possible positions to her career progression. Her checklist contains her personal and professional goals as well as the skills she possesses and those she must acquire to get to the next step on her plan. By honestly acknowledging her strengths and weaknesses, she says she has been able to evaluate the degree to which particular jobs will build her expertise and advance her career.

> *When I move into a job, a higher percentage of it has to leverage my experience, but a certain percentage also has to provide opportunity for me to develop new skills. The ratio I use is no more than 70/30 and no less than 60/40. Leverage your skill sets into new areas but make sure you accept new positions with the understanding that you should walk away with more skills than you came in with.*

Before she took control, Cathy said management moved her into positions that leveraged her prior experience 100 percent: Therefore she didn't acquire much more knowledge than she had going into the job. The company promoted her into positions that were a good fit—she had done similar jobs and done them well. But the company didn't take into account her need to expand and stretch when it lined up promotions for her.

> *When I choose jobs, I make sure I will learn a new skill I can take with me. I make evaluations based on a long-term perspective and on what I enjoy doing. I have turned down jobs, even though they were higher paying, because I wouldn't learn new skills—I enjoy learning and it motivates me. Using a ratio means you have to be willing to take risks. You will have to learn 30 to 40 percent of the job, which means you have to be willing to get a little uncomfortable.*

Cathy determined the skills she needed for particular jobs by asking headhunters to describe the ideal characteristics they looked for in potential candidates. She told me she had initially avoided talking to headhunters when they called, but her attitude changed after she saw how many transitions were taking place as Baxter merged with American Hospital Supply, her original employer. She realized recruiters could help her make better career decisions by providing her with valuable information about her market worth and the skills she needed to qualify for particular positions. Even as a general manager, she said she continues to evaluate her progress and thinks carefully about the professional and the personal implications and ramifications of each decision she makes.

> *I still use my list and one box yet unchecked is international, which entails making a pretty big decision. I have to ask myself if I want that box checked. If I don't, what does that mean? How does that affect my personal and professional goals?*

In addition to using her checklist to evaluate whether jobs will stretch her sufficiently, Cathy also assesses the environment and the person to whom she will report before she accepts positions.

> *I know what kind of a culture I thrive in and what kind stifles me. Having the right culture and the right boss is just as important as some of the other criteria. I look for people who surround themselves with good people, both men and women.*

When I asked her what other advice she could give around job selection, Cathy emphasized the importance of communicating goals during the interview process.

> *If you go into an interview not knowing what you want, it comes across so clearly. It makes a big difference for someone interviewing you when they see how well you've evaluated yourself and can articulate how well you fit with the job—what you bring to it and what you'll learn from it.*

In the process of planning and strategizing the best way to move her career forward, Cathy has also moved laterally. Cathy, who is a CPA, started out as the director of finance for one of her company's businesses, but as she contemplated her career growth she decided a move to marketing would enhance her understanding of the business.

> *I decided if I wanted to go on to be a controller, I needed to learn more about the business instead of just knowing the numbers. I started thinking about ways to get involved with the customer. This was right after the merger in 1985 and, at that time, people did not move from one function to another. But I began net-*

*working informally and took the opportunity whenever I had
interactions with people to let them know that I was interested
in moving.*

Once again, the women I interviewed show they were ahead of
the times in using leading-edge management techniques. In the
previous chapter, women like Shaunna Sowell and Carol Tuthill
intuitively initiated management processes such as teamwork and
cross-functional training in their areas; here, Cathy illustrates that
she, too, recognized the value of gaining cross-functional experience—only she applied it to her own professional development.
Viewing marketing as a stepping-stone, Cathy took a big risk and
jumped down from her managerial position in the finance department to a marketing position two levels down. It wasn't an easy
jump, and she said the people in finance let her know she wouldn't
be welcome back, while the marketing people were not waiting to
catch her with open arms either.

*Taking lateral moves can be risky, but it's also freeing to be
able to put yourself in a situation of sink or swim versus allowing the company to make that decision for you. I figured that if
I was as good as I thought I was, I could move fast. However,
the culture wasn't used to that type of move. Today the environment is different and there is much more of an open door policy, but, at the time, I was probably one of the first people to
move out of finance.*

Cathy's gamble paid off: She gained valuable experience that
opened up new opportunities for her. Before the concept became
popular, Cathy had realized how people from different functions
can learn from each other.

*The key is leveraging strengths. I appreciated what I could
learn from the people in marketing and knew how I could help
them understand the financial ramifications of their marketing
decisions.*

When Cathy first managed the finance department, she was only
22 and had 12 people reporting to her. By 23, she had 35 people.
She said her initial management abilities were "totally gut and
instinct" and stemmed from her family background—as one of
eight children, she had to learn how to negotiate well. When she

took her lateral move from finance into marketing, however, no one reported to her. Yet she saw this as an advantage.

> *I learned more about managing when I had no one reporting to me: I was able to concentrate on what motivated me. It gave me a whole new perspective because I was able to assess my own reactions to how others behaved, communicated with me, and set objectives. It was a really good learning experience.*

Managers often shy away from lateral moves out of fear they will lose time, prestige, or income, but long-term career gains can outweigh short-term losses—lateral moves can be opportunities to broaden skills that lead to better opportunities and to expanded networks of people.

As Cathy sought to learn more about her company's business and customers, she accepted a sales management position because she believed that directing a sales force would hone her managerial skills—different abilities are needed to manage people spread out over a territory as opposed to managing people in a corporate setting where interactions tend to occur on a daily basis. Cathy followed the sales management job with another marketing assignment and calculated that it would take 18 months to get the experience she wanted. One year later, however, the company offered her a regional sales manager's job that paid about $30,000 more—but Cathy turned it down.

> *I told them I did not want my resume to look like I simply took a coffee break in marketing. People thought I was nuts for turning down the regional sales job, but I was looking at long-term benefits. The marketing director's job would really round out my marketing experience and I am motivated by doing what I enjoy. And the sales job did not meet the criteria for my job ratio: It would not have sufficiently enhanced my learning and skills.*

The time Cathy stays in a particular job depends on what she is trying to learn and accomplish. As she told me, "Neither too long, nor too short is good." In her well-thought-out plan, she not only determines which skills require honing, but she understands herself and how much time she needs to learn skills and develop expertise. All this planning on Cathy's part not only helped her reach her present level, but along the way it provided her with a sense of security.

Cross-functional experience protects you against the frenzy of today's downsizing. If Baxter came to me tomorrow to say, "Sorry, you're out," the fact that I've worked in so many different divisions and so many different functions gives me the confidence that I could go out and find something else with much greater ease than had I stayed in one function or one division. With any restructuring we've undergone, I've felt comfortable knowing I had skills to take with me.

Cathy has held about 12 jobs in 14 years, rotating through finance, marketing, and sales. Prior to each move, she contacted people to set up informational interviews, letting people know the types of jobs that were of interest to her. After using this technique to move around, her visibility increased and people began calling her from other businesses to offer her positions. By deliberately and purposefully gaining a well-rounded view of the business and its customers, by expanding her functional and managerial skills, and by aligning with the right people, Cathy has steadily climbed Baxter's corporate ladder at the same time that she has widened her circle of contacts throughout the organization.

BETH DUDLEY: ASK AND YOU SHALL RECEIVE

Beth Dudley, the vice president of quality management and regulatory affairs at Baxter, also used a fairly precise plan to achieve her present position. But because Beth's interest focused on the staff function of quality, she structured her plan somewhat differently from Cathy's. Beth, 46, started out as a teacher and switched to a corporate career when her husband went back to school after returning from Vietnam. Once she entered the corporate world, Beth, with a background in science, knew how she wanted her career to progress and clearly articulated her goals to her managers. Beth has never been hesitant to speak out in order to get what she wants for herself or for her organization.

When I started with Baxter, I knew I wanted to be the quality manager for the plant. And so I sat down with my boss and said: "This is where I am today and this is where I want to be five years from now. What are the skills I need to develop to get there?" And through the years in my performance reviews, I always close by saying: "I heard the things that I am doing

*right; now, tell me what I am doing wrong so I can change it."
And that's always been my focus. Improve on the areas that
need improvement and have a long-term vision in mind of
where you want to go.*

*I firmly believe in spending time planning. People should
decide where they want to be three years, five years, and ten
years into the future. The first two questions I ask people during interviews are: What do you want? and Where do you see
yourself in the future? The job applicants who impress me are
the ones who have really thought about it. And you can pick
them out quickly.*

Interim goals such as three- and five-year markers not only
become milestones, but they can also be places from which to view
the corporate environment with a new perspective. A woman's
vision can shift as her environment changes and as she matures as
a manager, but, by making assessments and reevaluating goals
periodically, she can make sure her vision, goals, and present reality remain aligned. With planning, barriers can also be more effectively surmounted. After four years with Baxter, Beth said she ran
into a blockade, but it had nothing to do with gender: There were
too many qualified senior people in her plant and, in order to be
promoted to plant quality manager, Beth realized she would have
to relocate out of state. Once more she told her boss what she
wanted.

*I took control of my career by telling my boss I was interested in
learning and growing and that I would be very interested in
any opportunities for relocation. When an opportunity did come
up, they made me an offer.*

Taking constructive action provides control over career direction. Beth says she finds it frustrating to listen to people complain
when they haven't done the things they should to help themselves
succeed.

*Some people get upset because they have worked somewhere
for years and they are still doing the same thing. I want to
shake them. Is that their boss's fault? Is it the company's fault?
Or is it their fault? People who don't know what they want and
who are not willing to take a risk will always blame something
or someone else. You have to decide what it is you want to do*

and be committed to doing it. It's perfectly okay to change your mind and to make adjustments as you go along. But some people don't even have a vision of where they want to be, so consequently they just accept the status quo.

Beth hasn't been afraid of risk or of speaking out in defense of her strong beliefs. In fact, her feelings of success come from knowing that she has made a difference.

I am really vocal. I've never felt intimidated with the group because when I believe something, I believe it passionately. I take the risk and speak up. From that standpoint, it has been interesting to watch things change. I changed the culture in our organization around quality. And any difficulties I might have had, had nothing to do with being female: The person I replaced was so bad that the culture viewed quality negatively. So, I had to sell the worth and credibility of the quality organization and what we had to offer. I feel like I changed that culture and I am recognized for the impact I had. From my standpoint, I have so much influence on so many great people. I'm very, very happy and satisfied with where I am today and what I have accomplished. And I've gotten here because of good, honest hard work, loyalty and commitment.

Yet Beth has no desire to climb higher, saying she loves the quality area. Even though she has remained within one function, she has established a wide network of influence within the manufacturing environment at Baxter. Beth is responsible for 35 plants and believes in "management-by-walking-around." She told me she visits each plant at least once a year and, as well as meeting people who work during the day, she also likes to visit people who work the second and third shifts, because, as she says, "Everyone is important."

Beth not only tries to effect change in business situations, but she has also raised her voice to make changes in social networking activities in her organization. Historically, women have complained about their exclusion from some of the old-boy networks, such as the golf course. But Beth, who doesn't play golf, did not let male social practices stymie her.

When you go to a business meeting or strategic planning session or whatever, typically, the afternoon of entertainment is golf. For me, if I want to be honest, that's been difficult. I don't play golf. Yet, I play to keep the spirit of teamwork. I'll joke and ask the guys to let me drive the cart, but they insist that I need to learn to play. However, I don't feel like I need to learn to play—golf is not something I really enjoy. But I wanted to help because I knew I wasn't going to be the last one to be in that position. I wanted to influence the group and make a difference.

I don't think it's a "good old boys' club" or anything like that. They just don't think; it's ingrained in them. They play golf on weekends and I don't think they even think about the fact that somebody else might not enjoy it at all. I told them if they were fishing or bungee jumping or anything other than golf I would jump at the chance to do something—believe me I would much rather fish.

We need to feel comfortable about what we want, and it's our responsibility to give men honest feedback. I was perfectly okay telling my boss how I felt and I joked with the guys, and in that way I got my point across. There are a lot of different ways to give feedback.

Beth's willingness to speak out and make suggestions for change helped to raise awareness within her organization. Now, other activities are scheduled into social events, benefiting both female and male nongolfers. By speaking out for her personal career goals, the needs of her quality organization, and social activities for herself and others, Beth has moved herself and her organization forward. And as the vice president of quality and regulatory affairs, she has achieved her ultimate career goal.

LYNN CRUMP: THE RIGHT TIME FOR ROTATING BETWEEN LINE AND STAFF POSITIONS

In assessing the best ways for women to climb corporate ladders, the significance of holding line positions is often stressed. In a recent Catalyst study, 82 percent of the CEOs interviewed claimed that lack of operational line experience is a major reason women are held back from advancing vertically to a CEO position. The majority of the female corporate officers in this particular Catalyst study did, indeed, hold positions in staff functions, such as secretary or general counsel instead of CFO or COO. Yet slightly more than half the women in the study claimed it was male informal networks and stereotypes that presented the biggest barriers to advancement, rather than lack of access to the line.[1]

I find this line-versus-staff question particularly intriguing. Men and women seem to hold different beliefs about barriers. Is line experience so necessary? And if it is, what keeps women from it? Do women end up in human resources, public relations, marketing communications, and law because they are forced to remain within the confines of these staff functions, or do they migrate there because they enjoy the work?

When I was contemplating graduate programs, two areas interested me: communication and human resources. Later, while I was working in communication and heard the argument that women were forced to cluster in lower-paying "pink ghettos," I questioned the validity of that argument. I was there because I liked it. After working as the director of communication for a small market research company, I turned to the nonprofit sector in order to *make a difference* in the world. I spent one year as the executive director of a small foundation, where I was responsible for day-to-day operations, managing the budget and the investment portfolio, and working with the board. I am not afraid of numbers and created new spreadsheets and databases in order to improve the system and upgrade operational procedures. But I wasn't happy. I can work with figures, but I don't like them. I like to work with words and people. I returned to communication because I found it tapped my creative juices and turned me on far more than administration and finance did.

A key point the women I interviewed stressed—and one that is showing up more and more in popular business literature for both men and women—is that success comes when people work in areas in which they excel, areas that play to their strengths, areas that make them happy. Moreover, as the business environment rapidly changes, there is no surefire path to the top. In 1989, a survey by Korn Ferry, the largest executive search firm in the world, found that the best path for climbing was finance, but in 1996—a mere seven years later—another survey by the firm found that marketing and international experience outweighed the numbers route.[2]

Today, both line and staff positions *are* available to women, and women who want to climb understand they need experience in both functional areas. The corporate women I spoke to emphasized the significance of rotating through both staff and line jobs to develop a full perspective of the business without getting stereotyped in either area. The trick is knowing which position will provide essential experience within the right time frame. Knowing when to take particular positions calls for foresight, a thorough assessment of the variables, and a good understanding of timing.

At McDonald's, where careers progress through corporate staff functions or out in the field overseeing franchise operations, Lynn Crump, 39, faced difficult career choices several times in her career. But her ability to evaluate the variables and to trust her intuition enabled her to climb to the position of regional vice president.

Lynn had held mainly operational positions before becoming global director of training in 1991. Then, within the brief span of a day, she received two promotional opportunities: a regional manager's position and an assistant vice presidency in training. Lynn told me line responsibilities are valued at McDonald's and competition for them is intense. Field positions leading to an officer status proceed from regional manager to senior regional manager to vice president. Managers devote themselves to making regional manager—the first rung of the upper-management ladder. In choosing between the two, Lynn said she had to weigh the importance of giving up the "big kahuna" of running a territory, with its responsibilities for sales and profits, against staying in training but getting herself closer to her goal of becoming an officer.

> *It forced me to think really hard—I wanted to be an officer of the company, but everyone works towards the regional manager's position. I agonized over my decision. I struggled with what my peers would think. I finally took the staff position. My goal was to become an officer, and the board of directors had to approve the promotion into the vice presidency. It was the best move I ever made. I ran a global piece of the company with an officer status and by the time I finished doing that everything fell into place.*

Timing and corporate strategies were factors that weighed in favor of choosing a staff job. McDonald's had just formed a task force to examine a ten-year plan for the company, which included reengineering, global positioning, and tactical strategies. In her global training position, Lynn became one of several junior people on the task force. Working in a global training position while the company was focusing on developing global strategies put her in a visible position where she was able to spend time with the senior-most officers of the company. She was also able to demonstrate her organizational skills, initiating a new centralized training department for corporate personnel.

After she had been an assistant vice president of training for about two years, the opportunity to climb in a line position again presented itself. The zone vice president for the southern territory, which included Atlanta, offered Lynn the chance to manage the territory. Again, Lynn had to make a difficult choice. Several critical variables influenced her decision: Atlanta is one of McDonald's largest territories in the United States, the Olympics were coming, and the culture held line jobs in esteem.

> *The COO wanted me to stay in training and offered me a full vice presidency with additional responsibilities. So this was the second time I was being offered a corporate and a line position. Our culture truly values line positions. I had achieved visibility and established relationships. Before I took the position I talked to four of the eight executive officers. Several of them told me that in the future, being a regional manager was not necessarily going to be a prerequisite for being a senior officer and it wouldn't hurt me to stay in training. But I realized that cultures are slow to change and the culture still perceived the need to have that line experience.*

Other important factors that affected Lynn's decision concerned changes in reporting arrangements. The training department started to get lean and the COO, to whom Lynn directly reported, decided to bring in a new person, adding a layer between them. Sometimes transitions in reporting structures can be difficult and loaded with political fallout. Lynn weighed the new staff arrangement against the opportunity presented in the line position: If she took the territory, she would be reporting directly to the zone vice president, who at the time was one of the highest-ranking females at McDonald's. Lynn wanted an opportunity to receive guidance from a senior female executive, so, deciding that the timing was right, this time she chose the line, and, again, her choice paid off handsomely. She became vice president, running operations in Atlanta, and the 1996 Summer Olympic Games were played in her territory. Lynn says she had learned not to be afraid of doing things in a nontraditional way.

> *I have adopted a personal credo to always look for the piece that's different on which you can leave your individual stamp.*

Working in the field, Lynn oversees and approves site selection for new restaurants in her territory, which is strategically significant since McDonald's is one of the few fast-food restaurants that owns its own real estate. She is also responsible for making sure that marketing strategies are approved and followed by franchisees at the local level. Income is her responsibility and she says she is "the ultimate decision maker" with regard to how business is conducted in her territory.

Her advice to women who want to climb corporate ladders is to identify positions in which decisions are made and to get into jobs with authority. But she also cautions women not to get buried in the minutiae. Women, according to Lynn, can run into trouble trying to separate what's important from what's not.

> *Women have a tendency, unlike men, to think that everything is important. Men are awesome at merchandising and promoting only the things they know to be, or think can be made to be, important. They screw up so much other stuff, but what they talk about is the stuff that's important. And ears open. Women talk about all the little pieces of the puzzle and who cares, nobody is listening.*
>
> *Even if a hundred important things are put in front of you, you better know which ten, or which two, are really the most important. Once you can identify the important things you can put the lion's share of your effort there. Develop a knack for finding out what is really important when you are talking to your boss—what is really important to him and to the company's strategical and tactical plans.*

Lynn's own story provides a good example of how to tease out those important items: When she took over her territory, which covers 450 restaurants in Georgia, Alabama, and part of South Carolina, her peers advised her to visit every restaurant. Instead, she singled out the 90 franchise owners in her territory and spent quality time with them asking them how they approached their businesses and what they needed. In order to implement strategies and tactics, she told me she knew their support was critical: She needed to build good relationships with them that would help drive the business.

> *In my capacity, there are two things which are most important: customer satisfaction in our restaurants and income. I don't ignore other facets of business. I don't let anything fall off my plate, but I will delegate responsibility for the other things to someone else. My primary responsibility is to make sure customers are satisfied and to increase sales and income.*
>
> *To wind the process down to its lowest level makes no sense to me. I'm not saying every restaurant isn't important. The restaurants are where the rubber meets the road, but I had to make an impression on those 90 owners about the quality of the environment and the quality of service that we want to provide to our customers. Rather than touring 450 restaurants, I got more leverage out of spending time with 90 owners.*
>
> *So I strongly recommend looking for the highest leverage item. I tend to look for bigger pieces. If there is one small piece that is critical to the large picture, I'll deal with it, but I tend to focus on larger items.*

Understanding what's important and what isn't and knowing how to leverage the two are learned skills that Lynn says come from working in the organization.

> *A novice cannot say I'm going to deal with the big picture and go for it because a novice won't have the knowledge or the skill to understand which little pieces are the critical ones that need to be dealt with.*

One way to begin honing issues down to the few critical factors is to observe other successful people—the way they address problems and issues can serve as a model. I asked Lynn what other advice she could offer and she said women should be careful about the alliances they make.

> *Make sure potential mentors are going to be there for you and that they are well viewed by senior management. Find out if they have been successful in helping people move and in promoting people. Make sure you know their history of mentoring.*

I also asked Lynn, an African American, if she had any special advice for women of color and she emphasized the need for minority women to "have a strong sense of entitlement."

You are entitled to the same things in life that everybody else is. If you don't have a sense of entitlement, you will back off and not volunteer for projects; you will not recognize what you can truly achieve because you will see yourself as less than you are. Don't be arrogant. Be professional. Be sincere. Be all the things you should be, but have a strong sense of entitlement that drives you to take risk and to understand what you can achieve. And whatever you need to do, speak up and go for it.

Lynn's ability to go for it, to weigh the variables carefully in order to make the right choices, and to align with the right people has resulted in 21 promotions in 23 years. She says she has been "blessed" to travel on a two-way street to success: She has given the company her all and, in turn, she has been rewarded.

GLORIA SANTONA: HEADED TOWARD CORPORATE COUNSEL

In contrast to Lynn's rotation through line and staff jobs, Gloria Santona is strictly on a staff track. Gloria is the associate general counsel and secretary of the corporation at McDonald's and, unlike Lynn, she hasn't been pulled between the two functional areas. As a lawyer, she doesn't desire a line position. Her goal is to become the first staff woman on the top management team and she sees herself well-positioned to do so.

I've chosen law, so I don't feel trapped. At various points, I thought about the line, but never seriously. I happen to be a very good lawyer. It's very amenable with my personality and skill set. There are numbers of companies with CEOs who are attorneys so, in my mind, I don't perceive it to be a limiting factor, although I really have no desire to be a CEO. I like what I'm doing and I'm really good at what I do. I made a choice. Now the path I've chosen might seem more difficult to some, but in some ways it's easier for me, because it's more comfortable and I enjoy it.

This company has only one line of business: operating and franchising restaurants. For me to jump from law into operations would be a huge change, probably more so than in other companies that have more diversified businesses. Yet, I have a good friend in a staff function who chose to switch tracks and go into a line function. She is now on a fast operations track because she wants to break into top management, and she believes operations will help her to get there.

Actually, we probably have two or three lawyers who have chosen to go the operations route, but I've chosen not to do that. It might be a little bit tougher for me to make the break into the top ranks in a staff position, but I'm willing to do what it takes.

At 45, Gloria has learned to recognize where her strongest skills lie. In her early 20s, she told me she made two disappointing attempts to get into medical school, and when she didn't succeed she took a job in labor and employee relations, which called for her to work closely with several lawyers. One of the men recognized her capabilities and convinced her to pursue law.

He told me I had more skills than I was using in HR and he encouraged me, actually he badgered me, into taking the law boards. I took them and did very well, but since I had such a bad experience applying to medical schools, I was reluctant to go down the applications path again; so, I applied to schools as much to keep him quiet and off my back as anything else. Interestingly enough, I was accepted to all three law schools I applied to, and knowing at 24 that I didn't want to be in HR for the rest of my life, I decided I had nothing to lose by getting a law degree. I ended up loving it.

The feedback and extra push she received from him helped spur her forward and after finishing law school she was determined to make up for the time she felt she had lost trying to get into medical school. And, according to Gloria, the corporate environment helped to speed her law career.

I was very hung up on age. I thought if I went to a law firm, I would be two years older than everyone else when I made partner and that thought crazed me. I am very ambitious and aggressive. I thought a corporate environment would propel me forward faster. McDonald's provided me with just the right mix. It was the late '70s and the company was young and growing very quickly. The culture was energized. I could see the opportunities to move ahead quickly. When I interviewed for the job and was asked where I wanted to be in ten years, I said I wanted to be the general counsel. I was quite naive.

But I did have stretch goals and those goals have helped me move along.

The corporate world offered me a breadth of experience that I don't think I would have found in a law firm. I probably would have specialized in one area and stayed there for my entire career. At McDonald's, I have been able to function in a different context and get involved in the business, which is really appealing to me. I chose this company because it seemed to provide opportunities to move ahead quickly and I was right. I was out of law school for a year and I was working very closely with a senior executive vice president and chief financial officer as well as the treasurer; had I been with a law firm providing services to McDonald's, I probably wouldn't have met them for five or six years.

Gloria has worked for McDonald's for 18 years and, as associate general counsel, she is close to her career goal. Working in McDonald's supportive environment, Gloria has had the opportunity to develop her management abilities and has learned more about her own natural style of leadership. In one of her promotions she was given responsibility for the real estate department—the largest legal function in the company—and she learned to rely on her intuition to manage larger groups.

I was used to dealing with people on a one-on-one basis and winning them over on an individual level. This larger group was a real challenge for me. All of a sudden I had people whom I didn't know well and I thought "How am I going to do this?" So, I operated from instinct. To me, the most important thing is having integrity. If people know what you are about, and know that you are consistent with your values, they respect you. And it's fairly easy to be respected if you have integrity. Once I reminded myself of that, it was much easier than I thought it would be. People saw I was walking the talk; they had a sense I was going to be fair. They might not have liked me or wanted to invite me to dinner, but they knew they would have a fair shot with me. That was a very satisfying and gratifying experience.

Managers require practice and experience to hone their talents, especially if they have broad and weighty responsibilities, which is why it takes time to groom CEOs. As a lawyer with expertise in finance and securities, Gloria said she has concentrated on developing her technical skills, but as she has progressed up the legal track at McDonald's, she has found that her focus and approach to work have shifted and she now concentrates more on developing her leadership abilities.

> *I'm a very good corporate lawyer and I could continue doing corporate transactions well for the rest of my career, but now I spend more and more time looking outside at trends, at what's going on, at what the law is going to look like tomorrow, and what laws are going to impact our business two, three, and four years from now. We're in an era of change, and you have to embrace change and lead it, or you will be left behind. I plan ways to build a foundation to deal with that change. That's totally re-energized me: I realize I can be a change agent. Fortunately, I work in an environment where that is welcomed; so, it's been great. But it has taken me time to develop these leadership skills—I wasn't ready ten years ago.*

Female corporate counsels are making some of the best headway at the uppermost levels of corporations and their numbers in Fortune 500 companies have notably increased. The American Corporate Counsel Association estimates that women hold one out of five general counsel positions—the top in-house legal post.[3] Gloria recognizes that, because of the way the corporation has historically worked, it might take her more effort or even a little more time to reach her goal, but she wants to do it her own way.

LUCY BERROTERAN: GAINING VISIBILITY OFF THE FINANCE PATH

What I found striking about Lucy Berroteran, a 35-year-old communication manager in the finance department at J.C. Penney, is her strong personality and sense of humor. I interviewed Lucy over the phone, but somehow I have a vivid visual impression of her. If I ever get to meet her I will be very curious to see how well my image matches reality. What I can say from talking to her is that she is a vibrant, energized, outspoken, aggressive, Hispanic CPA who admits that sometimes she is even "loud."

Lucy started her career with J.C. Penney while she was in school, working part-time in the shoe department of a store in El Paso,

Texas. Two factors influenced the future direction of her career: She switched her major in college from music to accounting, and her very first boss took an interest in helping her develop a career.

> *He convinced me to fly to Dallas and interview with our account-ing center there. I hadn't thought about leaving El Paso, but I went because I was loyal to him and the company. I had spent four and a half years with people working around my schedule. My books were always back in the stockroom and I read when business got slow. People cared about me and wanted me to succeed.*

Another influential person and role model in Lucy's life has been her mother, who also worked at J.C. Penney while her four children were growing up. Lucy told me how significant her mother was in her professional development.

> *My father is really a wonderful man, but my mother has been my mentor. The entire time I was growing up, my mother told me how special I was, and there isn't anyone who can change that belief I developed in myself because of her. She has been a tremendous inspiration in my career. She worked at J.C. Pen-ney for 25 years selling fine jewelry. When I was working part-time in the shoe department during college, I used to tell people their children needed new shoes; my mother convinces women they need a new diamond.*

In the early part of Lucy's career, she followed a traditional finance track, moving from accounting centers in Dallas and Pitts-burgh to manager of financial reporting in New York, where she developed an overall understanding of the business as she compiled the company's financials and produced the Securities and Exchange Commission filings and the annual report. In her next promotion, to merchandise controller, she interacted with suppliers and came to love the retail atmosphere in New York, but it was her promotion to a newly created position as the director of the Minor-ity and Women Owned Business Development Program that cata-pulted her into the limelight. Working as the head of a program in a different function added new skills and put her in a highly visible position. The job brought her out of her finance track and into con-stant contact with customers, suppliers, and senior management. Because of the visibility she received and the relationships she established, she told me "the job was the best thing" for her. She became extremely active in J.C. Penney's diversity initiatives, helping to enhance communication and understanding throughout her company. She took part in the women's advisory team, the minority advisory team, the diversity task force, and the mentoring program.

> *My goal is to make people comfortable with the fact that I am a woman, an accountant, and a minority. If I can do that, then maybe the next person who comes along will find it easier. Unless we figure out how to communicate with different groups, we aren't going to continue to grow our business and attract the best suppliers to provide the kind of merchandise that we need. We have to figure out what it's going to take for men and women to work together effectively. And that ability to communicate well doesn't just affect our workforce, it also affects our customer. If you can't communicate effectively with the person—man or woman—sitting in the office next to you, you will more than likely have problems communicating with your male and female customers.*

Lucy headed the Minority and Women Owned Business Development Program for two and a half years. Working more closely with customers and suppliers and assuming responsibility for public relations activities, Lucy not only gained cross-functional skills, but she also acquired a broader understanding of her company and a deeper level of historical knowledge. She said the job also heightened her awareness about career planning, and now she wants to become even more of a generalist so that she can continue to grow with the company.

> *In retail, there are unwritten career paths: If you're a store manager, you grow up to be a district manager and a regional vice president; if you're a buyer you grow up to be a merchandise manager and a divisional vice president. When you're in an area like finance, you have to do something different if you are going to continue to grow with the company. In order for me to be competitive, I need to be able to bring something different to the table. I'm a CPA, with a finance background, and I can solve problems and do public relations. I gained a global understanding of the company through my financial reporting experience. In the Minority and Women Owned Business Development Program, I interacted with purchasing in every area in the com-*

pany. I also communicated with senior people and with people at all levels.

I've learned it's necessary to have extra experience that you can pull out of your career bag at the proper times. When we were little girls, we played jacks and kept our jacks in a little bag. We threw extra jacks into the bag so we would always have enough to play with. Well, you need to keep throwing extra experience into your bag, so you have enough skills to work with. When I went into the Minority and Women Owned Business Development Program, I threw my CPA into the bag, but I need to take it back out again now. Having credentials like a CPA helps. Education is important. You have to have something that makes you a little bit different.

Heading the Minority and Women Owned Business Development Program gave Lucy external as well as internal visibility: Headhunters and companies wanting to start similar programs started calling her. She said their offers were tempting, but pointed out that insider knowledge helps guarantee successful outcomes for this type of program.

The person heading these programs must know and trust insiders who understand the organization. If I walked into XYZ company, it could take me two years to figure out who the right people are—the movers and shakers are not always the people you think they are. I tell companies to find an inside person who thoroughly understands the company, its culture, and its power bases.

One of the skills that makes Lucy stand out is the reputation she has earned as a problem solver. And the manner in which she tackles problems once more shows how feminine skills provide an advantage in the corporate setting.

I have been placed in jobs that call for problem solving, which generally means change, and, unfortunately, people can have negative feelings when they know you are coming in to change things. When I start a job, I spend a lot of time up front just asking people questions. I start with a simple question: "If you could have anything you wanted in this department or this program what would it be?" I try to bring people in and make them understand they have a part in making the situation better. I analyze their answers, what they think is going wrong, and what they think the department or program would look like if the problems were fixed. Then I work on giving them what they want.

I'm very comfortable with people. I'd like to know their stories, what makes them tick, and what they think is important. I'm much more comfortable listening to people tell their stories than I am telling mine. I tend to get people to talk to me and to tell me what's going on. They end up feeling like they have contributed. I don't build new programs; they do.

Another skill of Lucy's, which has moved her career along, is her ability to go for what she wants.

I have a very aggressive attitude. I want to get things fixed. I don't have time to wait for everybody, so I get input and I act on it because I don't want to do a particular job forever. I've had people challenge my aggressive style, but I keep moving forward until somebody tells me to stop. When you take risks and things work out, it gives you a level of confidence. You've got to be willing to take a risk. You've got to be willing to stand up for what you think is right. You've got to have integrity. I have a reputation for honesty. People come to me when they want to hear the truth. I don't sugarcoat things. People respect you when you say, "This is what I think and this is why I think it." They may not always buy your ideas and that's okay. But, at least, you are able to say what you think is important. As long as people feel you are doing things because you believe in them, you gain respect.

Her latest promotion, which her mentors recommended, has brought Lucy back into the financial end of the business. They told her it will continue to build her credibility, preparing her for the next jump up, which will take her to a senior management level.

DIANA BELL: LESSONS FROM MENTORS AND CAREER DEVELOPMENT PROGRAMS

The concept of mentoring is as old as Greek mythology. While Odysseus was off sailing the seas surrounding Greece, Mentor, his trusted friend and advisor, counseled his son, Telemachus. In the *Odyssey*, Athena, goddess of wisdom, posed as Mentor in order to make sure Telemachus would heed her advice. This small snippet from the monumental epic presents us with two interesting thoughts: On one hand, it could mean that as far back as ancient Greece, men's words carried more weight than women's, and, on the other hand, it does show that women are wise enough to do whatever it takes to get the outcome they want.

Today, the words of mentors—both male *and* female—are required for successfully navigating corporate waters and understanding cultural currents. Without support and guidance, without someone to help read corporate maps or warn against dangerous moves, careers can get caught in the wake of political backfire and business storms. If your career is stalled or you take the wrong tack, mentors can help put you back on course.

Formal mentoring programs are being set up inside and outside companies. Many of the companies in this book have some type of mentoring program, and, although most corporate programs are inclusive, they tend to target women and minorities who have not had as long a history of mentoring as their white male counterparts. Some studies are finding that the gender of mentors makes a difference in career development and female executives make out best when they have both male and female mentors. A 1992 Korn Ferry study found that just 15 percent of women had been mentored by women during their careers,[4] and in the national survey I conducted that same percentage holds true. Many of the women over 40 whom I interviewed had male mentors simply because there weren't many women in high positions. And a good portion of the women who were in positions to mentor back in the 1970s were still too insecure to reach out to other women. These "queen bees" were afraid to lose their status or "upset the delicate balance they had established with men."[5] Women are no longer so insecure. Many professional organizations have started mentoring programs to help match women with other women. One of the professional women's groups I belong to even serves as a link, matching women coming out of local state and community colleges with businesswomen in the region. As more organizations and women appreciate the value of mentoring, and as more women fill those higher-level positions, a greater number of women are becoming involved in both ends of the process.

Mentors have played key roles in moving Diana Bell's career along at Hewlett-Packard and she has trusted their advice to help position herself and make specific job selections. At 44, Diana has been with HP for 20 years, and over the course of her career she has taken responsibility for finding a variety of mentors to guide her. Taking ownership of the mentoring process is key: It's the responsibility of each woman to find and nurture mentoring relationships that will help her move forward.

Presently, Diana is operations manager for Worldwide Remarketing Operations, and she has navigated her career through programming, financial systems, manufacturing, technical support, and product marketing. At one point, she was faced with two promotional choices—a management position in the technical support area in which she had been working or a management spot in the documentation and training area. Her immediate inclination had been to accept the technical support position because she perceived it carried more weight and prestige, but her mentor pointed out that learning how to manage people who have been peers makes mastering management that much more difficult.

The key is to make it as easy as possible on yourself. Why choose the hardest way? So I decided to focus on developing management skills without having to deal with the nuances of changing relationships, and I took the job in documentation and training. It was a good choice. It gave me a chance to develop more project management skills. Later, I ended up managing the technical support group after it had been restructured and made larger and my peers were no longer there.

As Diana's career progressed she again wanted to make a move that was countered by her mentor. She thought a position in marketing would expand her skills, but her mentor advised her to become a star performer in the technical area she knew best. As she relates her story, her mentor believed the high credibility she would gain by excelling in her area would benefit her in the long run.

I had been frustrated because I wasn't moving into the product management end of marketing as fast as I wanted, but was getting steered toward technical support, where I had experience. At that time, we were assessed on percentiles like a bell-shaped curve and the terminology was "be a 90th percentile player." If you were in the 90th percentile, you could write your own ticket. So I followed his advice and I became a 90th percentile player in the area where I had experience. I took the technical support position and I could see how my prior background in R&D and my MBA gave me an advantage over the other people who didn't have that kind of background. When my management promotion came, I had a choice of two jobs.

Since Diana always counted on her mentors for advice and guidance, when she found herself without trusted relationships, she realized how truly significant they had been to her. In the 1980s, when her software division had started on a downward cycle, there was a major shift in leadership. Many of the people who had supported her left the company. When she lost those valued relationships, she also lost a promotion she had expected.

I realized how easily I could be derailed without the right relationships. It had nothing to do with me and yet it had everything to do with me because I had stayed with this one group. The thing that works for you suddenly works against you. I had never worked in another group; other people didn't know me. They hadn't worked with me directly. I didn't have the right relationships.

Diana consciously set out to reposition herself, and, fortunately, there was a progressive program in place to help her: Diana took advantage of HP's Accelerated Development Program (ADP) for high-potential candidates, which has a formal mentoring component that matches participants with senior managers throughout the organization. Diana used the program to make new alliances.

The program worked for me because it gave me access to new individuals who would not have known about my skills. If I hadn't been in the program, my present boss wouldn't have had the opportunity to know me. There are plenty of jobs in HP that I could be qualified for, but if people don't have a way to get to know me, I won't get to interview. So the real value of this program is the access it provides. HP has a resume book, which lists all the people who have been in the ADP program, and general managers use it when they are looking for job candidates.

My goals were to use the formal mentoring piece of ADP to become familiar with another part of HP's business and to develop a new and lasting relationship. My present division manager was my mentor in ADP, and later he called me to interview for a job in his division. So, the program really worked for me because it helped me create a new relationship that I knew I needed.

She interviewed for and landed the job, and her relationship with her new manager flourished. One of the reasons Diana loves working for him is that she feels nurtured—she can count on him for honest feedback without wondering if he's holding back criticism or not telling her everything she needs to know. Diana functions with a deep sense of caring and operates from a basis of trust. She told me she specifically looks for these characteristics in the people with whom she aligns. She intuitively understands that in order to be significantly helped, anyone who mentors her must appreciate and respect her value system. Trust is, in fact, an essential ingredient in any mentor relationship. Relationships can't be artificially created: There must be some amount of personal chemistry. If both people in the relationship don't have the same set of values and beliefs, the relationship simply won't work.

> *On some level, there has to be some genuine respect for each other, some common ground, something from which you build. If it's forced, it won't last over time. That's one of the hazards in formalized programs—people can be disappointed because they have expectations that aren't met. They might be expecting to develop long-term relationships, while the assigned mentor has a different expectation. So, it's important to be clear about expectations on both parties' sides from the beginning.*
>
> *Real mentors become invested in you. If you follow their advice and it doesn't work, they feel responsible. And they will try to help you out of your dilemma. If their advice works, they feel great. The people I regard as mentors have become friends. They care about me and give me the feedback that I need.*
>
> *My mentors have provided me with different perspectives that I use to put a whole picture together. They have helped me to step back from situations and look at them in new ways. Sometimes you can be too close to see clearly. It's important that your mentors have a sense of your values and abilities so their advice is given in relationship to you.*

By listening to people she respected, Diana also decided to accept a position without direct reports. Up until that particular point in her career she had felt it was extremely important as a black woman not to take jobs without clear management responsibility: Having direct reports made her authority visible. She had been thinking of turning down the assignment, but Diana found that taking a position without direct reports provided space to learn. And she discovered that periodically it's good to be relieved of the responsibility of managing people.

> *If you are managing people, especially if you are a first-line manager, so much of your focus is on developing people. If you have a good-sized group, by the time you speak to them every day, write a couple of evaluations, and do some wage planning, you don't have time to learn new skills yourself. So moving into that position gave me time to develop more expertise and gain new perspectives. It really rounded out my marketing skills. I had approached marketing from the technical side and I knew my product area, but I didn't have the process skills in the way that someone who had come in as a product manager would have. So spending a year and a half in that position helped me do that. It was refreshing.*

With freed-up energy, she expanded her management and leadership skills by serving as the president of the National Black MBA Association. She told me she learned how external networks can be successfully used for career development. Rather than managing staff inside the corporation, directing the affairs of the association honed her managerial abilities and expanded her network of contacts outside the organization.

> *There are lots of ways to learn, lots of ways to develop yourself. Being on a board is one way. Being the president of the National Black MBA Association became a calling card for me. Plus, it was a lot of fun. I met people from all kinds of local corporations. I also learned how to motivate people when they are not getting paid, which is a great skill to bring back into the corporate environment. There are plenty of avenues for developing skills. And there are numerous nonprofit organizations and volunteer groups that are looking for people with those skills. These organizations can provide you with opportunities and broaden your perspectives. What you learn outside can help you in the future inside. The benefits are enormous, and the pay doesn't always have to be cash—you get rewarded in other ways.*

Not only was Diana fortunate because she worked for a large organization where she was able to work with trustworthy people who provided sound advice and assisted her with her career, but there were also structural supports in place, enabling her to build her management skills. HP provides a framework that allows top performers to compete more effectively for senior-level jobs. Established in 1992, the Accelerated Development Program at HP has three components: leadership and skills assessment, formalized mentoring, and external development. It provides participants with visibility, development of skills, and access to job opportunities. Development programs like HP's help women to gain a more thorough understanding of how the whole company operates and provide the connections women need to advance their careers. The company benefits as well: Formalized development programs help to sustain the organization by building its own core competencies through the preparation of a broader range of future leaders. As participants receive valuable guidance, organizational knowledge is built and transferred. These progressive practices—career development, formalized mentoring, and job rotation—not only advance women, but they also improve bottom-line results and market value.[6] When a company assists in the development of women as managers and leaders, it helps itself.

Through the external educational component of ADP, Diana was able to attend Duke University's two-week executive leadership program. In addition to the business simulations and on-line cases, the course included leadership training, where Diana had one of those "aha" experiences.

> *During the outdoor leadership portion, we did a ropes course and I learned in a new way the importance of strategy. In preparation for going up on the ropes, we talked on the ground about the strategy we would use to complete the mission that was given to us. We knew we just couldn't start climbing, we had to devise a plan before we got on the ropes.*
>
> *It seems so simple, but I realized in the business world you don't have a physical or a tangible result in a short term. The lack of a strategy isn't as obvious. So you can get into a lot of activity, but it might take a year before you realize that the activity is not producing the results you want. Energy is wasted. People often want to dive in immediately and get things done. So I use the story of the ropes to show how we should set aside time to give to planning and to decide how much time that planning should take. With a plan in place, you'd be surprised at what you can do.*

Diana says she has been able to move toward her goal of becoming a general manager partly because of the wisdom of her mentors and the developmental supports offered by HP.

> *I'm getting more general management skills now because I have multiple functions reporting to me on a smaller scale. My boss is helping to position me. Last year, he gave me dotted line responsibility for accounting and IT. On a mini-level, I'm getting exposure. I'm getting the right people in place and I think our strategy is right. When I make this business profitable, I can look ahead to the next position. And I feel good, because I can see it happening. I can see the possibilities and I feel I have the support of my boss and the rest of the management team.*

DARLENE SOLOMON, PH.D.: RISING IN RESEARCH

Although Darlene Solomon's career goals differ from Diana's, both mentors and career development programs at Hewlett-Packard have also enabled her to expand her knowledge and managerial skills. Darlene, 36, has a Ph.D. in chemistry and is climbing up an R&D track, which doesn't call for rotating and switching. She feels good about her management achievements and told me she hasn't personally experienced any kind of glass ceiling. Sitting in her busy office, with activity swirling all around us, Darlene said she has had "very supportive managers," three promotions in six years, and two kids. How high she wants to climb, she says, is still an open question for her.

Darlene manages the Chemical Systems Department of HP Labs, the company's central research division. The department conducts long-range research in analytical instrumentation for the Chemical Analysis Group. In this male-dominated engineering arena, Darlene doesn't see her career limited at all by the fact that she is a woman. Her concern is that it might be limited by the fact that she is a chemist who wishes she knew a little more about physics and electrical engineering.

> *I manage a department where chemistry is a component, but instrumentation is easily as important. And I know I could go one level higher with the background I have, but beyond that*

the issue becomes a question of whether I become an in-depth technical person who needs to understand what's going on, versus a really good manager who can deal with all facets of the organizational issues. And those are questions I haven't completely answered for myself.

I really like what I'm doing right now. There's a driven part of me that wants to keep going higher, but I'm not sure I would enjoy it as much as what I'm doing. I have a Ph.D., but I really didn't get any training in business or management. When I moved into management, I thought I would try it and if I didn't like it, I could go back to concentrating on chemistry. I like the idea of moving forward and I don't want to miss opportunities because they're not always present.

I have high levels of satisfaction with the progress of my career. Sometimes I still can't believe it. I've got about 30 people working under me who are all great scientists and engineers. I really like everybody and I feel I have a lot of responsibility. Some people say I'm the voice of the future of analytical instrumentation at HP. We're a small part of HP, but we're still the second largest company in analytical instrumentation.

I feel really lucky especially as a chemist, as a woman, to work in HP Labs at this management level, which is a level that still focuses on people's needs. The next level would be fun, but it gets more focused on upward management. I'm not feeling pressured yet since I've only been in this position for two years, and I'm not sure which way I'll go.

Like Diana Bell, Darlene has taken advantage of the developmental opportunities offered by HP for high-potential candidates. She, too, participated in the Accelerated Development Program and found each part of it to be helpful in different ways.

ADP provides you with a self-focused examination, with mentoring, with some formal education, and exposure. It definitely conveys the idea that HP wants you to be the most that you can be. During the assessment phase, you go through a host of exercises and receive immediate feedback about what you did right and what you could have done better. It was great. You don't normally get that kind of feedback, and if you do, it's never right on the spot, nor is it as in-depth. Working with people from all over the country, I learned how much we all have in common.

Darlene participated in the year-long program in 1995 and creatively used the mentoring component to step outside of her research mind-set to learn new ways of thinking.

> *I'm involved in long-term research, which is not high-risk, but we need to make a lot of changes if we want to grow the way we need to grow. For a mentor, I chose a general manager in the new video instrumentation division, which is a new, high-risk business for HP. I wanted to bring that model back to my analytical group and broaden my exposure to cross-functional interaction in manufacturing and marketing. Here at the labs, we are strictly an R&D environment and I wanted more cross-functional interaction.*
>
> *During my mentor's busy strategic planning time, we got together twice a week, and after that, about once every three or four weeks. I did a lot of shadowing at meetings, observing his behavior. Afterwards I would get to ask him what he was thinking or why he said or didn't say something. I also got to talk to his staff. After the meetings, I was able to ask a lot of basic, dumb questions because it's a different business than the one I know. It was really helpful.*

When managers in R&D can work more closely with people in higher-risk areas closer to the customer, the company gains competitive advantage. As more focus has shifted to the customer, these relationships have become even more important. Darlene understands how her department needs to think beyond its own usual way of operating: When R&D works more closely with marketing and manufacturing people in product development, for example, the company is more fully guaranteed that customers' wants and needs are being met, increasing revenue potential. As Darlene looks at her own career progress in the research arena, she has found that establishing credibility in a nonthreatening way has helped her to succeed. And one of the ways she has expanded her credibility is by learning about other functions and how best to interact with them.

> *In my area, broad technical skills are important because you're doing long-range research with folks from different backgrounds, but good people skills are important too. You have to be driven and credible. One of the reasons I think I have succeeded is that I am not an extremist. I've built up pretty good*

credibility and have been able to get the rest of the company to rely on HP Labs and to believe in us for long-range research. I strike people as reasonable: I'm a champion for the organization, but I don't go so far overboard that I'm unbelievable. I'm pretty analytical, pretty easygoing, and that makes it easier to fit in.

My advice is to establish your own credibility in a way that isn't threatening. You need to show your abilities and then you need to take credit for your contributions, while still giving credit to others—then people will start to listen and respect you.

Cochairing HP's first Technical Women's Conference (TWC) also enhanced Darlene's credibility and visibility. TWC was first organized by HP women in 1988 to provide the female engineers a means to network, share their knowledge, showcase their work, and advance their positions in the company. She told me her team worked for two and a half years on nights and Saturdays putting the first conference together, and through that process she experienced her own professional growth.

I am trained as a technical person and I got to work with people who had very different views than mine. I developed new relationships and experienced new ways of learning, operating on a grassroots level as opposed to a management level. As a consequence of my experience running the conference, I have been asked to be on other committees. And people who have presented have been invited to give talks in other parts of the organization. It stimulates different parts of the division to think of ways of working together. So the paybacks extend beyond the day of the conference.

When I asked Darlene to suggest ways for companies to help women advance, I wasn't surprised by her advice. Companies, she said, should "make an effort to understand and trust people." While I was interviewing the women at HP, I was struck by their commitment and loyalty. They echoed everything I had read about HP's deep values.

If management had said no to the concept of TWC, it would have put up a barrier. Sometimes companies think that if they don't address issues, there aren't problems. When problems are exposed, at least management learns what the issues are and they can learn what they are doing right and what they could be doing better. At HP, people are empowered to do a good job, not because someone tells them to, but because they want to. And there's a lot of trust in that. If I find out somebody works for HP, I'll be more likely to buy a car from that person than from somebody else. Some divisions have better morale than others, and some areas are rated more positively by employees than others, but we have common beliefs and a common set of goals.

HP has very little turnover. Many people have been with the company for 20, 30 years. HP invests in you and broadens you. I actually know more people who have moved around in HP than have left. There is definitely a family spirit.

The careers of both Darlene Solomon and Diana Bell were helped by HP's efforts to develop female leaders. Both women used a combination of mentors, networks, and the company's formalized career development program to advance themselves, and both utilized opportunities and took advantage of what the system offered to move their careers in the unique direction that each wanted.

JAN TOMLINSON AND ANN GINN: MOVING UP THROUGH HR

In 1977, Rosabeth Moss Kanter wrote that for most of the twentieth century the manager's image was defined by the "masculine ethic of rationality." Women were relegated to human resource departments because they were seen as the "social workers of management." Women's ability to handle people and their emotions made the area "more appropriate than in decision-making functions."[7] These images are, however, changing. As organizations become more knowledge-based, HR is gaining strategic significance. The personnel selected by HR to work in the organization and the way HR structures systems within the organization help determine productivity and profitability. As teamwork is becoming more critical to the efficiency and effectiveness of work processes, the human element, and, therefore, the HR function, is becoming more important to business strategy.

At Chubb, there is a focus on expanding skills with particular jobs built into a job rotation process in order to help managers develop. HR is one of those rotations and both Ann Ginn and Jan Tomlinson, who started out as underwriters, found that rotating through HR expanded their knowledge of the company, broadened their skills, enlarged their networks, widened their global perspectives, and helped to position them farther up the ladder. So, rather than being viewed as a staff function that traps women, these women told me that HR can legitimately be perceived as adding value to women's resumes.

At 45, Jan Tomlinson, one of two women who head divisions at Chubb & Son, is president of Chubb Insurance Company of Canada. Jan was climbing the traditional route up the insurance ladder, when she reached a typical turning point: She had to accept a relocation in order to keep climbing. Jan had been resisting the move because it called for her to work in New York City. She and her husband (who is in the banking industry) and their son lived in Connecticut, and the thought of commuting to New York simply wasn't appealing to Jan. Moreover, if the family moved, her husband would have to look for a new job. As the couple mulled over their choices, they decided to follow Jan's career, since, at that time, the banking industry was experiencing a dramatic downturn.

Following the advice of her manager, Jan took an administrative position in a downtown office in Manhattan, where she gained knowledge about different facets of the company. After a year and a half, she continued expanding herself and rounded out her skills by taking a lateral move to the financial institutions division. With greater understanding of the way the company operated, Jan was offered a promotion to branch manager, which at Chubb is a vice president–level job. Happy and expecting to hold the position for the typical five- to seven-year rotation, she was surprised to receive a call from corporate headquarters asking if she would be interested in taking a worldwide HR position. At first, she admitted to me, she was hesitant to accept because of the stigma attached to HR.

> *I wondered why they wanted me to do that when I was doing my dream job. I didn't think I had been working at the branch manager position long enough to do all that I wanted to do. And I wondered if it was a way for the company to move women into senior positions in convenient ways. I voiced my concerns and the president himself stepped in and explained why the company wanted me to take the position. I was told it would be a*

five to seven year assignment, and if I did well, there would be
a bigger job at the end of it.

The job gave Jan the opportunity to understand overall business operations better. As she described it, she was able to comprehend her organization more completely rather than just focusing on the management of her territory.

> *In the underwriting world, particularly in the U.S., you really*
> *don't talk to other industries much. In the HR world, that's how*
> *you find out what's going on. I had an opportunity to talk to HR*
> *experts and consultants, to take courses, to attend a week-*
> *long program at Harvard, to do things I probably would not*
> *have thought about or been able to do. It gave me much more*
> *than I ever thought I would get out of a job. It exposed me to*
> *Chubb's total operations and enabled me to interact with so*
> *many of our people around the world. So I learned to look at all*
> *possibilities, even when the benefits of a particular position*
> *were not immediately clear. I advise women to remain open to*
> *all possibilities.*

As management promised, after five years she was promoted to her present position as president. Rather than locking her into some feminine closet from which she could not escape, working in HR expanded Jan's understanding of her company and better prepared her to lead it. Jan told me she is a firm believer "that success depends on what you make of a particular situation."

> *You can go one of two ways: You can either burrow yourself in*
> *at your desk or you can spend as much time as you possibly*
> *can learning about the world around you. That's what I*
> *decided to do with the HR job. I didn't think that I would ever*
> *become the greatest technical expert on compensation or bene-*
> *fits, but I knew there were things I could bring in terms of*
> *understanding people better and figuring out how we could*
> *design systems better. It was a tremendous experience for me.*

In contrast to Jan's experience, Ann Ginn decided on her own that she needed the broader experience HR would provide. At 39, Ann Ginn is vice president and branch manager of the Rochester branch of Chubb & Son. Ann's early career path also followed a traditional route: She worked on the line as an underwriter, senior underwriter, supervisor, and manager until she reached the highest level she could within the division.

> *I had gone as far as I could go in the field. I was a vice president, but I didn't have any diversity of background to put me in contention for a managing director's job, for leading the division on a worldwide basis. So I looked for opportunities in our home office that would develop my ability to think more strategically and build on skills that would fill in the gap.*
>
> *I started to realize I had to take some lateral moves to build out my experience. I took a strategic staffing job in the HR division for 18 months. I had the opportunity to work with senior management and I got real insight into what the company was trying to do on major strategic issues. It gave me great exposure to the people from whom I wanted recognition, and it allowed me to learn their perspectives.*
>
> *Some people wondered why I took an HR job, but I developed relationships that otherwise I never would have. I worked very hard on developing those relationships and over time it paid off for me.*

When the branch manager's position opened in Rochester, the people she had met through her HR job supported her in getting it. According to Ann, women "need to be much more aggressive in starting and planning their careers, much more in control of their career decisions and choices." In offering career advice, Ann was adamant about the importance of gaining control so that the timing of positions can be geared toward family life. In her own career, she wishes she had taken international assignments earlier, before she started her family.

> *Once you are older and more established, those kind of moves make life more complicated. That's why it's good to get advice from mentors who can call your attention to particular jobs and say, "Take this job rotation now." The earlier you can figure out what is important to your future growth—what jobs will give you the ability to do other jobs—the greater competitive advantage you will have. Know which jobs will enhance your career and which ones won't. And get the jobs that demand more from you completed earlier, before you have family relationships that create complexity. Most of us want the families, but it is wiser to reduce complexity as much as possible by being proactive.*

Ann also believes that female managers now have greater opportunities than they did in the past. She said it's time for women to put all their energies into performance, which is where the true power of the future lies.

> *The positive change in the business environment towards a results oriented environment means that there is less subjectivity. If you get results, you're able to push ahead more easily today than in the past. It's time for women to move beyond worrying about comparisons, about our management styles, or about whether we are clustered in jobs or not. We spend too much time worrying about these issues.*

The business environment is continually evolving. I find it interesting that both Ann and Jan were prompted into the insurance business by early mentors who recognized opportunities for promising women in the 1970s. Jan went to a small Catholic college in Kansas and said she had an advisor "who was extremely interested in getting women into business." Jan says she still sends her old mentor notes and confesses, "I don't think I would have gotten into the insurance business without that early connection she made for me."

Ann's interaction with her first mentor occurred in high school. She was taking secretarial courses when she became involved in a corporate sponsorship program. One of Chubb's female managers took an interest in her and helped to guide her toward college and a Chubb scholarship. Ann is extremely grateful for that guidance and says, "I would not have had this opportunity had she not believed in me and recognized my abilities. She really influenced me at a very young age." Like Darlene Solomon and Diana Bell, Ann participated in a formal mentoring program at Chubb, and over the years she has used a variety of mentors. Her recommendation is to use "the best of a lot of different people." She identifies people's strengths and then goes to them when she needs advice in their particular area of expertise. In fact, many of the women I interviewed stressed the significance of having more than one mentor. Since advice is needed in more than one sphere of business, having more than one mentor is essential for success.

When I asked Ann if she had any final piece of advice to pass on, she counseled women to be flexible and open in their approach to their careers and not to be afraid to make mistakes. Ann is a strong advocate of learning from failing. And rather than continuing to compare women to men and focusing on how women have been held back, she says women must continue moving forward through persistence and hard work.

> *I have felt stalled at times in my career, felt as though I should have been moving ahead more rapidly, and I have had to put in extra work, but so have my male counterparts. This is not an exclusive female domain. You have to be prepared to accept disappointments. In my experience, men typically are less introspective about their failures. Some women have a tendency to give up. You have to be tenacious and persistent. You can't just take the first failure with resignation. You have to build from failure.*

Mistakes provide space for learning. The advice author Betty Harragan gave back in 1977 when she wrote *Games Mother Never Taught You* is still worth heeding. In her analogy to corporate life as a large playing field, she said that men have had the upper hand because they have been acclimated by their earlier participation in sports. Through their experience they learned a major lesson: You can't win all the time. "Thus *losing* becomes part of the larger game." She goes on to say that men are trained in sportsmanship in order to cope with the inevitable loses. Men have learned to lose with aplomb and have learned "to handle the evidence of failure" more easily than women. Her most important insight, however, is that failure, rather than being treated as a "demoralizing agent," should be treated as a "revitalizing force."[8]

The stories of Jan Tomlinson and Ann Ginn illustrate how new opportunities have arisen for women and new ways of thinking are replacing old ideas about the worth of functional areas. These women have found that the best way to make the system work is to gain knowledge and skills, and to get what you need from wherever you can within the organization. Rather than believing old organizational assumptions, they provide evidence that the best career choices can include charting courses through areas that others might assume to be less than desirable.

MAKING THE SYSTEM WORK

The women in this chapter used a variety of techniques and strategies to navigate the corridors that would lead to the functional areas and positions they wanted. But the method for each woman depended on her individual goals. These women sought out and relied on mentors to provide them with guidance and support, and they took advantage of networks and corporate programs that offered them systematized methods for gaining knowledge and education.

Women, in both line and staff positions, leveraged their skills and assessed each job for its value, determining how much new knowledge it would provide and how much it would increase their expertise. Women who were headed up the line understood that gaining a broad range of experience, especially in areas close to the customer and the company's products, was critical. During their rotations, these women sometimes surprisingly found that moving into a lateral spot, or into a spot without direct reports, provided the space to grow and learn, and in the long run provided greater advancement opportunity. Planning when to take particular positions was also strategically important—timing and events in the external and internal environments proved to be crucial factors in decision making. The determined women in this chapter assertively went after what they needed, used every support the corporate system offered to steer the course of their careers, and made difficult choices to get where they wanted to go.

BRAVE MOVES

I learned that focusing on excellent performance pays off. People who perform excellently will have doors of opportunity opened for them that they never anticipated. . . . I know how to learn, so I'm not scared anymore. I'm not scared of people saying that I'm not the right person for the job, because I have the confidence that within six to eight months I can produce results that change their opinion.

SHAUNNA SOWELL, Vice President
Texas Instruments

If you have ever participated in outdoor leadership activities, you know the courage it takes to climb ropes, scale walls, and jump off the top of 30-foot poles. These arduous tasks seem almost impossible, but somehow you create a strategy for yourself and then you just do it. That's how the women in this chapter struck me—they summoned their courage and then they just did it. They might have been scared, but they confronted their challenges and plowed through their fears.

I hesitated to use Shaunna Sowell's opening quote, concerned that the word *scared* might erroneously be equated with *weak,* but I decided to use it because being scared speaks to the heart of what courage is all about. It exemplifies the feelings of many women as they have progressed on their business journeys. Making progress takes courage, but courage doesn't come without fear. Courage is owning the feeling of being scared and overcoming that feeling by continuing to move ahead anyway.

The women in this chapter tackled issues, made risky moves, and took career paths that others less brave might shy away from trying. Marlene O'Toole climbed corporate ladders without a high school diploma. Shaunna Sowell went back to school to get a second bachelor's degree so she could switch from a traditional teaching track to the occupation she'd had in mind in the first place—engineering.

Julie England found herself in a declining business unit, but gathered up her strength and found a way to advance her career. Carol Tuthill moved her whole family to Venezuela to gain cross-cultural experience and Karen Moreno took a dramatic demotion in order to reposition herself for the future. Vela McClam Mitchell confronted harassment with a head-on, direct approach that resulted in a move to a better position within the organization. And Ann Delvin dropped out of high school to have a child at 17, but now has a graduate degree from Cornell and a successful corporate career.

The stories of these women illustrate that success comes in all kinds of packages, but regardless of how it is wrapped, inside is courage, tenacity, and a unique kind of intelligence that becomes visible in the quality and excellence of the women's performances.

MARLENE O'TOOLE: STREET-SMART AND DETERMINED

At 50, Marlene O'Toole is IBM's southern regional manager for customer support. Before moving to Atlanta, Marlene worked in the Boston area with one of my friends. When I was batting around ideas for this book, my friend suggested that I contact Marlene because she had such high regard for Marlene's management skills. And since Marlene had entered the business world back in 1963, she thought Marlene would certainly have plenty to say about the progress of women in management.

At the tender age of 17, Marlene dropped out of high school and began her career at the Federal Reserve Bank in Boston, where she made $32.50 a week. As the youngest of eight children, she knew what competition meant and she was determined to succeed in the business world. From the very beginning of her career, she took advantage of every opportunity that was offered. Calling herself a "hustler," she told me she was "always working, always trying to get ahead."

In 1967 Marlene left the bank and joined IBM as a keypunch operator; in 1997, after 30 years of service, Marlene is planning to retire and is looking forward to her vacation home in Florida, golfing, and time with her 11 grandchildren. Over the course of her long career with IBM, Marlene has received several highly respected awards for her outstanding work and dedication. When I asked her to look back and tell me what made her successful, she responded by saying, "You can do anything, if you put your mind to it."

A determined, gutsy, and aggressive woman, Marlene said she has set goals, worked hard, and sacrificed to achieve those goals. And she said her definition of success changed over the years as she grew professionally and her career progressed.

> *When I was young, I defined success by how much money I made. When I was first given the opportunity to buy IBM stock, it was a first in my family. I invested as little as I could, and it took me a year to purchase one share. I sold it the next day and made $100 and thought I was a millionaire. The money did drive me. Over time as I developed, I started being recognized as an outstanding performer and I received service awards and got a taste of the recognition that comes from working hard. And that made me feel successful. Today my success comes from watching those I've hired move up the ladder and succeed. It comes from coaching them.*

Marlene rose through the ranks at IBM and prided herself on the fact that she was often the only woman in her line environments. As keypunching faded out, she jumped at a transportation opportunity, doing administrative work in a branch with marketing reps and systems engineers. This gave her the chance to work on the line and interact with customers on a daily basis. In those early years, there were few women in line positions and Marlene took her share of ribbing from the men. But as with most of the women who came up through the ranks, she knew that having a sense of self and a sense of humor were necessary tools. Listening to her Boston accent as she described a turning point in her career, I was struck by the changes women have experienced. I could envision the scene that she described (which hopefully would never take place in today's office environment), but her determination to handle it enabled her to succeed and allowed her to continue climbing.

> *When I first got to the branch, the guys, who basically were really good guys, played tricks on me all the time because I was the only girl. After a while their humor began to get to me, but I wasn't sure how to handle it. At each monthly meeting, they put together a branch office skit and about 140 people would come. For one of the meetings, they wanted me to play the part*

of an Indian maiden since I was 23 and had long dark hair. I was insulted. Not sure where to go for advice, I turned to my father. He asked me if I had to do anything bad, which I didn't. He asked me what my lines were, and my one line was "How." And in those days that wasn't considered offensive. So, his advice was, "Marlene, just go and be one of the best damn Indians they ever saw." For 29 years, no matter what I did, I tried to be the best I could be. And I think that's how I got ahead.

Marlene was a groundbreaker who believed in excelling at every job. Working hard and setting goals for herself was the formula that she stuck to over the years.

I've had goals. I wanted to be better than I was. The only way I knew how to do that was with hard work and sacrifice. Every job that came up I raised my hand for it. I have always been a hustler. If I hadn't given up something, I wouldn't have been to the places and seen the things that I have as a result of my career. I traveled all over with IBM, and had wonderful opportunities, but when my manager looked out his door, no matter what time of day or night, I was there.

A no-nonsense kind of woman, practical and down-to-earth, Marlene described herself to me as "tough but fair, disciplined, results oriented, and very competitive"—she does whatever is necessary to get a job completed.

I start early and I stay late. I don't ask anybody to do anything I wouldn't do myself. We are measured on accounts receivable and I want to be number one or two. And I tell that to the people who work for me. After we consolidated in 1993, we were dead last, but we ended 1995 number one in every single measure. We worked people hard; yet, we had some fun.

Marlene also says she has "a lot of common sense and street smarts" and has never allowed male-dominated environments to silence her.

I'm not the most brilliant person you're ever going to meet, but I'm respected and admired for my experience and for my gut instincts. I've been very fortunate—I got in the door. But I wasn't given a gift: I worked hard and I stepped up to issues.

I'm outspoken and even a little opinionated, but it's never harmed me in any way. I would never allow my voice not to be heard. I usually have men working for me, so I've had to carry my own voice. Sometimes I've had to shut up and listen. And sometimes I've been told to do something and I do it without question, without getting into a debate. But my present boss will also call me in and he'll bounce ideas off of me and ask me what I think.

When I listened to her I couldn't help liking and respecting her for her forthrightness and determined spirit. Marlene emphasizes the point that women have to take responsibility for succeeding, and a key way to do that, she says, is to take responsibility for learning. Although she reached the ranks of upper-middle management without the benefit of a high school diploma, she is a firm believer in education and, more than anyone, does not recommend that younger women model themselves after her in that regard. What she does recommend, however, is that people accept the responsibility for their own development.

When people tell me they are struggling, the first thing I ask them is if they have a degree. If they say "no," they usually start apologizing, and then I tell them I don't have one either, but it didn't stop me. I ask them when they took their last course. You can't blame a corporation if you've stopped seeking knowledge yourself. People have got to keep growing. I tell them to take a course in something they really hate to see how much they can stretch themselves.

At IBM, Marlene says there are all kinds of on-line classes available to employees, which they can easily access right at their desks. Software programs inform users of the skills that are presently important to the company and provide workers with guidance about matching skills to courses. Employees can even borrow a laptop to take home for course work. So Marlene firmly believes that if people are held back at IBM, "it's because they have made a decision not to move forward."

Marlene has loved her job, her company, and the people she has worked with over 30 years, and her future still holds interesting possibilities. Her story demonstrates that gutsy women, without privileged backgrounds, without college degrees, could achieve success on their own terms if they worked hard, went the extra mile, and were the best that they could be.

SHAUNNA SOWELL: LEARNING LEAPS
AND EXCELLENCE

Shaunna Sowell, 42, joined Texas Instruments (TI) in 1984 after having returned to college in her 20s for a second degree. Her corporate career didn't even begin until she was 31. But it took her only 11 years to climb the ladder at TI and she is now a vice president of corporate environmental, safety, and industrial hygiene. Shaunna's story is intriguing because she admitted to me that as a young woman she allowed herself to be intimidated by a male environment. But her intellect and maybe even some Irish stubbornness would not allow her to ignore her natural engineering skills. Always good in math and science, Shaunna started out taking engineering courses in college, but switched to education because of the discomfort she experienced in the male environment of an engineering school.

> *In 1972, I found going to an engineering college very intimidating. First of all, I didn't know any women engineers or any other women engineering students. I felt like I was the only woman and I had no support systems. So, at 18, without the confidence and the maturity to be the only female, I dropped out, and got a degree in education. That was an easy path for me because, as the oldest of five children, I was teaching all the time anyway.*

Shaunna enjoyed teaching high school English for five years, but as she thought more about the future, the idea of engineering persistently returned. So with the support of her husband, she returned to college and acquired a second degree in mechanical engineering and, during that same period, she also had two children. When she graduated she had a number of job offers, but she told me she joined TI because the company was rapidly expanding and it presented her with a rich array of possibilities. She knew she would quickly be given project responsibility. As she put it, "TI didn't care if I was purple, green, female or alien as long as I could produce results, and that felt like a perfect place for me to be." Her career did, in fact, progress rapidly and she has repeatedly been promoted at TI sooner than she has expected.

I never expected to be a vice president in ten years; that wasn't on my road map. I never expected to run an environmental, safety, and health team; that wasn't on my road map. In each job, I concentrated on doing the job excellently. Other people recognized how my skills could be applied in a variety of forums. Once a door opened for me, all that I had to do was to have the confidence to leap across whatever gap I perceived was there. Sometimes, I had the opportunity to take jobs for which I didn't have the traditional, acceptable competencies. But I believed in the person who was offering the opportunity, his knowledge about the job and about me, and I was willing to take the risk.

Because TI has historically been a male bastion, Shaunna has never worked for a woman and she emphasizes the point that she would not be a vice president today without men who supported and mentored her. This point is often forgotten when glass ceiling issues are discussed—without progressive-thinking men, women would have had an even harder time gaining acceptance and advancing their careers.

During my career, I've been the "first" in many of my jobs, but I never thought I was a token. I have been supported by people who focused on me as a person, what I could contribute, and what potential I had. They nurtured me and gave me opportunities to demonstrate my skills. In my experience, the people who supported me were gender blind. That is not true of every single manager at TI, although it is more true today in 1996 than it was in 1988. But I have been very blessed at TI to work for people who valued me for the results I could produce and the value I added to the organization.

One reason Shaunna has come as far as she has as fast as she has is that the quality of her performance and her ability to build successful teams has been recognized. Some of her career jumps have required an enormous amount of learning on her part. In the first six months of her last three promotions, she told me she experienced huge learning curves, but she has learned to stretch herself using management and leadership skills that seem to come naturally to her.

Shaunna seeks excellence in others as well as expecting it from herself, and she sees part of the work of leadership as eliminating the barriers that prevent people from achieving excellence. If people don't perform well, she believes it is because some internal or external barrier is in the way. According to her, it's the role of the leader to help remove hurdles—whether those hurdles stem from beliefs people have about themselves or from barriers in the organizational structure. Her success, she says, is dependent on the success of her organization, and she doesn't believe people can succeed on their own. Thus, she emphasizes the importance of having good people to work with and sees fostering excellence as a responsibility of leadership. Shaunna has found that people can be trusted and don't have to be controlled, but they do have to be supported and encouraged.

> *As a leader I focus on developing people, defining the business vision, setting clear goals and creating good strategic plans so people know what's expected of them. Successful leaders have a fundamental philosophy about people that is positive.*

As Shaunna, who is now divorced and the mother of three children, climbed in the corporation, she also had to confront issues that single, working mothers meet on a day-to-day basis. Wondering how she manages so much, I asked her if her life is in balance and she told me that, from a psychological and emotional perspective, her life works the way she wants it to.

> *Life is about choices and about enjoying and being personally accountable for those choices. I made the choice to have three children and I love my children. I also made the choice to work full-time and I love what I do. Being a working mom really fits me. At work, I am highly focused and highly motivated and produce results around my core work. When I go home, my core work is my family life. Both jobs are highly demanding. To have both in my life right now means there's not a lot of personal time for me—I usually don't get more than five hours sleep per night. I totally subscribe to the notion that you can't have it all.*

Although her life is a whirlwind—she logged 125,000 miles in international travel in 1995—she admitted to me in her down-to-earth way that lack of balance doesn't upset her. She sees it as a "visionary stretch goal." Rather than taunting herself with it, she focuses on the satisfaction she gets as a result of her choices. Her life at home revolves around her children's school and sports activities, and her evenings are full of homework, athletic practices, and games.

> *I know this stage is a very short period of my entire life. My oldest child is 14 and I know in the blink of an eye she'll be grown. What I try to do is enjoy the chaos and deal with the everyday reality of combining work and parenting.*

Shaunna doesn't believe it's possible to succeed alone and, just as she emphasizes teamwork in the office, she emphasizes how important it is to have other people helping her combine her personal and professional life.

> *I manage work and family with a lot of help. I don't believe one can do it alone. I am fortunate because I've always been able to have a caregiver in my home. When I travel she either stays overnight with my children, or they go to their dad's house in town, or sometimes my parents will stay with them for the duration. Support systems and networks at all levels—in your personal life and your professional life—are vital. I don't think one can survive without them.*

Life often—not always, but often—has a way of making things turn out right. Rather than impeding her advancement, the delay in Shaunna's engineering career allowed her to hook up with TI at the right time, and her skills in teamwork and her demand for excellence catapulted her up TI's corporate ladder. Not willing to give up her true career desires and not allowing herself to be deterred by her own fears, Shaunna demonstrates how owning our choices empowers us to reach levels we once thought impossible.

JULIE ENGLAND: SPEAKING OUT AND MOVING ON

Julie England is also a Texas Instruments vice president with a unique twist to her story. Julie found herself in a dwindling business unit, but by mustering up her courage and raising her voice on issues of importance to her, she gained visibility and got her career back on a successful track.

Julie is 38, has a chemical engineering degree, and has been with TI for 17 years. Her career was in danger of stalling due to external market conditions. Sometimes even with the best planning, careers can begin to go awry for reasons beyond an individual's control. Markets and businesses can change for the worse, negatively impacting career plans. When this happens, seizing as much control as possible is critical for survival. Julie had been in the Defense Systems Electronics Group for about six years, but the business was shrinking because, as she explained it to me, "peace broke out around the world." She realized she had to do something or her career wasn't going to go anywhere—she needed to be in an area that was growing, where she could get better visibility. Rather than simply complaining about an external environment she couldn't control, she took calculated risks and aggressive actions to get herself in a more productive area of TI.

> *I really felt the need to change. I kept sending a message to management: "The business conditions have changed; this particular area is not going to grow. I have untapped potential. Please move me. Please move me." I started plugging back into old managers I had associated with in the Semiconductor Group, asking them about growth areas. They named managers who were in those areas and I went way beyond my comfort zone, making cold calls and introducing myself, trying to get on their calendars just for 20 minutes. I basically said, "Hi, I'm Julie England. You don't know me, but I think I have some skills that might be valuable to you as your business grows, and if an opportunity arises I'd like to be considered on a list of candidates." I made it open-ended: I didn't say, "I want job ABC"; I said, "Here are my competencies and please consider me." It was the most dramatic thing I did in my career.*

In the meantime, Julie also went to the division vice president and asked him to put her on a market research team that was seeking opportunities to convert defense technologies to commercial applications. Working on the team carried some risk because she became an individual contributor and lost her direct reports. She had been managing large groups of people, but she calculated that the short-term sacrifice had more potential in the long run than simply staying where she was. Her risks paid off.

> *In the end, calling all those managers made a big difference. One of those people ended up being the decision maker who brought me back into the Semiconductor Group. I got a call ask-*

ing me to be the quality manager for one of the divisions. So, asking for what I wanted, taking risk, and making short-term sacrifices paid off.

When I asked Julie if she could share any lessons she learned from her experience, she offered the following:

I have two pieces of advice around career planning: The first is to tell management what you want and where you want to go with your career. Upper managers continually tell me women don't tell them what they want. It's as if women are afraid to ask. I've always had the philosophy the worst thing management can say is "no." Learn to handle a "no." The second piece of advice is: Don't hesitate to go back and ask a second or third time. There's no harm in asking more than once.

Julie also cautions that it's important to act professionally and make a sound business case to support requests that are made. If Julie hadn't spoken up for herself, her career might be extremely different: The defense group was later sold to another company. Her ability to understand the business environment and position herself in relation to it benefited her enormously.

Another strategy Julie used, not only to overcome the feelings of isolation she experienced working in a shrinking unit but also to help make changes in the organization, was to engage herself in the Women's Initiative. Becoming involved with it helped her to link up with others throughout the organization.

I clearly see the ability to network as a critical success factor for my career. Working on the Women's Initiative helped me to network with other women across the company and I started to understand the whole company better. From a business standpoint, networking is well worth the investment of time. Delivering results makes you competitive, and networking facilitates the ability to deliver results. Through networking, people can help me accomplish my goals and I can help them accomplish theirs.

The culture at TI emphasizes teamwork, which calls for the ability to communicate well, to compromise, and to influence without authority. In an earlier chapter, we spoke about how women tend to exert their power by influencing others around them. The ability to influence a range of people, even when they are outside of a manager's formal area of authority, is exactly the kind of skill that is called for in a flattened, team environment such as TI's. Julie told me she has discovered that the ability to influence without authority has great value.

> *As a quality manager, I'm considered a staff person, but I need to influence line people in manufacturing and product development to do things differently. So knowing how to influence without authority, especially in the '90s when corporations are flattening and we're getting virtual organizations springing up inside of companies, is a very important skill.*

Julie's skills and her determination to get herself out of a bad spot and into a better one set her apart. I was particularly struck by her comment about making cold calls: She saw it as the most "dramatic thing" she did in her career. How many of us resonate with that thought? Making telephone calls to sell your own skills requires self-confidence and courage. Julie knew she had to get out of where she was and the only way to do that was to raise awareness about her strengths and abilities with people on higher levels who didn't know her. In order to move on, she had to be her own best promoter on cold, inside calls with senior managers—not an easy thing to do.

CAROL TUTHILL: SEEKING CROSS-CULTURAL SKILLS

Lots of things impressed me about 44-year-old Carol Tuthill, who is a worldwide vice president of human resources and organizational excellence at Procter & Gamble. Not only was Carol way ahead of her time in introducing cross-functional training and concepts similar to 360-degree feedback into her brand area, but before international assignments were as significant as they are now, she requested an international position simply because she wanted to expand her cultural horizons. Her desire to work in a different culture did not originate from any grand career strategy: She merely wanted the experience for her own personal growth. And she didn't view an international assignment as a complicating factor in her family life; she believed the experience would enrich all the members of her family.

My husband had lived abroad before we were married, but I grew up in Cincinnati and went to college in Cincinnati and I wanted to learn more about the world. I had an interest in understanding other cultures and wanted to develop a world-wide view of business. When I observed international managers, I was intrigued by the differences in their perspectives and I wanted the chance to experience cultural diversity and be in a place where I had to learn a new language. And I wanted my children to have a chance to see the world in a different way. So I made the request more for my personal growth than for thinking it was going to get me ahead in P&G. It turned out to be very beneficial to my career, but that was not why I originally sought the opportunity.

Her international request was complicated by the fact that her husband also worked for P&G. In order to make the move, the company had to find two positions abroad as opposed to just one. Dual-career-couples transfers were not common at that time, nor was it typical for a woman with children to ask the company to uproot her family, so Carol's request was extremely unusual.

Sometimes an international position is found for one person, but it is difficult to find a position for the spouse. My husband and I both wanted to work; neither one of us wanted to take an extended leave of absence. I also had an additional requirement: Because I had small children, I didn't want to travel more than 25 percent of the time. My boss was very supportive and aggressively worked on our behalf. It took about a year and a half before we were relocated to Caracas.

Carol and her husband moved to Caracas when their oldest daughter was four and their son was two, and their youngest child was born there. They lived in Venezuela for six years and her children attended a Venezuelan preschool so they could learn the language and make local friends. Carol wanted them to experience more than the expatriate community. Her children became bilingual and developed a bicultural way of seeing the world. Carol claims, "It was a great move from both a family and career standpoint."

Carol's risk taking and desire for new learning experiences paid off well. By the time she returned to the States in 1994, HR was becoming a function with greater strategic significance. P&G's separate personnel departments, which operated out of each functional area, were united into one function that focused on partnership with business. Carol became involved in the restructuring and reshaping of HR and was made a vice president.

> *In my first position in Venezuela, I helped the group establish performance development systems. After about a year and a half, I was asked to become the HR manager for our Venezuelan subsidiary. Two years later I came back and took over the entire HR operation for Latin America.*
>
> *I don't believe I would have the perspective and the capability to do what I've done without the Latin American experience. The jobs in the U.S. tend to be bigger in terms of responsibility and the scope of the people you affect, but they also tend to be more narrow in terms of the breadth of the business in which you are involved. Outside the U.S., you become involved in developing the operations of the company, and you tend to have a broader span of control. You can see your impact much easier. Working internationally was wonderful for me.*

Curious about Carol's feelings as a vice president of human resources, I asked whether she viewed the function as a "female ghetto," and she offered some good insights into the complex skills required of the job as well as some highly practical advice.

> *HR requires working from both sides of your brain: It requires good data management and analysis, as well as the ability to translate that data and understand how a system impacts people.*
>
> *Some people might think a staff role is in some way a second-class citizen role, but I don't see it that way at all. The CEO calls me frequently for input, which not only says to me that my role in HR is valued, but it also provides me with another way to make a valued contribution.*
>
> *There are lots of ways to skin a cat in corporations: There is more than one model of success. It's important to figure out what your personal lever is. How can you achieve results that are meaningful to the corporation? I am pretty clear about where my strengths are and I try to make sure I'm leveraging those. Other people can make an equally good contribution in a very different way. The key is to do what you are good at and to channel it into something meaningful to the company.*

Carol's work focuses on organizational excellence and the application of total quality methodologies to P&G's businesses around the world. She described her job as "rewarding, demanding and exciting" and believes that she has "an impact on the company in terms of direction setting." Carol is a woman ahead of management trends who is not afraid to make extraordinary moves.

ANN DELVIN: STRETCH GOALS

Ann Delvin was sitting next to me at a National Association of Female Executives satellite conference in Boston in 1996 and as we started talking and I heard parts of her story, I asked her if I could interview her for this book. Her story is striking because she dropped out of high school at 17 and went back to school 11 years later as a nontraditional student. Having taken that path myself, I know what a challenge it is to be in school with younger students while caring for a young child at home. In order to succeed, you have to have goals that stretch you and keep pulling you forward. Ann told me she has "blown by the goals" she set 15 years ago when she first went back to school. Now, at 43, Ann has an engineering degree from the University of Washington and a master of science degree in polymers science from Cornell. She is an individual contributor at GE Plastics and is in the leadership band one level below the executive band in her company's corporate hierarchy, which identifies her as having a strong future with the company.

Ann is continually trying to push her own envelope, and she reminded me that "having a personal, internal definition of success is much more important than letting others define success for you." She attributes her fairly rapid climb to several factors.

> *I have a lot of energy and drive. I am highly adaptable. For years, I worked in bars and met all kinds of people, so I work well with people at all levels—with operators, technical people, and managers. It's critical for women to be adaptable. If you are going to work successfully in a male environment, you have to be able to make the people who work with you comfortable. You need to be accepted by your peers. You have to be comfortable with them and they have to be comfortable with you. That was really critical to my success.*

> *My work style also fits the company culture. I believe in meeting business objectives. My maturity combined with my per-*

sonality and my ability to understand business needs and to deliver have all been important factors in getting ahead.

My entire eight-year career has been in a male environment. Aside from engineering and product development, I bought global commodities and I sourced materials. There are not very many women on either the sales or the purchasing side of these areas. But I have never found being a woman a disadvantage. A lot of it has to do with gaining immediate trust and the way to do that is to make sure you know the business and have the proper knowledge. I work really hard to make sure I'm up to speed on everything in the industry.

After working for three years in the technology end of the business, Ann realized her career advancement would be hampered because she had decided not to get a Ph.D. When she recognized that her initial decision to work in the technological organization was no longer right, she didn't allow it to hamper her growth and development. She pushed herself to get the support she needed to shift management tracks and obtain her present position in the materials sourcing organization.

You can't think: "Well, I made a decision, now I'm stuck with it for awhile." You can't sit back. You have to be confident and assertive, and know that it's okay to screw up. You can make career changes. You don't have to be locked in any track. There are opportunities out there, but you have to find the support networks, and that means you might have to dig for them.

I had to push myself to take risks, but I know it's okay to fail. It's not the end of your life. I've always pushed myself, but I admit my personality makes it easier because I don't find it difficult to go to people and ask for help. You need to build networks. I have developed a lot of confidence just by talking to the male engineering professors I met in college and graduate school. I don't think I would have done as well if I didn't seek out their advice. People are willing to give more than you think.

It isn't unusual for a woman to switch career tracks or to make a mistake in job choices. If this happens, the best thing she can do is to spend her energy figuring out how to get back on the right track. Ann admitted that she was cautioned against making the move into her staff function—everyone told her it would be disastrous for her career—but she felt the move would help her develop assertiveness and negotiating skills.

Whenever I find myself getting too complacent or too comfortable, I try to push myself to get out of that comfort zone to make sure I'm taking the next step.

She considered the move developmental and risky as opposed to safe and, in hindsight, she said she still thinks it was a good choice, since her staff position in global sourcing adds great value to the organization.

GE has done an excellent job of developing our whole sourcing role, which makes a key contribution to this company. About 75 percent of the cost of sales is the amount we pay to the supplier to make our product. The people in our sourcing group have done a lot over the last five or six years to build it up professionally. Although it is a staff position, it is not a passive function anymore. It has become very strategic and is now a sought-after function in terms of career development.

I know bottom line what I have contributed to the company over the last four years. I can tell you the dollars I have saved and put back into the company. That's the measurement we have for everybody in the sourcing organization from our general manager on down. We are very numbers driven and you've got to know your numbers. It's a very competitive situation.

My technical background has been a plus: Buying commodity chemicals you have to be able to talk the language and you have to know the industry. My technological knowledge and my background experience have been very helpful.

Ann also told me that part of her success comes from not being afraid to ask for help. She makes a point of identifying and targeting knowledgeable people across the organization whom she can call on to help her solve problems.

If I have a particular problem that I don't know how to resolve, I seek out one or two key people for advice. I think through a couple of solutions, and I tell them what the problem is and my ideas for handling it. I ask them what they think and if they can see what I might be missing. There were probably three or four key business leaders who helped me along the way and with whom I routinely touch base. I have not been shy about seeking men out and talking to them. I have found they want to talk. You just have to know the right approach. Timing is important: You have to be sensitive to their schedules.

If Ann hasn't worked with people she admires, she contacts them, introduces herself, and explains what she has noticed that is special about them. Usually that breaks the ice, and then she asks if they have time to sit down with her and talk to her about how they developed their special qualities. She has found that people—and in her male-dominated industry that generally means men—have been willing to engage in conversation with her and share their knowledge.

Making the men she works with feel comfortable has been critical to her success, and Ann believes humor helps to develop that camaraderie. She cautions women not to take themselves so seriously.

Guys like to joke with you and you have to have some flexibility. I never let anybody push me to the point of harassment, but people test you. You have to be able to take some of their humor and jokes. I push back when I need to and I stop it when I need to, but you have to handle and be comfortable with the way men joke.

Ann also knows how to remain cool while others are blowing hot air at her. She says she has had men yell at her, but she can walk away from masculine outbursts. Women, Ann notes, sometimes have a hard time separating men's responses to business situations from personal attacks, while "men have big, acid battles and walk away together as best buddies." The only time Ann has felt herself to be at a disadvantage as a woman is in social situations while traveling. At those times she says it's easy to be left out if you are the only woman.

You just have to be assertive and comfortable about stepping in and inviting yourself to dinner. Ease their comfort. Everybody is so sensitive about sexual harassment these days that everyone feels like they're walking on a fence. Most men are uncomfortable because they're not sure about where the boundary is. Let them know you're operating from a professional position and it's not going to be an issue.

*It's really case by case and you have to understand the cul-
ture you're working in because each is a little different. I've
worked with Japanese and Europeans and Americans and
what it comes down to is having them feel comfortable with you
and accepting of you. It doesn't work all the time, but I don't
know any magic tricks.*

Although she says she doesn't know any magic tricks, Ann's
career progress shows what can happen when a woman takes control of gaining the support she needs. With knowledge and credentials, with assertiveness and courage, a woman can, in fact, begin
to create her own success at any age.

KAREN MORENO: MOVING BACKWARD AND STANDING UP

Karen Moreno is a 40-year-old vice president of purchasing at
Gannett Supply Company, who opened our telephone conversation
by saying, "I am African American, so my perspective is unique."
And, as she went on to tell me her story, I found out how unique
she truly is. In fact, even as I write this I find myself smiling. Karen
has a tell-it-like-it-is conversational tone.

Karen's mother was a secretary with a college degree and her
father was a military man. The family lived all over the world, and
she credits her ability to get along with all kinds of people to her
family's nomadic lifestyle.

*My perspective is rooted in my ethnicity, my gender, and my life
experiences. I was born a year after Brown v. Board of Education, prior to the passage of all the landmark civil rights legislation. Race relations in this country were evolving, but I'm
convinced now as I look back that my parents never encouraged me to pick a career path because they were afraid to build
hope for success. All they had experienced were barriers
erected by a racist society. Thankfully, society has evolved and
we've all witnessed positive change.*

Karen had worked her way through three and a half years of college, majoring in education, when she realized she really didn't
want to be a teacher. She dropped out of school and worked at a
number of secretarial jobs before landing a position as an admin-

istrative aide in President Carter's White House Advance Office. As she described it to me, this was a significant period of growth for her, giving her the opportunity to travel and develop her skills, but when Carter lost the election, she lost her job. While deciding what to do next, a colleague she knew at the White House asked her to join a group at Gannett as an office manager. The group was tackling a new project, now known as *USA Today*, and Karen took responsibility for accounting, personnel, and purchasing.

In 1984, Gannett decided to move its corporate headquarters from Rochester, New York, to Washington, D.C., where Karen was working. A year prior to the move, Karen had a new boss, whom she describes as "a nice guy, but pretty much a dinosaur when it came to career women, a throwback from a bygone era." During the years before the "dinosaur" arrived, she had worked her way up to the position of purchasing manager and had been negotiating with suppliers and working with department heads on her own, but when he arrived, he used his position to make sure his footprints were visible. For instance, before going into meetings together, he would tell Karen to remain quiet during negotiations.

During this period, Karen married and had her first child, and while she was out on maternity leave, he hired several women inexperienced in purchasing. When she returned from maternity leave and looked around, she realized what was happening and, as she astutely explained it to me, "The learning curve had flattened." In order to continue advancing, she knew she had to leave the department.

Looking for other opportunities, Karen spotted a chance to work with someone she truly admired—but in order to do so she had to take some steps backward. In the group coming down from Rochester was a man she described as "savvy, competent and genuine." She had met him when she first joined *USA Today* and immediately recognized him as someone special. The corporate move meant he would be coming to Washington, and he needed a secretary.

> *By this point I was a purchasing manager, so it meant I would have to make a move that, relative to title and image, would be a demotion. I knew that if I took the secretary's job, he would help me advance because he knew my background. So, I moved into the job as his assistant and within a year became a buyer on his staff. That was 1985 and I've been with Gannett*

Supply ever since. I have steadily moved from buyer to agent, to manager, to director, and now to vice president.

As she climbed, Karen continually demonstrated her courage in handling tasks and challenges. Hard work and a commitment to excellence mean being willing to do the small jobs as well as the big jobs, to go the extra mile without complaining. Karen told me one reason she is now a vice president is that no job was too big, too small, or too insignificant for her. The other reason is that she had the foresight to recognize a good mentor and was willing to take the risk of a demotion to align herself with him.

I credit my success not just to timing, tenacity, and aggressiveness, but to an individual who saw potential in me and was willing to provide opportunity. The most important training I've had came from him. He was willing to show me the ropes, point out the land mines, and help me understand the company culture. I doubt that I could have achieved this level of success without his selfless interest in showing me the way. I use him as a model for my own management style—give those who have potential and who also show interest an opportunity for success.

In addition to working hard and seeking support, Karen also told me that as a black woman she has never allowed "ignorant, mean-spirited things" to stop her, and she says women "must set goals, stay focused and ignore and sidestep detractors." She believes in being able to "stand up and wage a good fight" and warns women: "Take constructive criticism, but don't accept abuse."

One of the most significant lessons Karen has learned over the course of her career is to give voice to her concerns. While working for her mentor—for whom she has the greatest respect—Karen had a jolting experience that proved to her how valuable good communication skills are and how it is crucial for women to stand up for what they want. When Karen was not given a major account that she had requested, she was flabbergasted. Actually, as she recounted it to me, she was really almost knocked over when it happened.

I had expressed an interest in handling a $20 million account to my boss, but during a manager's meeting he assigned it to a subordinate of mine. Now, I would walk over hot coals for this man, but when this happened, I was stunned. I left the meeting *quietly enraged. After taking a lunch hour to cool off, I went to his office to present my case.*

Usually, I have found that once a superior announces a decision, it seldom changes because someone disagrees. He didn't alter his decision immediately, but three months later I was given responsibility for the account. I now believe he was simply testing me to see if I would speak up, and since then I've never regretted voicing opposition when things just don't appear justified.

When a woman asks for what she needs, she gains respect, which ultimately brings her closer to her goals. When a woman stands up for her beliefs, she displays self-confidence and leadership. By pursuing the issue and making a logical business case for herself, Karen got what she wanted, and, now, as vice president of purchasing, her goal to become president is within reach.

You ultimately become what you think. That in many ways determines what your fate will be. You've got to be willing to recognize the reality of your existence, but you have the freedom to choose and to change that reality. In my field there are few women. I was the first female purchasing manager on corporate staff, but I've never felt like a token. I know that I have never gotten anything that I did not earn because in this area, at this level, people are not in the habit of giving—there is simply too much money involved. Yet, sometimes when I've said that I want to be president, people have looked at me like I've lost my mind because I came to Gannett Supply as a secretary. But I happen to be one of those people who view the glass as half full.

It takes courage to take a demotion, and confidence to see beyond a position to possibilities that others can't envision. Karen knows herself and her abilities. Others might be skeptical about Karen's goals, but even though she started out as a secretary, she clearly sees herself as the next president of Gannett Supply.

VELA McCLAM MITCHELL: OUTSMARTING HARASSMENT

Vela McClam Mitchell, a marketing and sales director at Worldspan, a high-tech information services company for the travel industry, is a vivacious and determined woman who attributes part of her success to her "guts." She claims she has been able to succeed in male high-tech and aeronautical environments, like those at Honeywell, Hughes Aircraft, and Northwest Airlines, because of her ability to withstand harangues from her male superiors. And, like Ann Delvin, Vela says she has no problem with masculine styles of criticism.

> *I don't take things personally. Men curse each other out, but they don't get mad at each other. After they finish cursing, they talk to each other like it's no big deal. One guy reams another one day, but the next day, they're both okay. That's what I think helps my success: I've had men ream me, but I don't take it personally if I know it's justified. If somebody starts yelling at me because I messed up, they're not yelling because they hate me, they're yelling because they are worried about the business. I can relate to that. I love the game as much as they do.*

Yet, even with Vela's resiliency, she encountered a harassing situation that almost got the better of her.

Over the course of a woman's career, she will be lucky if she doesn't meet at least one boss whom she can classify in the most euphemistic way as "nonsupportive." When male bosses become threatened by female strength, they can react in a variety of detrimental ways, and when those strong women happen to be from minority groups, the situation can be even more complex. Vela ended up using her supportive network of family and professional friends to help her think and act rationally and strategically and turn what could have been a horrible working experience into a win for herself.

In one of the companies for which she worked, Vela had a manager who was—to say the least—less than supportive.

> *He constantly badgered me. Constantly. When I was hired by this guy we agreed I would have six months to learn the business and another six months to be productive. I believed I was not only holding to that agreement, but more than fulfilling it. In six months, I had learned the business and was already being productive. I'd cut costs. I'd reduced staff. I worked until 10 at night to make sure I got everything done, to make sure I knew everything I needed to know. But he was driving me up the tree.*

Vela isn't defeated easily, but after six months of taking continual verbal badgering and belittling from this particular boss, she began to question whether the job was worth the aggravation.

> *I went home one night pretty distraught and called my mom and dad for some inspiration and love. I started crying on the phone, finally letting all my frustrations out, because I certainly wasn't going to cry at work. My mother reminded me I could walk out any time I wanted. And my dad said, "You are still alive and you are still talking, so you are okay. You think because you are well educated, you must be accepted, but some people are always going to have attitudes and you have to withstand it and get beyond it. So find out what you need to do."*

With the loving support she received from her parents, she regained her energy and spirit and realized she had to devise a strategy.

> *I needed to figure out how to win; so, I called my best friend from graduate school, who is the toughest white broad I know. And she said something similar to what my mother said: "Your goal is to remain happy in the job or take yourself somewhere else. You're doing a good job and he knows it. Call his bluff. He wants you to be his whipping boy. Go in tomorrow with a letter of resignation."*

Knowing that she could get another job and had enough money to live on if she had to go on a job search, Vela overcame her fear and decided she would calmly threaten to resign. The next day, aware that her secretary would spread the word, Vela had her type a letter of resignation. Then Vela went around her boss by two layers and asked for an appointment with the executive vice president.

> *I wanted to let him personally know I was resigning and why. Word started spreading. The senior vice president, who was one layer up, sent his secretary to get me. I was prepared one way or the other. I didn't really want to quit, but I wasn't going to work for someone who was abusing me. So the senior vice president and I had a very rational conversation in which I outlined my accomplishments and listed the kinds of aggravation and humiliation that I had been dealing with. I told him I had come to the job with my self-esteem and I was leaving with it,*

even if it meant leaving that day. He agreed with me completely and asked me to stay until the end of the week while he worked something out. By the end of the week, my whole department was reporting to a different manager.

Later, Vela had a face-to-face exchange with her former boss, who, needless to say, was not pleased with the outcome of events. And Vela frankly told him that if he had treated her like a human being in the first place, the organizational changes would have been unnecessary.

Perhaps Vela's ability to make brave moves developed over time. Earlier in her career, her instincts to go with her gut enabled her to move her career forward in an unexpected way.

Vela held a master's degree in physiology education. Her first job was in social work, which she followed with a stint as a legislative aide on Capitol Hill. When she entered the business world several years later, she sold software services for a small high-tech firm. The company custom-designed programs for businesses and government, and Vela learned marketing concepts, computer technology, contracts, and purchasing on the job. After several years of gaining knowledge and experience, she set out to find something bigger and made a conscious decision to work for a company that would help finance her MBA. One night while she was out with a client, the opportunity to work for a corporation that would pay for graduate school presented itself.

I happened to be out one night with two friends. One was a customer with whom I had developed a friendship. She is a lieutenant who heads the unit responsible for developing computer operations for the Navy, and the other friend worked for Digital. We were having a drink in a Washington, D.C., bar, where everybody tries to sell something to someone in the government. And the three of us were talking business.

The guy sitting at the table next to ours overheard our conversation, introduced himself as a recruiter from Honeywell, and asked to buy us a drink. Of course, my friend from Digital thought he was giving us a line. But he handed us his business card and sure enough he was in HR. He invited us to a recruiting reception he was having the next night at Howard University and asked us to bring our resumes. My friend was skeptical, but I figured I would check it out; so, the next night, I went to the hotel where the reception was supposed to be held, and sure enough, there was a reception and he was in charge. And he was really pleased when he saw my resume. The following week the manager of HR at Honeywell called me and asked me to come to Minneapolis to interview for three different positions in Minneapolis, Boston and California.

When we are alert to opportunities and trust our intuitions, good things occur. The fellow Vela met was legitimate, was doing his job, and followed through on his word. Had she not trusted her instincts and taken the risk of being wrong, she might have missed out on getting an MBA at no cost to herself. Vela was offered all three jobs and chose the one in California. She started working for Honeywell in April, began her MBA work at Pepperdine University the following January, and completed the program in two years while working full-time.

Getting my MBA was one of the best things that happened to me besides having good parents, having a father who encouraged me to deal with money, and growing up in a small business environment.

Vela's capacity to go with her gut gained her additional credentials and advanced her career. Her ability to muster her troops, cast off her fears, and boldly take action not only moved her out of a harassing situation, but also relocated her under better people, strengthening her position and her alliances.

WOMEN MOVING FORWARD

The stories of Vela McClam Mitchell and Karen Moreno, both black women, contain harassing incidents to which most women can relate. But their ability to move forward, despite the behaviors they encountered, demonstrates the progress minority women, who make up only 5 percent of *female* corporate officers,[1] are making. Yet, because of the possible removal of affirmative action programs, minority women still hold concerns about the future. Although Vela acknowledges that her success comes from her own skills and guts, she also believes that affirmative action helped to open doors for her.

Affirmative action forces companies to look at you. That's all I want. I don't want companies to give me anything; I just want them to look at me. I want them to talk to me. And once they talk to me, they'll realize they're not giving me a darn thing. Affirmative action doesn't do anything once you are inside the door; it doesn't get you promoted and it doesn't get you more money. But it gets you in. Without affirmative action, I think people will suffer because they won't get interviews. The insidious thing about discrimination is that it's really subconscious. I see it every day. People are just not aware of it.

In today's changing environment, mandated programs supporting women and minorities are at risk of being scrapped as they were in California's 1996 Proposition 209 ballot question. Arguments are raging around the pros and cons of keeping affirmative action programs. There is fear that, without these systemic measurements, it will be more difficult to redress grievances and the work environment will become less supportive of women and minorities. As Vela points out, affirmative action only gets people in the door—what happens afterward depends on the company.

The good news is that research indicates that black women in management represent the fastest-growing segment in corporate America, and this growth offers hope. Corporations are beginning to institute diversity programs of their own accord because they are beginning to realize that diversity is connected to the bottom line[2]—in a multiracial global world, companies need to be able to relate to a wide range of customers. The Glass Ceiling Commission reports that corporate leaders say it is "easy to find top-quality black women."[3] Over and over again the women of color I interviewed said they are pleased with the efforts that progressive companies are making. They see discrimination operating on an individual, rather than on a corporate, level. What's even more encouraging is that the women themselves are hopeful about the future and are satisfied with their personal achievements.

Whether black or white, each of the women in this chapter tackled her career and faced her challenges in her own unique way. Whether she had to find her way out of the quicksand of a failing business or make leaps across chasms of learning, whether she climbed untethered by the security of a degree or had a late start climbing, or whether she had to confront harassment, each woman stared down her fear and accomplished what she set out to do. And each time a woman overcomes her own fear, not only does she move herself forward and create success for herself, but she also adds to the collective success and progress of all women.

In the next chapter we'll meet even more women who have brought their own individual brands of success to their organizations, and, in facing the challenges that confronted them, they actually changed the structures of their jobs and introduced new ways of working into their organizations.

NEW WORKING STRUCTURES

The psychology of the American workplace has focused more on the idea that work should be everyone's primary commitment and every-thing else should be secondary, which leads to a quantity versus quality orientation—how many hours people work versus what they do while they are at work. This is a particularly important issue for women because women have been expected to make the utmost commitment of both quantity and quality. In a reduced schedule, you may not be the one player in the single event, but you're still part of a relay team and you're still a serious contributor. And it's important that people know that.

ELIZABETH (BETH) RADER, Director
Deloitte & Touche, LLP

Donna Eidson, 43, opened our interview saying, "I've gotten to the point where I am more willing to say, 'This is what I want and it's okay.'"

Her comment resonates with our need to give ourselves permission to create success on our own terms. Success doesn't mean a woman has to be a full-time CEO, a vice president, or a general manager. And it doesn't mean she has to make more than X amount of money. For the women in this chapter, success means working within a nontraditional, flexible structure—at least, during this period of their lives. These women decided it's okay to do things their own way.

Donna is presently the executive director of the Polaroid Foundation, the philanthropic arm of Polaroid that decides which charitable causes deserve the corporation's dollars. I've known Donna since the early 1980s when she worked for a city newspaper in Massachusetts. I was going to march in Tallahassee, Florida, for the passage of the Equal Rights Amendment, and she suggested that I write about my experience for her paper. After three days of rallying, I wrote my story on a yellow legal pad while sitting in my hotel room and called it in to her over the phone. It was my first published piece. Since then I have paid close attention to Donna's suggestions, particularly when they pertain to my career. And every time I have listened to her, I have benefited. Her success as a part-time executive at Polaroid actually planted the seed in my mind for this book. When I looked at how she combined her personal and her professional life, it prompted me to think more deeply about what success means to women and to investigate further how women structure and fulfill all the varied dimensions of their lives.

As I researched women, it came as no great surprise to find that sometimes the demands of being a full-time career woman and a full-time mother can simply be too much and something has to give. In this chapter you will meet innovative and determined women, like Donna, who decided it was the nature of their professional jobs that had to change. These women found ways to alter the structure of their work in order to fulfill their definitions of success. When they couldn't find the balance that mattered so much to them, they joined with their companies to create new working arrangements and schedules that ranged from part-time to flextime to telecommuting to job sharing. They designed new ways of working in their companies to create win/win situations for themselves and their employers. Their stories illustrate that success can be achieved when creative women and enlightened senior management collaborate.

DONNA EIDSON: PART-TIME SUCCESS

Donna came to her decision to work part-time while she was trying to get pregnant. She was the manager of employee communications at Polaroid in the late 1980s, when the company was in the midst of a takeover attempt. Because the company was in a crisis situation, her position was highly visible; she had access to senior people, and she was developing her reputation and positioning herself for the future. But she was also trying with great difficulty to start a family, and, unfortunately, she experienced medical problems and miscarriages. Caught in the pull, which is familiar to many of us, she unconsciously began questioning where she should put her energies. The situation at Polaroid required her to spend six or seven days a week at work, putting in 10- and 12-hour days. As she described it to me, her job was both a "fishbowl" and a "pressure cooker."

> *It was a miserable scene. And I got angry. I knew it wasn't entirely in my control whether or not I could carry a child, but I wanted to do everything I felt I could possibly do to increase the chances of having that happen. No one told me to reduce my stress level or anything like that. But I must have felt in my gut that I should, because during a performance review, my manager asked me what I wanted to be doing in five years. I honestly wasn't conscious that I was going to reply the way I did, but I said, "I want to work part-time and I want to have a family."*

At that time, however, Polaroid didn't offer managers part-time arrangements. But Donna's male manager, who was extremely supportive, responded by saying, "How can we make that happen?" and assisted her in creating a flexible arrangement.

> *My manager was great. I started calling people in various areas of the corporation for informational interviews. I was fortunate because I had the blessing of two of the most senior people in the company. I was well-regarded and people were willing to talk to me.*

Donna contacted everyone whom she respected, telling them she was looking for a part-time position. During the process, one of her female mentors advised her to search for "the kind of work you really want to do." Since she was essentially creating a new type of structure for managers, her mentor believed she needed to be cautious and find the right position. Donna ended up with three possibilities and chose the Foundation job—it had stability and required community-building skills she possessed, and the Foundation's director was one of the most admired female executives at the company. The director was assuming additional responsibilities and needed someone to assist her three days a week. Donna began working as the associate director in November 1990, and, without knowing it, she was already pregnant. The following summer she gave birth to a healthy, beautiful boy.

Then, in the spring of 1996, the director, who had been a tremendous role model for Donna, retired, and Donna took over as executive director. The timing worked out wonderfully—Donna's boss retired just as she was beginning to desire extra responsibilities and challenges and as her young son was getting ready to start school. Donna still works on a reduced-hours schedule, but has increased her time commitment to four days a week.

Donna honestly acknowledges that her career has not advanced at full steam; nonetheless, she feels successful and describes her job at the Foundation as a "plum" assignment.

> *Everybody in the community loves you because you're giving away money. I tell myself jokingly "I'm such an important person—people return my phone calls." Yet, as much as I've enjoyed it, I also recognize that I'm working on the periphery. I'm moving forward and getting raises, but I'm not in the thick of things like I was before. Sometimes I do look at women who have incredible careers and I think, Wouldn't that be exciting to have that kind of thing? Yet I feel successful. I have balance in my life between my family, my friends and my work that feels really good. I also have tremendous control over my workload. I rarely have to do work at home. I don't feel like I need to make a lot of compromises in terms of my values and I feel like I have a lot of options. The Foundation job has been the greatest job for me during this phase of my life.*

Before assuming the position of executive director, Donna had contemplated other directions for her career, but had decided she didn't want to jeopardize the balance she had so successfully achieved. For now, she has decided to keep the Foundation job rather than seek a full-time, upward-moving position.

However, should Donna decide to put her career on fast-forward again, the benefits she has derived from her part-time position over the past seven years are numerous: She has been working in an area that she truly enjoys and has had a chance to improve her management skills. Because of the nature of her job, she has also had an opportunity to develop an extensive network, both inside and outside the company, maintaining her visibility. When I asked her what other directions she might take in the future, her attitude and belief in her abilities show that anything is still possible.

> *In terms of the future, there has never been anything that I've wanted to do that I haven't been able to do. I've been given a lot of jobs that I've never done before, but I've always been able to*

do them. I don't feel like a door is ever closed to me that I didn't close myself. I'm clear about my skills and know they are transferable. I'm a "doer." I take in information and know how to get things done. Tell me where you want to go and what you want done, and I'll get it done.

I enjoy people and I believe it's important to leave behind a trail of good relationships. I love problem solving and I'm not afraid of tackling tough issues. I've been told that I am good at being able to deliver negative news in a way that enables people to hear it. I'm also a good writer and communicator and I've noticed that the theme which runs through all my work has been community building in one way or another, so there are lots of possibilities.

Donna has also had the opportunity to work for "an extremely smart, very talented, incredible manager," who was highly regarded at Polaroid. In describing the training she got from this female mentor, Donna says, "I told her I felt like I was getting an MBA in management by working for her." So Donna can bring the knowledge and expertise she has gained from her mentor and her own experience with her to future jobs. Moreover, she gained that knowledge and expertise while achieving the balance that was so important to her and her family.

ELIZABETH (BETH) RADER: PART-TIME PROGRESSIONS

Every one of the women in this chapter demonstrates how success depends on being able to ask for what you need, whether it's skills and training, promotions or pay, or new working arrangements. When Elizabeth (Beth) Rader was looking for a way to balance her career as a partner at Deloitte & Touche LLP with being the mother of two young boys, she thought a reduced schedule was a good option. Beth started telling me her story in a way that I imagine must come from her accounting background: When she went back to work full-time after her second maternity leave, she "discovered pretty quickly that two are much more than twice one."

I was already a partner when I got married in 1986. Although we are both career oriented, we decided we would like to have a family. Our first son was born in 1991 and our second son was born in 1992. There were not enough hours in the day. I just didn't have enough time to devote myself to a full-time career in a way that I felt those responsibilities required and to have a reasonable amount of time with my children. I wanted to be there while the kids were growing up. At the same time, I realized that being a full-time, stay-at-home mother was just not me—it wouldn't be the best thing for me or the kids.

She decided the best way to find out if part-time work were possible would be to create a well-thought-out plan and ask for the firm's support.

In late 1992, I decided to take the leap and draw up the proposal. I figured the worst thing that could happen would be they would say "no," in which case I would regroup and figure out what else I might want to consider. In mid-January of 1993, the board of directors approved the concept of a reduced-schedule partner, and I submitted my proposal several weeks later.

Beth's needs coincided with the firm's decision to reduce schedules for partners as a partial solution to the high turnover rates of women. In the early 1990s, turnover for women at Deloitte & Touche hovered at 25 percent. Not only was the firm losing talented women, but it was also losing dollars the firm had invested in the women's training and recruitment. Client services were suffering as well: Relationships that had been developed over time were being severed, with continuity disrupted. New people had to be quickly trained to fill in the gap. When the firm quantified the cost factor for retention, it found that, by some measures, the cost of turnover affected the bottom line by $3 to $5 million.

In 1992, when CEO Michael Cook, the father of two young businesswomen, realized women were leaving at a higher rate than men, and at a crucial point when they should have been reaching partnership level, he formed the Task Force on the Retention and Advancement of Women to find out why. And a year later, he launched the Women's Initiative with the following goals: development of programs to enhance working relationships between men and women; enhancement of career opportunities for women through mentoring, networking, and career-planning programs; and development of criteria to measure progress. Between 1993 and 1994, about 5,000 people—every partner, senior manager, and manager—went through the program. By 1995, the firm had flexible work arrangements in place, turnover had dropped, and the number of female senior managers had increased. As a result, Deloitte & Touche won the prestigious 1995 Catalyst Award and was listed as one of the 100 Best Companies for Working Mothers for 1994 and 1995. The firm's goal for the year 2000 is to have women at all levels of the organization in close proportion to their representation in the labor pool, while enhancing productivity and client services.

Because of the Women's Initiative, the timing was right for Beth's ideas, yet she wouldn't have had the opportunity to become the firm's first part-time partner if she hadn't asked for reduced hours and hadn't carefully prepared herself by working out the details ahead of time.

Beth's reduced-hours agreement is somewhat open-ended: The firm has fairly flexible guidelines and the duration of her reduced-hours status was not predetermined. However, at some point, she is expected to return to full-time work. A reduced schedule at Deloitte & Touche remains a viable part of a career progression. It is considered neither a time-out nor a dead end. For example, after Beth reduced her hours, she advanced a level and received a pay increase. So the progress of her career has not been slowed by taking time out for her children. Since the Women's Initiative has been in place, not only can women and men switch to part-time after they have been made partner, they can also make partner from a part-time status and can continue to maintain a reduced-hours arrangement, with schedules varying from 60 percent to 80 percent of a full load.

According to Beth, women shouldn't hesitate to draw up proposals for reduced hours, but they should make sure their proposals represent a win/win arrangement. Flexibility won't sell if it is based solely on convenience to an employee. Proposals, she warned, need to meet both the company's and the individual's needs. Showing the company how it will gain an advantage by allowing the creation of a new structure, and how it will gain value by retaining the unique skills of the woman, helps to sell proposals.

Beth also pointed out that work/life programs make good business sense, but she urges women to communicate their needs for flexibility to management.

> *Flexible work programs will not be created just because they make sense. Women need to push forward on their own. In ad-*

*dition, the women who have gotten to upper levels need to work
to be part of the solution rather than silent in the process. We are
in a position to wave the banner a bit and move the cause along,
and I think we need to do that.*

Just as Beth thought she had one problem solved, however,
another one popped up: Her husband became the CFO of a client
company. Dual careers can cause complications that call for an
enormous amount of creativity and compromise. After discussing
options with her husband and the firm, Beth decided to resign as
a partner in order to avoid any conflict of interest. She now works
as a director, essentially doing the same kind of work she did as a
partner, but without the complicating aspects of partnership. As
she says, "It was a real dual-career dilemma, and one for which
there was no easy or ideal answer."

KIM HAINS: FLEXTIME STRETCHES OPTIONS

Kim Hains, 31, a senior vice president at NationsBank, has taken
full advantage of the bank's flexible working arrangements, and it
hasn't hampered her career at all. Even though she has worked
both part-time and flextime, she told me her ten-year career has
progressed just as fast as the careers of most of the people who
were in her original management training class.

At NationsBank, 54 percent of the bank's officers and 43 percent
of the top wage earners are women. But, like Deloitte & Touche,
NationsBank started losing high-potential females during the
1980s. In an attempt to find out what was causing the drain of its
female talent, the bank surveyed employees in 1986 and found
that women wanted time to adjust to family changes and flexibility
in how and when they did their jobs. As a result, the company took
an extremely progressive stance in formulating new family policies.
It established child care programs and more flexible scheduling
policies. By 1990, NationsBank had "SelectTime" options and
extended leaves in place, including maternity and paternity plans.

Kim, who is presently director of work/family programs, has
taken advantage of half a dozen different schedules and worked in
both staff and line positions during the course of her career. She
told me she has been using her present flextime schedule (5:30 A.M.
to 2:30 P.M.) since she returned from maternity leave in 1994. This
is the same schedule she used in 1992 when her son was born,

and, at that time, she was a production manager, managing three shifts at four different bank operation locations.

> *It was great for the company because usually third-shift people who leave at 6:30 in the morning never see the department head, who would normally come in at 8:30 A.M. So I saw the third shift before they left, and because I came in when they were balancing out the bank for the day, I was there at the time when they often needed a decision maker.*

As Kim explained it, not only did flextime ease the pressure on her family life, but her schedule also benefited the company, providing coverage the bank would not otherwise have had.

Flexible arrangements also help men. Kim and her husband, who is also a vice president at the bank, divide their parenting responsibilities to achieve an extremely balanced lifestyle. Between the two of them, they have a total of 12 weeks' maternity/paternity leave: 6 for her and 6 for him. When Kim's second child was born, her husband took part of his paternity leave to care for her, the baby, and their five-year-old. After Kim recovered from her caesarean, he returned to work, and when she was ready to go back to work, he took the rest of his leave to care for their new infant.

The culture at NationsBank has shifted to the degree that even men at the top are taking advantage of these supports. The bank's chief economist, one of the top people in the company, has three children and has taken advantage of paternity leave. New parents at NationsBank can also phase back into work as long as they return to their permanent schedules within six months. And upon their return to a permanent schedule, flexible schedules like Kim's are possible. With Kim's schedule she is able to pick up her children at school in the afternoon, while her husband takes care of the kids in the morning and drops them off at school before beginning his workday at 9:00 A.M.

Kim says that she has seen managers "be incredibly creative in trying to make flexible scheduling work." If an employee's scheduling needs can't be met working at one job, the bank tries to find another job that provides a better match elsewhere in the company. Even the company's busy discount brokerage desk, which deals directly with customers, has women working SelectTime. When a coverage issue did arise due to skyrocketing volume, the manager and the team brainstormed for a solution. The women altered their schedules: Two of them started job sharing, and the company helped arrange for additional child care. According to Kim, three or four years earlier that scenario would have been highly unlikely.

In providing guidelines for women, Kim, too, emphasized how important it is for women to be assertive in communicating their needs.

> *When I first began working this schedule, I had worked in more of a project capacity on operational consolidations and mergers. When they asked me to come into production and head the department, the timing was right: The bank had already introduced the flexible policies. So, I said, "Here is what I need to be able to do this job."*
>
> *They agreed to try out my requests. And 99.9 percent of the time that's the way it works: If you want to take advantage of opportunities, you need to tell your manager what you need. Outline a plan with regard to how you will accomplish your job on a particular schedule, what the benefits to the company are, and what the pros and cons might be.*

Working a flexible schedule hasn't detracted at all from Kim's career-planning strategies. She continues her upward progression by evaluating potential jobs for the knowledge and skills they will bring her. And she listens to her own instincts and to the advice of trusted mentors as she makes her decisions. She was emphatic when she said, "Trust yourself. Act on your gut. Think smart and say what's on your mind." According to Kim, women shouldn't get "hung up on male/female issues," but they should give their careers "the same amount of dedication, commitment and thought" they give any other major decision in their lives. And rather than being concerned about whether women can climb, Kim cautions women against climbing too fast.

> *Don't get caught up in worrying about where you fit on an organizational chart or how fast you are going up the ladder. Make sure you understand there are a lot of side steps on that ladder which involve building skill sets. It's important to move from one function to another. Find an area where you can transfer a skill set and then learn something new.*
>
> *You have to calculate how much risk you want to take. Make sure you bring enough other skills to the table so that you don't set yourself up for failure. At one point in my career, I was told I would be perfect for a particular job, and I can remember think-*

ing there was no way I could do it. I told one of my mentors, who knew the job and knew me pretty well, it didn't feel right. I was advised to be careful about being perceived as having unlimited potential and about letting people put too much on me too soon.

The trick is to stretch, but not to the point that the difficulties to adjustment and learning become demotivating. You don't want a job that is too far over your head, but you do want to keep progressing quickly. That's a hard balance to strike. So I didn't take the job that didn't feel right, but I took a similar job at the same level, where I had more experience with the work.

By carefully choosing jobs that provide her with learning and jobs that offer the flexibility she needs, Kim is able to balance her life successfully while continuing to progress in her career. A primary payoff of flexible work *is* continuous career momentum. A Catalyst study backs up findings at NationsBank and Deloitte & Touche: Flexibility and reduced hours increase retention rates without jeopardizing advancement opportunities. And, as with Kim and Beth, the women in the Catalyst study initiated discussions with their managers, speaking up about their professional goals and their plans for advancement.[1]

SARI CHAPMAN: TECHNOLOGY AT WORK

Sari Chapman's interest in telecommuting grew out of her own professional frustrations: She needed to inject some forward motion into her stalled programming career. Sari, a 35-year-old technology manager at Bell Atlantic's Federal Systems group, helped her company investigate telecommuting as a flexible work alternative, while gaining some much needed visibility for herself.

I drifted into information systems in college and during my first seven years at Bell Atlantic, I was a programmer. I was good at it. And, at first, it was a challenge, but it lost its edge after a while. I wasn't picking up any new knowledge. I was feeling frustrated: I didn't even have an opportunity to learn about PC-oriented or leading-edge database applications.

I decided I wanted to move ahead, but I didn't see any real career opportunities in programming. I realized I needed to become more aware of other job possibilities in the company. I hadn't really had a mentor during my programming years, so

*that was frustrating for me. I started reading company commu-
nications in more detail to find out what was going on in other
parts of the company.*

Through her reading, Sari learned about some technical opportunities that were opening up in the marketing organization, but
soon came to the realization that she didn't have the right telecommunications background. She discovered that she needed a master's
degree in telecommunications management to fill in her knowledge
gap and help her career gain momentum.

*School enhanced my visibility. For my master's degree, I did a
feasibility study of telecommuting in Federal Systems, which I
ended up presenting to the president and all of his direct
reports. They recommended that we do a pilot program to figure
out what is needed to support telecommuting. As a result, I was
also invited to join a Bell Atlantic–wide task force that is rewrit-
ing the company's policy and guidelines.*

When Sari started examining telecommuting, Bell Atlantic did
have telecommuting guidelines in place, but, as often happens in
large organizations, there were misperceptions and miscommuni-
cation about its use and application: People didn't know about or
understand their telecommuting options. Employees in her group
held the perception that they couldn't telecommute because of
their need to be available to customers. Sari says that people are
confused about the concept of telecommuting and don't have a
good understanding of what it actually means. When a manager in
the United States works via telephone, E-mail, or voice mail with
colleagues and customers—whether they are in the next city,
across the country, in Europe, or in Asia—she is telecommuting.
Instead of traveling to those sites to get her work done, she's using
technology.

*If you're telecommuting, you could be working from your home,
from your car, or you could be at a customer's site. Telecommuting doesn't mean you are less reachable. In fact, telecommuting
helps to overcome communication and distance barriers.*

In the feasibility study that she conducted, Sari said she discovered that managers often don't know how to handle a mobile workforce—in order to be confident their employees are working, man-

agers often feel they need to see their people. Another problem she uncovered is hesitancy on the part of employees who think telecommuting will have a negative impact on their visibility. According to Sari, people overlook the fact that in most offices employees don't sit at their desks all day, five days a week. People are at meetings and conferences and traveling, so there are times when those working traditional jobs aren't visible either. In order to make telecommuting successful, Sari's research indicates that companies will need to have proper training in place so that managers will learn how to handle a mobile workforce. Managers and employees will also have to agree on the schedule and the number of telecommuting days. And the company will need to set up the infrastructure and create policies to deal with issues such as who pays for equipment and how technical support is provided.

Sari's thesis on telecommuting gave her an entrée—she was viewed in a new light as an expert, was given access to senior management, and made contacts throughout the organization by working on the task force. Since she transitioned from programming into marketing and completed her master's degree, she has more opportunities and job options. Sari also began telecommuting one day a week as the demands on her personal life expanded with her marriage and the birth of two children. She finds telecommuting the best flextime choice: Job shares and part-time work reduce income, and flextime options are limited by her husband's schedule and day care hours.

> *I normally catch a train to downtown Washington, D.C., from our suburban home in Maryland, which is about 22 miles away. It's frustrating for me to work that far away. If the commute were shorter, I wouldn't feel as torn at the end of the day knowing I have to leave to catch the train. And in the morning, I have to rush my two kids out of the house to day care and preschool.*
>
> *I try to keep Thursdays free of meetings and other activities so I can use it as my telecommuting day and work on my laptop at home. I always have work that can be done independently whether it's planning or creating documents or returning phone calls.*
>
> *However, telecommuting is not a substitute for babysitting. When I telecommute, my kids still go to day care, but we can be a little more relaxed. We leave the house a little bit later and I can still start work earlier.*

Moreover, Sari told me, because she has a laptop for telecommuting, if she needs to finish work she might not have been able to complete during the day, she can work at home in the evenings. This gives her the freedom to leave her office in time to catch her train, and knowing that she can finish a project at home reduces her stress.

The response at Bell Atlantic to telecommuting has been very positive. A survey conducted by the Georgetown University School of Business for the company found that three-quarters of the employees who responded said they were more productive when they telecommuted, and over 80 percent said it improved their home lives.[2] "People have been really pleased," Sari says. "I've gotten a lot of great feedback. It is definitely growing and we are moving forward with it."

Telecommuting permits people to live farther away from their offices, creating more options for women and enabling managers to oversee geographically diverse groups. Sari claims Bell Atlantic has people in Pennsylvania reporting to managers in Virginia, and she says, "What difference does it make if the people work in the office in Philadelphia or at their home in Philadelphia? Either way they have to rely on voice mail or E-mail." Moreover, telecommuting enables people working internationally to have greater flexibility in overcoming time differences—making phone calls late at night or early in the morning is much easier to do from home.

Bell Atlantic is also examining the concept of having full-time telecommuters—people who would not have any assigned office space. With this approach, the company could reduce its operating expenses. As awareness of the benefits of telecommuting increases, companies and people will learn how to use technology in different ways to become even more flexible. As numbers of the women pointed out to me, all of our work doesn't have to be "face time," nor should face time be a requirement for success—the key is learning how to think and work differently.

Companies like Bell Atlantic are beginning to understand that it doesn't matter where the job gets done as long as it's done well. Telecommuting is proving to be beneficial to organizations in terms of improving attitudes and the efficient use of people's time. It lowers stress, heightens morale, reduces turnover, and increases competitive advantage. In fact, recent studies have even indicated that telecommuting enhances strategic planning skills because people have more time to think at home where they are less likely to be interrupted, and productivity has been said to rise as much as 20 percent.[3] Telecommuting even one or two days a week can make a difference in women's lives, helping them to maintain balance and a healthy perspective and fulfill their definitions of success.

CHARLOTTE SCHUTZMAN AND SUE MANIX: JOB-SHARE MANAGERS MOVING UP

I heard about Charlotte Schutzman and Sue Manix from Marilyn Mecchia, manager of work/life strategies at Bell Atlantic Network Services. Marilyn had been quoted in one of the articles I had read on flextime programs. I called her to see what was going on at Bell Atlantic, and she gave me Charlotte and Sue's number. After hearing their story, I became excited about their accomplishments and the job structure they had created at Bell Atlantic. Women can give birth in more ways than one.

When Charlotte, 37, and Sue, 38, first forged their job-sharing trail at Bell Atlantic, they were met with skepticism and fear. But, using their determination and expertise, they built a balanced space that gives them room for succeeding at home and at work. Their job share was originally the brainchild of Charlotte, a CPA with an undergraduate degree from Wharton, who was the CFO of one of the small companies in Bell Atlantic Enterprises. Problems in her first pregnancy caused her to take maternity leave earlier than she had expected, and the extended amount of time that she had to be away from her job did not sit well with her boss. While she was out on maternity leave, the corporate office unexpectedly called and offered her another position closer to her home, which she quickly accepted. But soon after she began this new job, she realized she no longer wanted full-time employment.

> *After my maternity leave, I worked in corporate for about six months, but I was really feeling the pain of working full-time— I wanted to be home with my child. My sister, who is a part-time lawyer in a firm, seemed like a good role model. So, after looking at other women and trying to decide who had the best of it—whose kids were happy and who was happy and fulfilled as a businessperson—I decided to ask for part-time work. But my request was turned down because the company said I had*

a six-day-a-week job, which couldn't be done in three or four days. That made me start thinking about job sharing. If most jobs at my level were really six-day jobs, why not divide the work between two women?

In the process of looking for a solution, Sue's name was mentioned as a possible job-share candidate. Although the women worked on the same floor of the same building, they didn't know each other. However, a short time after Sue returned from her maternity leave, Charlotte ran into her in the ladies' room, introduced herself, and the two women started talking.

Sue was thrilled to be back at work, talking to real people and I thought, "Forget it; this is not the right person." About four months later, I was getting ready to either quit or ask for part-time again, when I walked into Sue's office and she said, "It seems like it's getting harder, Charlotte. Tell me it gets easier." And I thought, "I've got her."

Sue had been hired into a management training program at Bell of Pennsylvania after graduation from William and Mary in 1979. The goal of the Bell program was to provide participants with high-visibility, high-risk, high-reward assignments in their first year. If participants made it through their first year, they were tracked to make middle management within a fairly aggressive time frame. Sue moved through her job assignments rather quickly and made middle management shortly after her fourth year.

In 1986, I finished a two-year MBA program at Wharton sponsored by Bell, and was ready to start a family. In tune with my plans, in August of 1987 I got pregnant with my first daughter and took six months off when she was born. I came back from maternity leave to a regional job and that was when I met Charlotte. At that point, I wasn't really ready to do part-time. But about three or four months later, we caught up with each other and said, "What are we going to do?"

The women made a date to go out to lunch and discuss the possibility of a job share. They wanted to see if they were at all compatible and discuss a possible course of action. Charlotte told me they knew that if they couldn't work well together creating the proposal, the job share would never work. Although their recommendations for beginning job shares include knowing each other well, they jumped in immediately, and over the course of lunch divided up responsibilities for putting their job-share proposal together.

> *I wish that I could say that I made the decision on my trust level of Charlotte, but we joke that our union was like deciding to get married after the first date. We didn't really know each other and we didn't know what we were getting into. I think I made my decision more on knowing that part-time work was the thing for me to do. Charlotte claims I said something like "Somebody is going to be the first to do this job sharing and it's really important that it be done right—I want to be part of doing it."*

Their proposal had to be approved by the head of HR for the entire corporation, but they first presented it to Charlotte's boss because they believed the more flexible culture of Charlotte's organization (which was the unregulated side of the corporation) would be more open to a job share than Sue's. Thus, they proposed working on a modified version of Charlotte's job, with responsibilities for compensation, HR issues, and business planning. Charlotte believes the company would not have been as hesitant about their proposal had the women, who were middle managers, been working at a lower level, but, as women in management, they were breaking entirely new ground.

> *The company's big fear was that everyone was going to want to do it and we would open floodgates. We emphasized the point that not everyone would want to job share—mainly because it cuts your pay in half. We were met with a huge amount of skepticism, which made us even more determined— there was no way we were going to fail, even if it killed us.*

Senior management was willing to give them a small window of opportunity, but their proposal was initially accepted with several conditions attached: Their job performance would be reviewed in six months, no one could report to them even though they were in middle management, and they should not expect to get promoted.

Charlotte and Sue emphasize the points made earlier: If they hadn't had the courage to ask for flexible work arrangements, they might not be with the company today. Charlotte adamantly believes in making stretch requests.

> *Don't be afraid to ask for what you want. You have nothing to lose and everything to gain. If they turn you down, they turn you down. If Sue and I had never asked for job sharing, we wouldn't be here. If we hadn't pushed at different levels along the way, we wouldn't be here. If we gave in after a year or two, we wouldn't be here. But you have to plan out what you want. And you have to have someone looking out for you, helping you to build those networks and relationships.*

Contrary to complaints often aired by women about men, it was men who helped Charlotte and Sue push that window of opportunity wide open. Charlotte credits two important male mentors for helping them to break ground.

> *We had to prove ourselves to our first boss in the job share, but he was extremely supportive, especially in getting us promotions. We still go and talk to him. Our other mentor was the fellow we reported to after our first promotion. He was a very tough individual, a perfectionist. We had our hardest time with him; he wouldn't take anything less than perfection. But to this day he is an unbelievable, tremendous supporter. These guys told others how our job share worked for them and really promoted the benefits they derived from having two perspectives and two backgrounds.*

Job shares can be arranged in a number of ways, and doing whatever works best for the company and the job-share partners is probably the best guide to use. In Charlotte and Sue's job share, each of them is technically scheduled to work two and a half days. Charlotte works Mondays and Tuesdays. Sue works Thursdays and Fridays. And they alternate Wednesdays. They share all their work and simply pick up where the other person leaves off.

> *Each week on the night before Sue takes over, I'll prepare a list of things she needs to know and a list of things she needs to do and provide her with any supporting material she might need to bring her up to speed on our projects. And she'll do the same the night before I take over. So we talk to each other on the*

phone the night before the transition. We try not to call each other on our days off unless it's really necessary.

They are also flexible about their schedules. Since Charlotte is Jewish and Sue is Christian, they swap holidays to accommodate each other and joke that they have all their bases covered.

Their first job-share position lasted for about a year and a half until they both became pregnant for the second time. Charlotte said the only thing worse than having to tell her first boss that she was pregnant was having to tell the team's new job-share boss that *both* of them were pregnant!

Needless to say, our simultaneous pregnancies opened us up for a tremendous amount of joking, but here's where job sharing paid off. My second pregnancy proved to be even more problematic than my first, and I had to quit working three months early. So Sue worked full-time for both of us until she had her baby. And our kids were born three weeks apart. In turn, I worked full-time in 1996, while Sue was on maternity leave with her third child.

When they returned after having their second children, Charlotte and Sue moved forward and upward together. People began reporting to them and they continued to break down barriers. The stipulations that the company had imposed on them at the beginning of their adventure fell away. They were given a new job, reporting to a senior manager who helped them get promoted into a position as assistant secretary of the corporation. This was an important promotion for them: It increased their visibility, enabled them to build important relationships, and gave them the opportunity to work with the chairman. As their skills became known, particularly their planning skills, they received larger assignments, and in their latest assignment heading employee communications, they reengineered and restructured the department. Within two years, they succeeded in turning it into an efficient operation, paring it down from approximately 50 to 15 employees. Having achieved their goals, they are now looking for new opportunities as a team.

They said the one factor that has complicated this job is their three-hour commute to Arlington, Virginia, from their homes in Philadelphia. They decided to make the long commute because, as

Charlotte says, they simply didn't want to lose a unique chance to move forward.

> *We felt if we passed up the opportunity at this level of a promotion, it might never have come our way again. So we decided to do it and to take advantage of what it offers us.*

Their willingness to adapt themselves to this arrangement exemplifies how sacrifice and resiliency are required for success. In order to take a job so far away, the two women rent an apartment in Virginia. With the job share, each woman has to stay overnight only one or two nights a week; without the job share, the promotion for either woman would have required a relocation. Although Sue admits that travel and being away on a regular basis is "a real pain in the neck," it's worth the reward of keeping her home life and professional life in balance. The only area that still leaves her uncomfortable is handling the feelings she experiences when she's away.

> *Those weeks when you leave the house at 6:00 A.M. on a Wednesday morning and get home at 8:00 P.M. on a Friday night are the killers. I don't like being out of the loop for that long. We've had a live-in au pair since my youngest daughter was six months old and that really helps, but I don't like turning over the reins for that long. My kids have mixed feelings about my absence. But I also think it's important in raising young women that they understand that sometimes it's hard, but mommy really likes her job and she has work responsibilities.*

If she ever did give up her job, Sue, who says she takes care of "zillions of things around the house" compared to her husband, worries that he would lose some of the understanding he's gained about what it takes to work, run a household, and care for children.

> *If I were home full-time, he wouldn't have a clue and he should have a clue—it makes him a better boss and it makes him a better peer. I have a fear that if women stay home, we are going to lose another generation of men.*

Charlotte's husband has also had to bear more responsibility for their two sons, and, in the process, Charlotte says he has developed even closer bonds with their boys. When Charlotte first started staying overnight in Virginia, she confessed she left menus and two days' worth of notes, but over time she says the couple's roles "changed somewhat." She admits it's been hard for her to give up some of the control, and both she and her husband are adapting to sharing the load.

> *I hope I raise a different generation of boys. I hope my sons will be more accepting and more balanced by seeing the role models that they see at home. In fact, we had to laugh—a couple of years ago when we were making our New Year's resolutions, my husband's resolution was to achieve a better balance for himself, and my son looked at him and said, "Dad, why don't you share your job with someone?"*

JEAN BRENNAN AND ERIN ANDRE: THE UTILITY OF JOB SHARING

At the same time that Charlotte and Sue were making their bold move on the east coast, Jean Brennan and Erin Andre were making their plans to become the first women at their level to job share at Pacific Gas & Electric (PG&E) in San Francisco. Erin and Jean joined forces in 1990, and seven years later they are running a department of 30.

Like Charlotte and Sue, Jean and Erin presented a proposal that was accepted on a trial basis. As with Bell Atlantic, at first, PG&E had reservations about the women's ability to cosupervise and believed the women would have a greater chance of success handling a smaller number of direct reports. Yet both teams have proven that job shares can manage larger groups.

When they started the job share, Jean and Erin had each been with the company for seven years and, like Charlotte and Sue, they worked on the same floor, but didn't know each other. Jean was the director of career management and was having her first child. She had the idea for the job share and was looking for someone who was politically well positioned to help her sell it. Erin was a prime candidate. Erin, who was already working on a part-time basis on special projects, had worked in labor relations, in the field as an HR generalist, and for the vice president of HR, with whom she had a good relationship.

Jean compares their alliance to a marriage or a business partnership in which both partners must work very closely with each other. In fact, the women's husbands jokingly refer to them as "work spouses." Jean now has two children and Erin has three, and both of them told me how thankful they are for the balance and happiness job sharing has brought into their lives.

Unlike Charlotte and Sue, Jean and Erin have stayed in the same job as directors of staffing and succession planning. Their responsibilities include staffing, recruiting, internal placement, relocation, succession planning, and executive development. Both Jean and Erin have HR backgrounds and are presently comfortable working in a staff function. Jean describes herself as having a "strong social, people commitment" and HR, she says, fits her personality well. She has had opportunities to work outside of HR and has been asked about taking line management positions, but she simply hasn't been interested.

> *I like the kind of work I do. I get really excited about changing the organization. To me that's been my primary motive and the reason I went into this field. I like having the ability to influence the organization and I don't have a high ego need for being seen as the person who did, and I think that's what it takes in HR. Since I started in HR, numerous changes have been made at PG&E. I no longer have to prompt officers to talk about the movement of women and minorities. These topics are being discussed and the officers are now leading the discussions. I feel like I've made a difference.*

Erin agrees that the work she and Jean do on women's issues is valuable. She says, they "are partners at the table, solving business issues in succession planning," and their skills are valued and utilized. In contemplating the future, though, Erin says other areas do interest her and when she is ready to go back to full-time work, she might pursue jobs in other functions. Rather than seeing their job share as a sidetrack, both women view it as a wonderful benefit, enabling them to have the best of both worlds.

Jean and Erin work as a unit and are technically considered six-fifths of a person. Each woman works three days a week with one day overlapping. They took over Jean's job, dividing the client base in half while maintaining some shared responsibility. Jean remained the primary contact for particular business units and Erin became the primary contact for others. Erin told me one of the challenges for her was to establish credibility with clients who had previously worked only with Jean. Clients had to become comfortable dealing with her and develop trust in her abilities. However, as clients became familiar with both women, they were amazed at how well the job share worked.

> *If an officer calls Jean on a question and Jean isn't in, I respond. If I meet with a client and issues come up, everyone knows Jean is my job share. They know if they can't get me, they can talk with Jean and they don't have to miss a beat because Jean and I brief each other on what's happening with our client groups. We also switch primary responsibilities from time to time. On days when we're not working, we still talk. We spend anywhere from a brief conversation in the evening to one to three hours of our non-work days on the telephone.*

In addition, each woman has primary responsibility for her own direct reports, but they confer with each other and keep each other informed of what's happening. Jean says she appreciates having "two sets of eyes" for performance evaluations.

> *I've given the best performance feedback to employees since I've done the job share, because I have somebody else to talk my assessments over with, somebody else to help me choose the right language. It really helps.*

However, an area that merits caution, according to Erin, is clarifying people's perceptions of coverage. Erin says that job sharing can increase coverage for the company, but it still doesn't mean that someone is in the office every day. If one partner is off-site for a meeting or conference or is taking a vacation day, it doesn't automatically mean the other partner comes in. On the other hand, for extended leaves or long vacations, coverage tends to increase. When Jean took her second maternity leave, Erin increased her time; when Erin went on her third maternity leave, Jean did the same. And when Jean takes vacation for the entire month of August, Erin works full-time, which provides PG&E with coverage the company would not otherwise get.

Erin claims that once managers have worked with the women and understand how the job share operates, they become strong advocates. Two people can provide more quality work than one person working alone. Erin says she and Jean can see the transformation of attitudes and she's amazed that the concept hasn't caught on in more companies.

JOB-SHARE PARTNERS: WHAT IT TAKES TO MAKE IT WORK

Charlotte, Sue, Erin, and Jean all agree on the key characteristics managers must possess to make job sharing work—and the top two traits are excellent communication skills and flexibility. Job-share partners must be good communicators because information exchange is constant and understanding each other is an absolute necessity. Each partner has to hear what the other is saying and understand the priorities and issues. Beyond the flexibility that is essential for compromise, the women are also flexible with their scheduling and child care arrangements. Sometimes both partners need to be at a meeting or days must be switched to meet clients' needs. Jean and Erin end up switching days several times a month. "The key," Erin says, "is to do what's best for the good of the organization, not the job share."

All four women acknowledge that a job-share partner must be able to give up her individual ego for the good of the team. Teamwork, they agreed, is essential. One person cannot have a need to look better than the other person. As Sue says, "You cannot be threatened. You cannot have a need to have something be yours. You really have to know how to share." Erin told me her job share with Jean has worked well because they both have "about the same level of ambition and need for recognition." Neither of them has "the need to grab credit." Yet the women are not without a sense of self. In fact, it is each woman's strong sense of self that allows her the freedom to put aside her individual ego. Charlotte says, "Ego is still there, trust me, and it's very strong, but it's not individual ego, it's team ego." And Jean's theory is that since women are socially conditioned to compromise and reach agreement, it's easier for them to make the psychological connection to the shared concept of "our product" that's needed in a job share.

> Lots of women have really strong egos, yet they seem to have the ability to transfer their own individual ego gratification and satisfaction to the product of the team. Actually, a new ego— the team ego—arises.

Other characteristics needed by job-share teams include complementary skills, similar values, and trust. Jean and Erin are very different personalities, but, according to Jean, they "almost always reach the same decision." And they don't have many disagreements on how to do things.

> *I think it's wonderful development for both of us because Erin is much more Type A and I'm much more Type B—so together we calm down or speed up. We have different skill sets in terms of background and human relations and that helps because I learn from her and she learns from me. Like any partnership, we give and take, and we compromise.*

Charlotte and Sue also have few disagreements. They might approach an issue somewhat differently, but Charlotte, similar to Erin and Jean, says they "almost always end up with the same decision."

> *Our opinions on people are almost exactly the same. There's a give and take between us. If we do have a difference in a business decision, we're not that far apart that we can't easily compromise. We know each other's hot buttons and we know when the other person has a strong preference on something.*

According to Erin, having a different management style from Jean benefits the job share. She and Jean are both strong managers, but they have different strengths that balance the relationship and fortify them as a unit.

> *Jean is very patient and easy to speak to. I think that I tend to be more direct and we use that to our advantage. I'll initially push hard on something and then Jean can soften it. I'm more comfortable playing the devil's advocate. Our differences give us flexibility. I learn a lot from her. Sometimes, I might want to push too hard, and she might not feel the issue is worth the energy. Together we come up with the right approach and it works out really well. We have developed a natural ebb and flow in who talks and who pushes. It's almost like a married couple where you can read your partner's mind. We use a variety of techniques in building agreement by using each other.*

Similarity in work ethic and values creates the trust needed for Sue and Charlotte. Sue believes it is critical to have the "same inner standards in terms of your work product."

> *You also have to be willing to delegate and have faith in the other person. You have to be really comfortable telling the other person what's expected and then let her go do it.*

These characteristics seem to come naturally to these women. Charlotte claims many people, particularly men, ask her how she could put such blind faith in someone else. And Sue points out that job sharing won't work for everyone, but all four women believe job sharing has brought balance into their lives. Charlotte says that as hard as she works on the days she's at work, when she's off, she's off, and she doesn't have to worry because she knows that Sue is there. The job share keeps Sue from being "a total nerd about work," allowing her to spend time with her kids and do the things she loves. Jean also admits the job share saves her from her tendency toward being a workaholic. She and her husband made a conscious decision when they married to make their children a priority, and the job share provides a vehicle for Jean to accommodate both sides of her personality.

> *I feel very comfortable with the balance I've achieved. My husband and I wanted to combine work and family without driving ourselves crazy. By job sharing, we've been able to do a good job of balancing. I can do chores like shopping during the week which allows us to do family activities on weekends. I look at job sharing as a gift to myself. Life is too short to be an absolutely frantic person and I do have frantic tendencies. I know myself well enough to know that this provides me with the kind of time that I really do need. On the other hand, I made the decision that work is a very important part of my life and I can't imagine not working, so to me it's been a great combination.*

The job share enriches Erin's life by giving her the flexibility to work in her son's classroom on a weekly basis. Both she and her kids love her arrangement and call her days at home "mommy days." Yet Erin admits that she is not without her psychological pulls and tugs.

On most days I'm satisfied. Sometimes, however, I see appealing jobs that I don't pursue and wonder what it would be like to run a different organization. Then, the next day is a "mommy day" and I'm working in the classroom and I realize that I have the best of both worlds.

If I were at home full-time, my kids would probably be sick of me and I would probably go crazy. If I worked full-time, I'd worry that I'd be making too many compromises. Other women can do it well. I'm sure I could too, but I feel fortunate that I don't have to. When the kids are a little older, it will be different. Right now, job sharing allows me to feel like I'm being a good employee and a good mom. It lets me try and do what I want in all areas without feeling like I'm failing or not meeting my own expectations.

These four women have been crusaders, blazing new trails for others. As difficult as forging new paths can be, these women have found a great deal of satisfaction in knowing they have succeeded. When Sue looks back over her years of job sharing, she says, "The single most satisfying aspect of my work has been making job sharing a good, acceptable working arrangement at Bell Atlantic." And Charlotte concurs.

Some people call us trailblazers. But I wish somebody else blazed the trail; I would have been happy to follow. My greatest satisfaction from the job sharing is having done it successfully. We have made tremendous strides. We have broken barriers. There are now probably two dozen job-share teams, but the dam didn't break like they feared. We're seen as the matriarchs and it cracks me up sometimes because I don't think I'm old enough to be in that position.

Job sharing enables women to remain an integral part of their companies and allows companies to retain highly talented women who bring a wider range of skills to the job than one person alone could. The job shares of Charlotte and Sue and Erin and Jean serve as models for what can be accomplished when companies like Bell Atlantic and Pacific Gas & Electric provide creative, talented managers with enough autonomy to set their own courses. By trailblazing flexible work arrangements, these women have proven that doors once tightly locked can be opened and new ways of working can be created.

FLEXIBLE STRUCTURES STRETCH INTO MANAGEMENT RANKS

The groundbreaking women in this chapter overcame skepticism within their companies and proved that flexibility works, even at management levels. Experts are now advocating the adoption of flexibility as an effective, competitive strategy—a new way of doing business. Flexibility adds value. When women work in flexible structures that help them fulfill their own definitions of success, companies benefit from managers who operate under less stress, with more energy, and with an enhanced sense of loyalty and commitment. Flexible work arrangements underpin balance and provide multiple paths from which women can choose how they wish to pursue their careers.

Many companies are incorporating flexibility into work schedules through a variety of arrangements, including flexible or reduced hours, compressed workweeks, job sharing, and telecommuting. For example, at PG&E, in addition to job sharing, people can work four 10-hour days or what is known as "nine/nines"— employees work 9-hour days and get one day off every other week. Numerous studies conducted by research institutes and companies instituting work/life programs during the last decade reveal the positive impact of flexibility on employees.[4] Creative work arrangements boost morale, commitment, performance, and retention rates, while lack of flexibility not only drives up attrition rates and increases employee stress, but also lowers productivity.

NationsBank's studies found that workers had higher morale and greater loyalty because they appreciated the bank's commitment to helping them balance work and family. And since flexibility has been introduced, there has been a significant decline in turnover in the professional ranks. The more autonomy and control women feel over their ability to create flexible work schedules, the less burnout they experience and the longer they tend to remain with their employers. A recent *Working Mother* magazine survey also found that flexibility has a greater impact on women's happiness than any other work factor. Seven out of ten of the happiest women enjoyed some degree of control over their schedules.[5]

Some alternative arrangements provide greater career progression than others, and there are limitations to flexible structures. Part-time work and job sharing reduce pay, restricting these arrangements to women who can afford them. Conflicts in family schedules can prevent some women from taking advantage of flex-time, and the nature of particular kinds of work will keep others from participating in telecommuting arrangements. Sometimes companies have the best intentions, but they meet with obstacles to implementing flextime. Even after policies have been changed, cultural attitudes and beliefs can impede the change process. While many companies offer flexible practices, they are not always fully utilized because individual managers do not support their use and employees fear negative consequences. A 1993 Rodgers & Associates survey of 80 large companies showed that fewer than 2 percent of workers use job sharing, telecommuting, or part-time options.[6] And a 1994 Conference Board study backed up those findings in the companies it surveyed.[7]

Yet there is tremendous potential for structuring new working patterns. Technology has helped people around the globe communicate and work together more effectively. It can be utilized in corporations more than it presently is and, in the process, help people to achieve better balance. As the stories of these executive females demonstrate, flexible scheduling can successfully stretch up the corporate ladder. Management jobs and flexible schedules are not antithetical—creative arrangements can benefit both the organization and its managers. In fact, a Ford Foundation research project in which Xerox participated found that "the beliefs and assumptions that create difficulties in work/life integration also lead to unproductive work practices."[8] So, by tackling work/life issues and uncovering deeply held assumptions about the role of work, companies can change corporate cultural views and construct more productive organizational practices and structures.

A key to success in structuring flexibility in the workplace is to make sure the offerings match the needs of employees. By reviewing and refining work/life policies to fit the changing requirements of both the company and employees, corporations are more assured their efforts will be rewarded. Marilyn Mecchia, manager of work/life strategies at Bell Atlantic Network Services, says companies have to communicate with their employees and find out what is truly important to them.

> *What the company might think is flexible may not be what is really needed. So, we've got to ask the people. Companies might think they have made a great policy, but when it goes out to the people, the response is "Why did the company do this? We don't need this."*

Managers and employees are also responsible for making flexibility work. Women who desire flexible working patterns must be flexible themselves and clear about their individual choices. Not all women have the same feelings about balancing careers and motherhood. Each individual brings her own experience to the workplace. Differences of opinion, if not handled well, can cause harmful chasms. Open dialogue around flexible working arrangements is essential if new ways of operating in a diverse workforce are going to be successfully implemented. If we respect each other's decisions and show concern for the well-being of all employees and their children, we can help to incorporate programs that help employees balance their lives.

As we look at women's progress, one of the deeply held beliefs that comes under scrutiny is women's role with regard to family. How can women be both managers and mothers? These questions reflect cultural concern about the well-being of children and deeply rooted, instinctual beliefs. They are crucial questions that deserve our continued attention. Unless both women and men have the proper supports, unless there is corporate flexibility, and unless the organization and the society within which it resides make sure the children are well taken care of, we are all in danger of losing ground. Both our larger cultural system and the organizational system benefit when the well-being of families is integrated into the system's value structure. Both men and women must work together, inside and outside the corporation, to create environments that will support flexible structures and the transition of roles without threatening the well-being of our children.

The innovative women in this chapter demonstrate what can be achieved even when others say it can't. And their creativity and determination show how women motivated by excellence and balance can meet organizational and personal goals while working flexible schedules. These women have proven it's possible to succeed by doing it their own way.

BALANCING ACTS

Historically women have been like the canaries in the coal mines, warning of danger. Women are the first to recognize issues that need attention. Right now women's voices are being raised around work/life balance issues and they have been its strongest proponents. Like the canaries, they are warning that we were all dying under the stress of not having that balance. I think that's positive and is influencing what's happening.

JUDY BEAUBOUEF, Chief Legal Executive
Barnett Banks, Inc.

Harriet Nelson and June Cleaver never had to worry about balance. They always looked calm, controlled, and pretty, their hair coiffed and their aprons starched. Work for them consisted of taking care of the boys. Although a few women I know still function within that traditional and perhaps even mythological family, the reality for most of us is far different. Most of us have thrown out our aprons, but we still care about our looks, and we still seek a calm, controlled demeanor. Yet our days are hectic, filled with family *and* work, and, despite the difficulty of meeting the demands of both, the majority of us seem to enjoy the combination.

Studies show that women like their jobs and work boosts their self-esteem. In fact, researchers have found that parents who are happy at work and have high levels of satisfaction have the happiest and most well-adjusted children.[1] Women *have* found ways to fulfill their personal and professional needs. In the national survey, a whopping 92 percent of the women were satisfied with their career choices and almost three-quarters of them were satisfied with the level of balance they've achieved. But in order to feel fulfilled and meet the demands of family and work, women require support from society, from their companies, and from their families. Women want balance—it's part of their definition of success, but they have come to realize they can't find it on their own. Without support, someone or something—people or performance—suffers.

In the last chapter, we met women who created flexible schedules or reduced-hours arrangements in order to find balance. But not everyone can work a flex or part-time schedule and not every woman wants to. The women in this chapter discuss balance issues and share strategies they used for creating better balance in their lives while working full-time jobs. Balance means having a sense that the "right" amount of time and attention is being given to work and to the personal side of life—that a woman feels as though she is covering most of her bases the way she wants to most of the time. Yet, as every woman working full-time knows, finding balance isn't always easy. Women who consider themselves successful don't expect the impossible; they accept the fact that at certain times they will experience less than perfect balance. They also understand that balance requires some amount of compromise, some amount of sacrifice.

The vignettes on the following pages present methods women have used for controlling their time and setting limits. Of the 45 women I interviewed, 33 have children. They sought balance by making decisions with their children and families in mind. They weighed all the factors in their definitions of success and established their own routines for working. And their decisions enhanced their feelings of success.

LEARNING FROM THE PAST

In looking back on their careers, some of the older women I interviewed wished they had set more boundaries around their activities, and several told me they would do some things differently. Corporate America wasn't especially welcoming to them when they started in business—just maintaining their jobs was a feat, never mind asking for balance. If they had it to do over, they said they would not make as many compromises on the personal side of their balance sheets. However, when they first entered the corporate world, they saw few options: If they wanted to succeed they just had to hang in there; it was too soon for them to try and change the culture. So, they had to go along with the model that was in place. Women no longer have to go along with old models; women can lead the way for shorter hours and greater balance. There are lessons to be learned from women who didn't have the opportunity to raise their voices on balance issues the way today's women do.

US WEST Vice President Teresa Wahlert worked until the day before she had each of her three children and admits she didn't have "a whole lot of balance," especially early in her career. She acknowledged to me that if the clocks were turned back, she might not make the same choices, but she says, "At the time, that's where I was." If she had it to do over, she might turn down some of the jobs she took and work fewer hours.

> *Having three children, I was eventually able to see the first tooth of somebody and the first step of somebody, but I didn't necessarily see all those important firsts with each child.*

When Teresa, who is 47, reflects on the 1970s and remembers the lack of support and even the criticism with which she had to deal as a working mother, she attributes the negative attitudes she encountered to the times. Teresa joined Northwestern Bell in 1970 and married in 1975. Not only did she have to take corporate flak, but her husband, who worked for the same company, was also the recipient of negative fallout.

Working inside the same corporate family as her husband presented the couple with complex challenges, but Teresa claims it also put her in the unique position of being able to use her husband as a mentor and a "male network translator." She took advantage of his viewpoint and benefited from having his masculine perspective, and together they studied the successful men in the company, using them as models to copy. However, trying to keep both careers on track in the same geographical location at times tested the couple to the extreme and, as they both climbed, they moved back and forth across the country with their children and went to great lengths in order to keep climbing. As the following story illustrates, Teresa made fairly dramatic sacrifices.

> *When we hit barriers, and we did, we had explicit conversations about what the next move should be in relation to what happened. He brought the subject of barriers up as many times as I did. And because we were both pursuing careers, and had to follow one another, when I hit a barrier it impacted both of us. We took a tour at AT&T in the early '80s because I had hit a brick wall with career development and we thought we needed to take a drastic step. I felt if I was going to go further, AT&T would be good to have on my resume. We both searched for AT&T opportunities and decided we would follow whoever got*

the first job. I got it, and my husband became the trailing spouse, but we both landed great new positions. I ended up working in New York City and he worked in New Jersey. It was fairly traumatic moving from Nebraska to New Jersey—the kids were four, two, and six months old. I ended up commuting four to five hours a day and we had to hire a live-in nanny. It was a true learning experience in many ways.

After the divestiture of AT&T, Teresa and her husband were faced with another traumatic relocation, which became a huge turning point for the couple—both personally and professionally. They were still living on the east coast, but had to decide whether to uproot their family again.

We thought we had figured everything out and decided to stay with AT&T when Northwestern Bell called at the last minute to offer me a promotion. We had to rethink our decision: Not only did we have to decide if we wanted to pursue our careers at AT&T or at the Baby Bells, but we had to decide whose career would become the major one. It was a definite advantage for me to go back west, but it wasn't for my husband. It was a big decision and a real growth experience for both of us. My husband had to have enough self-esteem to be comfortable with the decision to give my career first priority.

After moving back west, Teresa's career continued progressing, but once again, the family was faced with a relocation decision. Teresa had let management know that she wanted the company to provide her with a graduate fellowship in management from the Sloan School of Management. She already had one MBA, but as she says, the Sloan program had "a different aura"—because the company sponsors and pays for the program, it demonstrates a visible commitment to a manager's career. Her fellowship called for returning east to spend a year at MIT, which also meant her husband had to once again put his career on hold. He took a year's leave of absence in order to make sure the entire family could go to Massachusetts together. And, at the end of that year, at the young age of 49 but with 30 years of service to the Bell System, he retired and Teresa became the sole breadwinner.

Yet, with all the moves and stresses of trying to climb at a time when most women didn't climb, Teresa believes she did find ways to adapt her situation to meet the needs of her career and her family. She told me, "My husband and I spent a lot of fun time with the kids in the evenings and on weekends. We didn't do anything unless we did it with them." Another way Teresa has stayed connected to her family while she has been at work is through the use of a private phone line in her office that is only for her family.

> *As the children grew older and needed help with schoolwork, if I wasn't at home, I would do homework and study for tests with them over the phone. So we participated even if we weren't face-to-face.*

In the past, she interrupted whatever she was doing to talk to whomever was calling, but in recent years, Teresa says she has given these interruptions even greater priority and has placed more value on balancing family needs. Her mother now has Alzheimer's disease, which is another family issue that calls for Teresa's attention on a day-to-day basis. Teresa acknowledged that if she had it to do over, she might do things differently, and when I questioned her about the future, she said, "I still have many career aspirations." But she cautiously added that the direction her career takes will depend on "where the opportunities are, what the requirements are, and what I am willing to give up at this point in my life."

When Judy Beaubouef, chief executive counsel at Barnett Banks, looks back at how she meshed work and family, she wishes she had spent more time with her oldest son. When Judy's marriage was in trouble, she became extremely focused on work. "Any ordinary fear of failure," she said, "was heightened because I was scared knowing I had to support us." Now she is much more cautious with her time and splits it between work and her youngest son. She also makes sure she schedules vacations into her calendar—something she didn't do when she was working 80-hour weeks for the law firm before she joined Barnett.

> *When I look back, I realize I basically had blinders on. You get so caught up, particularly in litigation. I had deadlines and hearings and it just isn't easy to juggle a schedule because of the nature of what needs to be done and clients who expect you to respond quickly. And I was traveling much more then too. I think the balance issue was driving me to reevaluate private practice, which then led to getting this in-house position.*

Some women in law are finding corporate life more amenable to family life than private practice, but each woman still has to make choices about how she will meet her family obligations and fulfill her professional desires.

> *A couple of years ago, I was waffling about taking the kids to Olympic National Park in Washington when a friend reminded me that if I didn't take them then, a time would come when they wouldn't want to go. So we went. And every year that advice rings in my ears. Over the last few years, I put vacation days and days for my sons on my calendar just like a business appointment. I don't let anything get in the way. I found it takes some courage to do that, but I am convinced that otherwise we can get sucked into a vortex and we can't get out.*
>
> *I am also convinced that if people schedule time for themselves and their families, it will not affect their careers. The people at Barnett are highly motivated to do a good job; they are not going to slack off. They will still get their work done, even if it means finding a different way to do it. The company is not going to suffer.*

Marlene O'Toole, the IBM regional manager for customer support, raised five children during the course of her career. Reflecting the commonsense and down-to-earth way that she approaches work and life, Marlene stresses how important it is for women to take their lives in stages and to accept the responsibility for shaping the way they want their lives to unfold.

> *Women have to map it out—they have to know where they want to go and what it costs. Some of the women I've seen torture themselves. It's just not possible for women to have everything all at the same time. You have to pace it. I try to emphasize the point to the women I coach that they have time—they don't have to do everything in 90 days. You have to segment at what time in your life you're going to do what. And you can't hold the corporation responsible for meeting all your needs. The women who think they can do it all end up burning out, and then wonder why. Make a choice, and live with your choice. Some of the pressure women experience is self-imposed. It's up to women to decide how far and how fast they want to go.*

Marlene preaches what she practiced: She first started working in 1967, but didn't immediately try to climb into management ranks. She keypunched during the day and gave time to her personal life without the distractions of management responsibilities. During her early working years, Marlene took in a foster child and then married a man with four children. Later, her parents, who lived in the same two-family house, became seriously ill, placing more demands on her time. It wasn't until the late 1970s—after the death of her parents, and after the five kids were older—that Marlene had the time and the energy to give to a management career.

> *My line managers ask me how I did it with so many kids and the answer is simple: I had a deal at home. My husband and I agreed I would do certain things and he would do certain things. Some of my line managers tell me their husbands won't take on household responsibilities and my response is: "Then tell your husband he doesn't get your money. Tell him you're quitting. Ask him if he's going to get a second job."*
>
> *Many women don't have partners or they don't have good partners, and those are the ones we have to worry about. Women cannot have it all without a great deal of compromise and help. I don't see how you can raise your children and work 60 hours a week. There are only so many hours in a day. I also realize some moms have to work. Twenty percent of the people who work in my organization are single parents.*
>
> *But we're creating an awful lot of problems. This will sound terrible to some people, but someone has got to stay home with the kids. I don't care if it's the mother or the father or an extended family member. We should support fathers who want to stay home. We need to teach that it's okay to have dad at home. I'm not so sure we are sending the right messages. Staying home with young children is rewarding. While women are at home with children, they can give something back to the community or they can take courses until their children are in school full-time. They can take a hiatus and come back to their careers. They can do constructive things and enrich their portfolios a little while they wait.*

Sometimes a woman's career will call for more attention; other times, her family will. Gloria Santona, associate general counsel and secretary of the corporation at McDonald's, combined her career and motherhood by using what she describes as a "flip-flop" pattern. Unable to have children, Gloria dedicated herself to her career, but when her biological clock started sending its final warning signals, she decided to do something about it. And, now, at 45, she and her husband have adopted a baby boy. Having her child after her career was well established enabled Gloria to feel balanced and successful.

I'm at a stage in my life where I can afford to have a child in more ways than one. I was always a perfectionist. Now, I'm more comfortable with my career, which I love, so I can afford to be more relaxed about it. I don't feel that my son is going to impact my career. I can enjoy him fully without feeling like I am making a sacrifice. I can afford to be more relaxed about raising my son, because if I had done this at 25, I think I would have made myself and everyone around me crazy. I was not ready. Because of my increased maturity, I'm able to appreciate motherhood so much more and to enjoy the fun and excitement of having a child. I'll be older than dirt when he goes to school, but I figure it will keep me young.

Women's lives simply don't flow in one set pattern—women have too many demands that are different for each individual. Becky Allen, CEO of Barnett Banks Private Client Services who stayed home when her three children were young, reminded me that it's okay to proceed according to individual needs—there is more than one pattern for success.

Technology, job shares and flexible hours are making balance easier. Women can enter the workplace after their children are in school and still have plenty of time to work. They may be coming in at a much lower level and may have a lot of competition in front of them, but it doesn't mean they can't succeed—I was 30 when I started my career. I went to work because I had to—I had no choice. The family unit is extremely important. But you should prioritize. When you have a choice, you need to make choices that are in the best interests of your family unit.

Her advice is to sit down as a family, draw up family goals, and make decisions about what's best for the family unit. And she warns that if a woman's husband is not supportive, the woman is in trouble. "The husband," she says, "has to be on board." Her comments also support Marlene O'Toole's—it's okay to stay home with children while they are young. The point of the feminist movement was to give women equal opportunity to succeed, not to force them to conform to a particular model of success. True equality stems from making choices that work best for each woman and her family. "If you have babies and you can afford to stay home and nurture them and be a full-time mom," Becky says, "I think that's wonderful."

We are looking at the beginning of a new paradigm. Recently, the value of "traditional" family life has received recognition and companies are looking for ways to help employees meet their personal and familial needs. The concept of *wholeness*, of being able to mesh the personal aspects of the self with the professional aspects of the self has entered corporate conversations. And now that women have reached a critical mass, they are speaking out to make changes in their organizations. We need to make sure that we keep the volume of our voices tuned up on balance issues, so that women and men in the future won't look back and wish they had done anything differently.

DOING WHAT'S RIGHT FOR YOU

Procter & Gamble Vice President Carol Tuthill admits there is pressure to juggling career and family, but says she feels good about the balance in her life. She usually leaves her office by 6:00 P.M. in order to eat dinner with her family and be involved in the activities of her three children. Carol works between 55 and 60 hours a week, but not all of her work is done at the office. She brings work home and does it after the children are in bed.

> It's impossible to do everything perfectly. It's a constant battle of choices and priorities, but I really believe my role is to make those choices. If things start to feel out of balance, it's in my control to do something about it. The big thing for me is just being clear about what is important to me.

Repeatedly, the women I interviewed stressed the point that it is the responsibility of the individual woman to let management know what she wants from her career and what kind of support she needs to help her maintain balance. Yet women also admit that asking to have their needs met is not always easy. Carol acknowledges that many times it was difficult for her to ask for help, but when she did, she received the support she required.

I was my own biggest barrier. Women do that to themselves all the time—they don't want to ask. People do not have crystal balls in their heads. I wish I had one. A magic wand would be great too, but that's not standard issue equipment. So be articulate about what you want from your career and about the balance in your work and home life.

Carol also stresses the importance of good communication between spouses. She told me her husband is truly an equal partner and they are "very clear" with one another about their needs and wants. Both of them are actively involved in their children's lives and they take turns taking time out from work to go to their three children's events or take them to doctors' and dentists' appointments.

What matters most, Carol says, is "being in control of doing what is right for you." As she puts it, that also means knowing how to negotiate an "exchange." Balance has a price tag. Getting what a woman wants for herself requires giving up something in one area to gain something in another.

If I choose to ask for flexibility from my boss, which I do, then I need to be more flexible with him when he makes requests. If my boss asks me to meet with him and I want to say "no" because one of my kids is in a soccer game, then I've inconvenienced him. It's not a big deal to him, but it means that when he asks me to meet a deadline or provide him with something he needs, I have to be willing to adjust my schedule for him. That is a normal give and take of an exchange.

I've chosen to be different from my peers many times in my career and I don't mind paying the price. If you choose to have children as I did, and take maternity leave, you cannot look over your shoulder to see if you are moving at the exact pace as a peer who has never left the workforce. That's not fair. I want to be judged on my contribution, but if I'm not around to make a contribution, that is probably going to count in some way. I have taken maternity leave four times and I don't feel I have paid an unreasonable price. If anything, despite those leaves, I've leaped ahead.

Carol suggests women look at the exchange process from a positive, rather than a negative, perspective. So, rather than feeling like they have to pay a price, if women focus on the value of the trade-off, they will feel better about balance issues and career advancement.

When you are asking for something, think it through. What is it worth? What is a reasonable thing to give in return? This doesn't mean the company has an obligation to meet every request either. Companies are not social service organizations: They exist to make a profit in a way that is healthy for their employees, their customers and the community. But you need to know what you are going to do to support the business if you want some special consideration on your end.

Carol also pointed out that "hours can be a sticky subject"— women who succeed often tend to be "accomplishment oriented" and "driven to work more whether they are working on something at work or at home." Therefore, imbalance can be a result of internal versus external forces, and women need to take responsibility for how they spend their time as well as for the results they produce. In addition to asking for help and knowing how to negotiate a good exchange, in order to set limits, women need self-knowledge and an awareness of their tendencies toward perfectionism or workaholism.

For some women, self-knowledge and getting a handle on what they want for themselves is one of the first difficulties they encounter. Pulled between mothering and working, some women struggle with their own emotions, unsure of where to put their energies. For Jan Tomlinson, president of Chubb Insurance Company of Canada, the idea of combining work and parenting came as somewhat of a surprise. Jan, who is 45, grew up at a time when women expected to get jobs, get married, have children, and leave the business world behind—all in that order. When she was hired in 1973, her boss asked her how long she was going to work, and she said two years. However, nine years passed before her son was born. Those nine years gave Jan a taste of the satisfaction that comes from meeting business goals and making things happen, and after Jan stayed home with her new baby for ten weeks, she realized that she truly didn't want to give up working. In giving advice to other women, Jan says, "You never know until after you have children what your decision about work will be."

However, coming from a family of 11 children and raised on a Midwest farm, Jan had some nagging concerns and wondered if she was doing the right thing by going back to work. And, naturally, she called her mother for advice.

After that conversation, I understood that my mother had sub-consciously influenced my career choice more than I had real-

*ized. In my conversation, I reminded my mother that she was
always home when we got home from school and how great it
felt for us knowing she would be there. She asked me what I
specifically remembered. And I answered that I always remembered having home-baked bread when we came home from
school.*

*She responded by telling me that she wasn't always there:
She was helping my dad run the farm—she just gave us the
impression that she was always there and home-baked bread
was one way. She said that I needed to figure out what I really
wanted to do, and if I wanted to go back to work, I needed to
give my son the sense that I was always there for him.*

*So I don't make bread, but I do I take him to school every
morning and I try to create rituals that are constant in our lives.
I have also been very open with everyone I've ever reported to
about my expectations: If I am in town, I never miss a sporting
event, and I take time to go to school for teacher conferences. I
tried very hard to do those kinds of things with him and I think
it's worked. Once I decided to go back to work, my husband
and I made some very conscious decisions about how we
would structure our time. Chubb has never been a nine to five
company; so, we decided we would be as busy as we possibly
could be during the week, but the weekends were for our son.*

By creating rituals, Jan maintains consistency and provides the
feeling for her son that she is always there for him, even though
she is not at the door to greet him. This helps her balance motherhood with managing her company. And by acknowledging (with a
little help from her mother) what she wanted for herself, she was
able to structure a balanced life.

SAYING NO TO LONG HOURS

Whether women are married or single, whether they have children
or animals, they want balance and by actually setting balance as a
goal, women have found ways to be just as productive, while
increasing efficiency at work and harmony in their personal lives.

Connie Van Zandt, director of planning and fulfillment services
at Gannett Company, is separated with no children, and is on a
quest for balance. For a long time she worked 60 to 70 hours a
week; now, she works between 45 and 50. Unless she absolutely
has to, she no longer works on weekends—something she used to

do on a regular basis. Connie told me there is a general underlying assumption that the people who work longer hours get the promotions, but she acknowledged there was a cultural shift taking place at Gannett. Connie echoed other women in saying there is always more work to do than hours in the day. Her advice to women is to learn how to prioritize time, determine what to say no to, and schedule reasonable commitment dates; otherwise, she claims women will find themselves getting buried. "If you don't schedule properly," she says, "you end up working incredible hours and not giving the right priority to things."

Cathy Spotts, a general manager at Baxter Healthcare Corporation, is another reformed workaholic who is consciously trying to reduce the number of hours she works with each promotion she gets. At one point in her career, Cathy worked for three months straight without a day off. Then, she learned that many tasks really didn't need the attention she was giving them. Now she works between 45 and 50 hours a week.

> *I worked 15-hour days including Saturdays and Sundays. I gave 150 percent to everything, and finally I realized that I didn't have to do everything 150 percent—some things could be done at 70 percent and some things didn't need to be done. So I set a goal to try and strike more of a balance. Now, I don't work on weekends unless I absolutely have to. My approach is to do what absolutely has to get done first and I plan out the rest. I'm much more efficient, have a much better perspective about what needs to get done, and I prioritize much better.*

Cathy also wants her staff to lead balanced lives: "I tell my staff I want them to spend time with their families, and then I do too." She has instructed them not to send voice mail or E-mail messages to her or to each other at home or during holidays or vacations unless it's an emergency.

Allegiance Healthcare Executive Vice President Gail Gaumer is another female leader who holds her workweek down through discipline and good organization. She has set limits on her time by refusing meetings or, if she has to, she admitted, she will even "walk out of meetings." Yet, she says, no one has ever questioned her work ethic. Another way she sets limits is by hiring "good people," who, she says, are "the answer to many issues in the workplace." When a manager hires key people she can trust, she can effectively delegate work, knowing that it will be efficiently carried out.

Commuting taught Diana Bell, an operations manager at Hewlett-Packard, how to utilize her time more efficiently. Her 40-mile drive between Oakland and Palo Alto was so long that she car-pooled in a van three days a week. Therefore, she had to leave her office at a specified time on those days. As a result, she learned how to put boundaries on her responsibilities and duties so that she wouldn't miss the van. Moreover, her colleagues, knowing that she used the van, scheduled meetings not to conflict with its departure time.

> *The van helped me focus on the ways I used my time, how I packaged my days, and it helped me prioritize activities. It gave me structure and sent a message to other people about how they used my time. I learned that people will respect your time restrictions if they understand them and you share them. I learned to speak up to people about my time. I started noticing that these jobs don't necessarily require all this time. There's always more to do than you can do, but it's often how we use our time during the day that determines our need for extra hours.*

Diana used her time in the van wisely as well. She caught up on her reading or actually held one-on-one meetings with one of her direct reports who also commuted using the van. Now Diana prior-itizes all her activities and writes all her commitments, even per-sonal ones, onto her calender. She told me she "honors" whatever she writes in and won't infringe on it or overlap activities—she even blocks out thinking time.

> *I plan with my administrative assistant to leave a day each week free. I may choose to do something different that day or a meeting might be called that can't be avoided. But in general I know that I have that free block of time that is thought time. If your calendar is full of meetings, you end up doing your think-ing work after work.*

Scheduling her time so precisely helps reduce Diana's stress level and enables her to get the work that needs to be done com-pleted in a reasonable time frame. As Diana has spent time reflect-ing on balance issues, she has put balance itself in a new perspective.

I believe in personal ownership and preach it to my team. We have to be careful about giving up the ownership for our lives to anyone. Instead of talking about career management, we ought to think about it more in terms of life management. What are you trying to do in your life? How does your career help you get there? Our lives are more than our careers. There are benefits from being in a corporation, but what does that mean in the scheme of things? How do you balance your life as opposed to balancing your career?

BUILDING TIME FOR YOURSELF WHILE COUNTING ON DAD

Stress can influence effectiveness, and some women find the best way to reduce stress is to set aside time for themselves. Darlene Solomon, manager of the Chemical Systems Department at Hewlett-Packard, told me she needs some time for herself each day and, by running for 45 minutes (often at lunch), she gives herself the "downtime" that she feels enables her to function at her best. When I interviewed Darlene, her desk was in the middle of a busy office and she was surrounded with a hubbub of activity. I had expected an R&D facility to have a sterile quietness about it, but hers did not, and I could appreciate how taking time out for herself in the middle of her day—even running—would be relaxing. Darlene said she also tries to schedule occasional lunchtime tennis games with her husband—she candidly admits that in meeting the needs of her children and work, her relationship with him sometimes has a tendency to get sacrificed.

I put the kids' needs higher than ours when we're at home. Sometimes the stress shows when my husband is worried about his work and I'm worried about my work and neither of us is thinking about each other. Sometimes we try to play tennis at lunchtime and get some "real" time together. Little things like that help a lot. You have to be committed and do what you say you're going to do.

Although Darlene says the responsibilities for children and household duties are not a 50/50 split, she appreciates her husband's contributions and considers his efforts critical for maintaining balance. He makes breakfast every morning and they grocery shop together on weekends. Darlene has two children, one in elementary school and one in preschool. Having a second child was a big decision for Darlene, who had successfully combined working with one child, but was hesitant about whether another child would upset the balance she had achieved. She overcame her concerns by networking with other female engineers. Talking to them boosted her confidence and assuaged her fears—since they had successfully managed their careers with more than one child, then she felt she could too. Darlene admitted to me, however, that she takes things one day at a time. She keeps her workday to a normal 8:30 A.M. to 5:30 P.M. schedule, but she usually puts an hour or two in at night and a couple of hours on Saturdays or Sundays. She is pleased with her children's day care arrangements and her mother provides backup when her kids are sick or when she has to travel. However, travel does increase her stress level and she no longer accepts last-minute trips, knowing she has to have time to plan arrangements.

Without support, especially from husbands and fathers, wives and mothers say career life would be so much harder and there would be far less chance to find balance. I was surprised to hear how much support the married women I interviewed received from their husbands. Almost every married woman commented on what a critical role her husband plays in her success. Ellen Gabriel says her husband is "Wonderful. Incredible. He's the best." And she says that, whenever she talks to women and they ask her about the key to success, she tells them, "You have to find the right husband." Marlene O'Toole says her husband is "one in a million." Cynthia Danaher claims her husband is "great," and bluntly adds, "If you don't have that support at home, forget it." And Kim Hains, a senior vice president at NationsBank, says her ability to balance her life comes in part from her husband's full participation as a parent.

> *My husband and I both take full responsibility for parenting. I could never say that I come home to another job. Our work at home is clearly 50/50. When I travel, he adopts the flex schedule. When I'm out of town, he leaves early and picks the kids up. It is our partnership that causes balance as much as the bank's flexibility.*

When women speak this highly of their husbands they reveal the heights that can be achieved when men and women work together in collaboration for the good of the unit—both the family and the business unit.

Some women attributed part of their success to role reversals in their families. According to the Bureau of Labor Statistics, 205,000 men were keeping house in 1993, an increase of 49 percent since 1989.[2] Karen Moreno's husband is one of those men. He's a Native American ex-Marine who has no problem being a househusband and stay-at-home dad for their three children. When he and Karen decided to start a family, they agreed that one of them should stay home with the children; since Karen's career looked the most promising, they decided that he would take care of the kids while she continued climbing. He makes dinner for the family during the week, and Karen takes over on weekends because she enjoys it. They both do household chores and are both avid gardeners.

> *My husband is my light. He gives me tremendous support. Without him as a partner, I couldn't possibly have come this far. Yet, balance is not easy. If you seek balance in your life, you need to understand that at some point in your career path, you may stall. I believed that if it became necessary to step off the career path to have a baby, there was nothing to prevent me from stepping back on. I stepped off three times to have children. But I'm extremely fortunate because I'm able to come to work without worrying about how my children are being cared for. I don't have to send them off to school when they're sick because I can't afford to take time off. It's an incredible life and I'm lucky.*

Even with her husband at home, Karen confessed to me that sometimes her own aggressiveness makes her "a little crazy" because she wants the house clean, she wants to be involved with PTA and her children's soccer and ballet, and she wants to give her husband personal attention too.

Karen, who works about 50 hours a week, arrives at the office early in order "to get a jump on the day, to plan and focus." The key to balance she says, "is what you do when you get to work." She does not micromanage her staff and believes in flexibility, but she told me, "I expect results and those who work with me understand that." She wants her managers to "work smart, maximizing their time so they're not forced to work late," and believes that managers who know how to balance their lives make better performers.

At Beth Kaplan's house, there is a 65/35 split of domestic responsibilities and her husband carries the lion's share of the burden. When Beth headed Procter & Gamble's Cosmetics and Fragrances USA, she traveled 40 to 50 percent of the time, and her husband just took control of family matters.

> *Our situation works because my husband is more than supportive: He digs in and just assumes total responsibility. He takes care of all the domestic details. We never have a debate about who is going to do what. We hardly ever discuss it. My career takes general priority.*

Beth's husband makes sacrifices to make her career work. When Beth was offered the opportunity to head the Cosmetics and Fragrances USA division in Baltimore, they had to relocate from corporate headquarters in Ohio to Maryland, which meant her husband had to close his business and start over again in a new state. When she tried a long-distance commute during the transition and found leaving her young son too difficult, the family moved sooner and her husband took on the long-distance travel.

> *We decided that since my husband wasn't quite ready to wrap up everything in Cincinnati and since we had a great nanny and had just moved into a new house, I would commute on a weekly basis. I left on Monday mornings and came home on Friday nights. My son was fine. I was a mess. I would leave very early on Monday morning to catch my plane and would sob all the way to the airport. After about three months, I couldn't do it anymore. So we moved to Baltimore sooner than we anticipated and I was much happier. My husband commuted while he wrapped up his business in Cincinnati and then he started a new business in Baltimore.*

In fact, because management at P&G knew that Beth's husband's real estate business was firmly established in Ohio, Beth almost missed the chance for the promotion. If she hadn't had an enlightened boss who wouldn't allow the organization to make assumptions for her, she might not have been given the promotional opportunity. If she didn't have a supportive husband who puts her career first, she would not have progressed as far as she has.

> *My husband and I had never discussed relocating because I had worked in headquarters for 13 years. I was still on the same floor, parked my car in the same spot, and took the same*

drive to work. Up until this point relocation simply hadn't been a factor, but I was almost taken off the list of potential people. My son was only a year old. We had just moved into a new house and my husband's business was firmly entrenched. Everyone just assumed I wouldn't want to move. But my boss stood up for me and said, "Don't make that assumption—ask her first."

I didn't know any of this was happening. Out of the blue, I got a call from the head of U.S. operations to come up to his office. We circled around the subject for awhile. Would I be willing to relocate? Would I move to Baltimore? Would I like to work in cosmetics? We went around and around, but by the end of the discussion, he offered me the job. It took me very little time to say "yes." I remember calling my husband on his car phone. When he answered, I said, "You better pull over."

Beth told me that when she worked at P&G she wasn't the only woman in her division with a helpful husband. She said that virtually all of the senior posts were occupied by women and several husbands stayed home caring for the kids. With such support at home, Beth has found that travel has been the only factor in her career that ever caused her to feel out of balance—no matter how much her husband helped at home, she still had to be away.

I will do almost anything to sleep in my own bed. I have been known to take the 9:00 P.M. train home from New York, which arrives in Baltimore at midnight, and take an early plane out the following morning to another city. I do prioritize travel because I could travel even more than I do. If my schedule has been crazy, I will say "no." When possible, I get people to come to me. I use the phone as much as I can and I've been encouraging the advertising agency and others to use the videoconferencing center. But there is still a certain amount of required travel that is not discretionary.

Travel does add hours and stress and represents the ultimate challenge to finding balance. By assessing corporate travel requirements more thoroughly, companies can help managers trim travel time and fewer hours can become the norm for both men and women. Other women I interviewed concur with Beth about travel and they try to use other communication methods—videos, faxes, E-mail, teleconferencing, and even rotating staff members for trips—to reduce travel. The women claim that more managers are accepting this new way of working, and as more women demonstrate how well technology and creative problem solving can substitute for long hours away from home, less travel can become a new corporate norm.

In 1996, Beth took another promotion and accepted an offer from Rite Aid Corporation (which she had previously turned down twice because of her commitment to P&G) to become an executive vice president. Her new senior management slot required no relocation and, in fact, will actually help her reduce some of the stress she experienced around travel in the past. In her new position, a corporate plane provides her with greater flexibility—no more late night trains—and her travel will be all domestic, cutting down on travel time. Travel, as Beth points out, is not just an issue for women.

Many men don't like traveling either. To be honest, I think it is somewhat easier for me as a woman to say "no" to someone, than it is for a man. I don't do it often, but if there is something important happening with my son, I will ask someone to shift a date or time. I think it is easier for a mother to do that than it is for a father.

Unfortunately, Beth seems to be right about attitudes toward men and flexibility. Kathleen Gerson, a professor of sociology at New York University, conducted research on men in the workplace and found that almost a third of the 180 men she interviewed wanted to be more involved with rearing their children, but were reluctant to ask for flexibility out of fear of being penalized.[3] Hopefully, as more male leaders—such as former U.S. Labor Secretary Robert Reich, former Assistant Attorney General Deval Patrick, and former American Express President Jeffrey Stiefler—quit demanding jobs to find more flexible work,[4] the message that men as well as women want more time for their families and better balance between work and home life will penetrate deeper in the masculine psyche, which still entangles the hierarchical structures of corporations. The more clearly this message is heard, the more men and women can seek to alter the ways they work.

CAREER CHANGES FOR BETTER BALANCE

Sometimes balance requires giving up a particular career goal and trying a different career path. Florence Williams, who told me she had "gotten pretty far in a short period of time," thrived in the fast-paced manufacturing environment at Xerox. She also said she worries that if she does ever have to slow down, she'll "lose her mind." Florence's original career goal was to become a plant manager, but she had to shift her career plans because family and balance issues unexpectedly interfered.

> *At my ten-year mark, I could have been a plant manager if I had chosen to take the job, which is exactly where I wanted to be. I am 100 percent satisfied with the opportunities I have been given and what I have achieved. I turned the job down because the timing was off. Being a plant manager consumes you and I have a daughter who is a year and a half old and I have a stepchild who is 13. My husband was offered a tremendous job opportunity in Boston, so he and my stepson moved down there, and my daughter and I commute from Rochester to Boston on weekends.*
>
> *I had numerous conversations with the people involved with nominating me and everyone understood my situation. I would have been consumed at work and would have needed to be in on Saturdays. That would have left only Sunday to somehow see the rest of my family. It was really an impossible situation, just not the right balance at this point.*

Florence and her husband, who had also worked for Xerox, had believed they would retire together from a company they found so supportive, but when he was presented with this great job offer, the couple decided he should take it and they would try living in two houses. So, even though Florence did not accept the plant manager's position and accepted a staff position instead, she stayed with Xerox. But eventually two houses became one too many and the commute simply became too much. Florence became the trailing spouse and she is now happily employed in the Boston area, again working in the same company as her husband.

Becoming a plant manager at Xerox was also Diann Monroe Jones's original career goal, and she had carefully laid out the order of the management assignments she needed to achieve her goal.

> *I knew how crucial the manufacturing supervisory role is—it's the ultimate key position that you need to build from if you want to be a product manager or a plant manager. I also knew how demanding it is, so I decided to get it behind me while I*

was young. During the six months that I was a manufacturing supervisor, I learned so much that I immediately sought it as my first permanent assignment and, for almost three years, I supervised on the manufacturing floor. I figured if I got married or had kids I would not have that type of demand on me when I was in a critical stage of my personal life.

After she finished her three-year supervisory stint, Diann took a two-year job as a manufacturing engineer, followed by an 18-month job in quality control, and from there she moved into a supply and demand role. But then she began shifting away from her original career plan.

I was building an operational path toward becoming a plant manager, which had been my original goal. But by the time I reached supply and demand, I was married and I had a child and I started to migrate away from the notion of becoming a plant manager. But I had a wealth of operational knowledge, so I thought I could utilize it in a planning capacity. In my current position, I do strategic planning for international business and I'm happy with it.

Diann's decision to steer away from operations did not leave her feeling that she made a detrimental career move. She was wise enough to understand the time requirements of the manufacturing floor and got the really demanding work finished early in her career. But as her own life changed, her attitudes about where and how she wanted to work changed as well. As Diann's family grew, she found balance harder to achieve and moved into a staff role to reduce her time commitment. Yet, because she is now responsible for business development in Canada and Latin America, she needs to travel internationally, which tags hours onto her working week.

I have been able to get out of two trips to Brazil this year. We try to work through faxes and teleconferences, and so far it has not had a negative impact, but it is something that concerns me. At some point, you do have to be physically there in order to make things happen. You are already dealing with the language and the cultural barriers, and it complicates it more when you are not physically present at key meetings.

Therefore, Diann is leaning more toward alternative paths and has started contemplating reducing her work status to a part-time level. Although her career plans have changed and she works in strategic planning rather than plant management, she still feels successful. Working in jobs that require less time, or shifting from line to staff positions, doesn't make women any less successful or reflect lack of progress in business. To Diann, it is more important to her at this point in her life to be with her children than to be a plant manager.

> *Success is achieving what I want on my own terms. At this point, I feel I have contributed a lot to Xerox, and the company has contributed to me. Before I had my kids, I thought I would figure out a way to balance everything, but I didn't anticipate the level of demand on my time as I moved from position to position. Women have had the opportunity to climb the ladder and now we are finding that many of us are choosing not to because we are finding what happens when you mix the two.*
>
> *When I was working 12 hours a day I began realizing that my family was not getting the kind of time I would have liked to give them. With my first child, who is six, there were times when I wasn't there for him, and I don't want to repeat that with my daughter. After my son started kindergarten, I began to realize how crucial and how important establishing a foundation is. It impacts the rest of their lives. I don't want to be the cause of them not having a successful life because I didn't establish the proper foundation. I don't want them to suffer. Not being there at key times can negatively affect them.*
>
> *My ideal at this point would be to work part-time, but I don't want to decommit on my current position. So, when it comes time to change assignments, I will look for something more flexible. As long as I can contribute at a satisfactory level and not degrade my performance, but take on manageable assignments that don't take time from my family, I'll be happy.*

THE SEARCH FOR SKILLED NANNIES

Women who try to balance work and family without supports find themselves like Sisyphus—in endless uphill struggles. A nanny makes the balancing act easier, and skilled, trustworthy nannies are highly valued and deeply appreciated. One-third of the women I interviewed who have children also have nannies on whom they thoroughly rely; in fact, some women consider their nannies a part of their extended families.

However, recent negative nanny stories, particularly the tragic case in Massachusetts of the young British au pair accused of killing a baby by shaking him too hard, draw attention to the situation in which we find ourselves as we attempt to meet the demands of family and professional life. If we recognize that women are entitled to careers and all the fulfillment that accompanies feelings of professional success, why haven't we done more to upgrade training, pay scales, and the professionalism of nannies, au pairs, and day care providers? Have we fallen prey to a model of thinking that looks down on those who care for children?

Cynthia Cannady, a divorced mother of three, finds the issue of caring for her three children her biggest concern. Before joining Apple Computer as vice president of law, manufacturing, and development, Cynthia left her position as a partner in a 100-person law firm to set up her own part-time practice. She was looking for a way to gain greater flexibility and balance. However, like many other self-employed women, Cynthia discovered that in order to maintain a client base big enough to meet her financial needs, she ended up working long hours anyway. So, when a headhunter called her in 1993, she decided to go for the interview and was drawn to Apple, not only because she liked its products, but also because she liked the people she met and she found the culture to be open and supportive. But Cynthia, who says she is reconciled to working full-time, admits she doesn't really have balance.

> *The single biggest emotional upset for working women is caring for their children. Having a problem with your husband is manageable, but finding the right child care is a major problem. It's very distracting and very disturbing.*
>
> *I have a live-in nanny for my three children, which is wonderful. As my mother says, "She's a saint." I get home at about 6:30 or 7:00 P.M. and she fixes dinner. She takes the kids to their dentist and doctor appointments and things like that, but I like to go once in a while to make sure I know what's happening. I go to school conferences and occasionally I leave the office in the middle of the day and go to my daughter's violin lesson, but I count on our nanny and live in fear that she'll get another job offer or something. Beyond the logistical problems, having someone else care for your children raises issues around your feelings of adequacy as a mother. And you wonder if you have all the bases covered.*

Teresa Elder, a general manager at AirTouch Cellular, agrees that child care is a disturbing issue that causes problems for working women who are concerned about the well-being of their children.

> *Child care is one area where I think there are male/female differences and it's still a huge issue in society. Even with the resources that my husband and I have, it's a challenge to find good child care. I think it's an American cultural issue. We've had great nannies, and so-so nannies, and horrible nannies. I get distracted from work when I am not totally comfortable with my child care situation. If that piece isn't in place, it's hard for me to focus and do anything else. It's so critical.*

Without a nanny, Teresa would not have been able to take a promotion she wanted. Thinking that a strategic planning job in Portland, Oregon, was going to last less than a year, she and her husband decided she would try flying back and forth on a weekly basis between her new position and their home in Omaha, Nebraska. They had already survived one long-distance commute and it hadn't worked out too badly, so they were willing to give it another shot. Early in her career, Teresa had worked in Nebraska while her husband, a young lawyer, commuted to South Dakota, where he clerked in the Supreme Court. But now the couple had a very young baby.

> *I didn't know it was going to be a whole year when I started or I don't know if I would have done it. It was really hard, but it worked out. My husband ended up bonding very closely with our son during that year because he would take care of him in the evenings on his own. He became a totally competent father, changing diapers and handling all the problems that accompany a new baby. I now know that whatever happens, he can take care of our kids. During that year, I commuted home every weekend, but sometimes I missed my son so much that I had the nanny bring him to stay with me during the week at a Residence Inn. They would do whatever they do during the day, and I'd be able to spend the evenings with them.*

Teresa "feels a huge responsibility" to help out other women in her organization with child care issues, and she has even developed a template of questions on how to interview a nanny. Not everyone, however, can afford a nanny, and Teresa acknowledges that she is fortunate to have both a nanny and a fully supportive husband, calling single parents without good financial resources "the real heroes."

> *I don't know how they do it. If I were ever to change industries, or to change what I wanted to do, I would work on solving the child care issue in the U.S.*

She also feels a responsibility to communicate to her peers the importance of *never* making assumptions about anyone else's job aspirations. Teresa almost lost this particular promotional opportunity because of false organizational assumptions that her baby was too young and the distance was too far—people thought she wouldn't be interested in the job. But having a nanny whom she trusted to commute with her child enabled Teresa to succeed in her own way.

> *I go ballistic when I hear people make assumptions. One thing I emphasize is never second-guess what people might do. I tell my peers never to withhold an offer from somebody because you never know what people really want to do, what they can work out, or what their situation really is. So don't ever assume anything. I happened to be promoted both times I was off on child care leave. When I came back the first time, I wanted that strategic planning position and almost lost a vital chance.*

Hearing stories like Teresa's underscores the degree to which women are committed to their careers. I was struck by her energy and determination to make her life work the way she wanted it to. Teresa did admit, however, that she doesn't know if anyone has a totally balanced life, but she feels good about the way she has managed to find balance. She now has two children, whom she described as "pretty happy kids."

> *We have a good relationship. I'm not good at being a stay-at-home person. I really love being a mom, but I'm a happier person working. I realized if I do what makes me happier, my kids are happier. They never complain and ask me to stay home.*

When she's not traveling, she's in the office by 7:30 A.M. and leaves at 5:30 P.M. because she "absolutely wants to be home by

6:30 P.M." so that she can read to her two children in the evening, help them with homework, and put them to bed. She and her husband also spend all their weekends and vacations with the children, and she admits, "Perhaps, my husband and I don't take enough time just for the two of us, but we take our kids with us wherever we go because we enjoy them so much." She says she is very involved in her children's lives and puts time on her calendar to volunteer for projects for her son's school. And like the other younger female executives, Teresa performs her job according to her own standards and not her predecessors'. So, even though she has gone to extraordinary lengths and at times stretched herself across miles, she says she adheres to limits and does things her own way, weighing what she thinks is best for herself and her family.

> *When I look at the people who are the next step above me, I know they sacrifice a lot. In many cases, their travel is just crazy. I know that every time I move up to the next level, I don't have to manage the job the same way the person who was in it before me did. I can balance my life. My two young children and husband are very important to me. I'm not going to miss my kids growing up.*

DAY CARE AND CORPORATE COMMITMENT TO KIDS

What happens to the women that Teresa mentioned—women with children, who don't have the financial resources to afford a nanny or who don't have a husband to help out at home? Four out of ten women with children in the United States work full-time. Over 12 million families are maintained by women,[5] and approximately 15 million children under age six in the United States are involved in some type of day care arrangement. Yet studies show that most day care is mediocre.[6] In fact, preschools have been found to be among the least regulated institutions, and finding good care can be a real hassle.[7]

Progressive companies are learning the benefits of assisting mothers with child care needs. At NationsBank, which is 75 percent female, affordable, quality day care was a major issue, particularly for entry-level employees. In response to employees' needs, the company committed $35 million to dependent-care initiatives, including a child care subsidy program. Over a five-year period, it established more than 35 programs around the country and created two child care centers, in Charlotte and Atlanta. NationsBank offers these programs as a means to develop commitment and retain workers. In studies conducted by the bank, two-thirds of the employees said they continued to work for the bank because of the child care benefits. At Motorola, child care centers have been recognized as a necessity. The company presently runs five centers and more are in the planning stages.

Other concerned companies are banding together to develop cost-effective programs. Even major powerhouses with huge bottom lines realize that joining together in efforts to make working environments more friendly to families can be better achieved through cooperative efforts. In 1992, major corporations formed the American Business Collaboration for Quality Dependent Care to support the provision of quality care for dependents of employees. CEOs of these companies recognize they "can accomplish more by working together than by working alone." Driven by business strategy and the need to meet business goals relating to retention of valued employees, productivity, and competitiveness, the Collaboration launched a $100 million initiative in 1995 to develop and strengthen dependent-care projects in cities across the country. Funding will finance research and development of model programs and projects.[8] In Boston—my own area of the country—Hewlett-Packard, Texas Instruments, IBM, and Deloitte & Touche, all part of the American Business Collaboration, are funding projects for transportation, emergency backup care, and training programs for child care providers for employees in Massachusetts.[9]

Day care is one area that can strike a discordant note in Jacqueline Sinclair-Parker's carefully orchestrated plans. Jacqueline is a 31-year-old electrical engineer and an award-winning senior project manager at Xerox. She thoroughly planned how her career would interplay with her family life. As she told me her story I noted the precision with which she had scheduled her personal and professional activities. Yet her manner is warmly relaxed, open, and welcoming, and her conversation is splattered with humor and her rich laughter. In fact, I was laughing so hard at one story she told me about her aunt's advice on husbands (which I won't share) that it was hard for me to imagine how she could maintain both her tight schedule and her great sense of humor.

If you want to do something, you find a way. I am always thinking ahead and planning. You have to be quite determined and make some sacrifices. And you have to establish a vision.

Her plan included having her children before she was 30, and her children are now 5 and 2. Her five-year-old son goes to YMCA, and her two-year-old daughter is in a home-care setting. She also decided to complete her education and her family before immersing herself in her career—with several more MBA courses to take, she is presently not seeking management positions with direct reports, knowing that managing people requires additional energy and extra time at work.

I don't want to have too much of a problem juggling things. As a new manager you have a lot to learn.

The drawback to my plan is that finances are tight when the kids are young. My husband is very supportive and we make the best of our lives together, but we don't get to do a lot of things together, which sometimes puts a strain on our marriage. Fortunately, I'm pretty jovial. You've got to laugh to keep yourself sane. I'm a pretty low-key person, but I'm very ambitious and determined. I eventually want to become a vice president. I set my goals and constantly evaluate them to make sure I am on the right path.

Jacqueline also told me she is flexible, but she does set boundaries, working a 40-hour week, and she tries to get out of the office every day by 5:00 P.M. in order to pick up her daughter. But getting her two children to their day care arrangements has at times been complicated. As children's needs change, day care requirements also change. While one type of facility might be adequate before a child is school age, once children start school they need other kinds of supports such as transportation between school and day care settings, or between school and after-school activities. When her son started kindergarten in the fall of 1996, after-school care and transportation had to be arranged.

When there are two kids and two parents available, two different day care locations can work out. Jacqueline's husband drops their son off in the morning, while she drops their daughter off, but without that extra pair of adult hands, mothers face a tough challenge trying to juggle everyone's schedule and get everyone where they need to be. Another problem is timing: If local day care facilities don't open early enough or don't stay open late enough, it causes stress and hassles for everyone. Parents worry about picking their kids up on time and day care providers are provoked when parents are late. Children, too, get frustrated and upset when they are hustled to various interim spots before day care centers open or are left sitting with their coats on at the end of the day, waiting for their parents. On-site day care can make caring for children much easier. Xerox has been a leader in addressing work/life issues and is a member of the American Business Collaboration, but Jacqueline's manufacturing site doesn't offer on-site day care, and she wishes it did.

> *From a financial perspective, we don't have an alternative to day care. As a new mother, I struggled trying to find a place that made me feel comfortable. If we had on-site day care, it would be much easier. The kids would know that I work close by and at lunchtime I could see them. Now they're in two locations and having them together would save time and make them feel better being physically closer to each other.*

When companies help alleviate women's concerns about the well-being of their families, women can turn their attention to workplace issues and use their freed-up energy to solve business problems. Studies also show that increased levels of employee satisfaction through workplace policies translate into reduced turnover, and reduced turnover translates into increased retention of customers—better performance leads to better bottom-line results. Practices that benefit employees' personal lives enhance productivity and yield significant bottom-line results by unleashing creativity and energy.[10]

At Texas Instruments, when lack of balance between work and family was identified as a key barrier to success, the Semiconductor Group formed a work/life volunteer team and surveyed employees across the company. As a result of its findings, TI developed a corporate work/life strategy and the company now has summer camp for kids, flextime and alternative schedules, parents' E-mail networks, and even "mothers' rooms" with refrigerators in all buildings so that nursing mothers can pump their breast milk. Women need to continue to raise their voices about dependent-care issues in their organizations and use companies like those mentioned here as benchmarks for demonstrating the benefits of these programs.

The Role of Leadership in Work/Life Balance

The problem of balance and long workdays is pervasive. Most managers agree there is more work to be done than time available. Cynthia Danaher, general manager of Hewlett-Packard's Medical Products Group, draws a connection between leadership and the amount of time workers put into their jobs. Leaders set the pace for norms and ultimately determine how employees perceive the acceptability of shorter workdays.

> *If the leader is insecure, then everything is more complex. And, if everything is more complex, then people are changing their minds more and things take longer. Insecurity goes right down the chain and people end up working too many hours. So, if people are secure and if people understand they are valued, then people know what is important and what isn't. They can focus on a few things, do them well, and go home at night.*

Cynthia says people who work long hours are "grumpy, burned out and horrible to be near." When Cynthia first took over management of one group, the people worked long days, actually ranking themselves by how many hours they worked. She introduced a new way of working by telling them to "forget the hours."

> *I was interested in results and I didn't care how the hell they did it. We started working on a work/life balance program. And when people started figuring out that I was serious, results became the currency. And men as well as women started balancing their lives more.*

The corporate culture is exhibiting change, and CEOs, such as Lew Platt at Hewlett-Packard, are providing innovative leadership in this area, questioning the value of long workweeks. If managers can't complete their work in reasonable time frames, maybe they aren't prioritizing and delegating their work as they should. The abilities to delegate, organize, and prioritize are management skills that can be evaluated. When leaders learn that problems stem from the way work is done, actions can be taken to reorganize and restructure work. Long days should be the exception rather than the rule. As companies undergo reengineering, they can ask questions to uncover whether long hours are based on necessity or on assumptions that have no basis in reality. Results are more important than time, and, as Cynthia says, leaders are responsible for setting the pace.

Balance is no longer a woman's issue—long hours and dependent-care issues are everyone's concern. Yet both corporations and the government have been slow to act. The Family and Medical Leave Act (FMLA) passed in 1993 after ten long years, 17 hearings, and 13 votes. It guarantees up to 12 weeks of unpaid leave to full-time employees to care for family members. But the law applies only to companies employing over 50 workers. Passage took so long because of corporate fear that leaves would be abused and costs would be high, but follow-up studies found that implementing FMLA cost companies little and is valued by workers.[11] In fact, companies report that it has resulted in enhanced employee productivity and a willingness to go the extra mile.[12]

The future health of the country, both economically and socially, rests on the well-being of people and most especially on the well-being of our youth. Families need to be cared for while women and men are at work. If methods to care for children properly are not created, companies will have to deal with a distressed and absentee parent worker in the present and the lack of a well-functioning adult worker in the future. Recent studies are showing that the quality of care children receive when they are young affects their cognitive and emotional development.[13] If more companies begin tackling dependent-care issues, the well-being of employees and their children will increase along with loyalty and commitment.

Through their need for balance and their desire for relationship, women are helping to create a better, more humane working environment. A 1995 study conducted by Deloitte & Touche and *Fortune* magazine found that "men and women agree that the presence of women in the work force has had positive effects on business,"[14] affecting changes from consensus building to better teamwork to better communication to greater emphasis on families. For years, men worked long hours, denying their own human needs and missing out on family life. Immersed in a macho culture, they didn't know how to voice the issue of balance. Women have given them access to a new way of thinking and speaking, and, for the first time, female managers are giving men a shoulder to lean on and an ear that listens to them and allows them to speak about their needs. As Texas Instruments Vice President Shaunna Sowell says, "The presence of women in the workplace makes the discussion of work/life issues more acceptable for everyone." Shaunna has had men tell her that she was the first manager they felt free to talk to about family responsibilities.

They felt comfortable telling me it was their turn to stay home to care for a sick child and were relieved to know that I would be flexible and supportive in helping them balance their professional and personal demands. This is a way managers can help make a difference in the quality of employees' worklife.

As discussions on balance have become more open, and as men have benefited, working patterns are changing. Barnett Banks Chief Legal Executive Judy Beaubouef says she sees a difference in male behaviors at Barnett Banks.

More and more men are beginning to fix their boundaries and make an effort to be with their kids. I've been very impressed with the men in this company at the most senior management levels. Some of them are on their second families with younger wives and a second round of children and they realize they have a second chance to do things right and they're doing a real good job of it.

Empowered women in management serve both women and men in the organization, helping everyone achieve better balance in their lives. Although changes in technology and bottom-line issues also drive work/life issues, women's presence and influence have pushed efforts to make the work environment more accommodating to people's lives and to create career paths that intertwine in harmony with family needs.

Younger women have learned their lessons well and have their eyes open to balance issues. Twenty-seven-year-old Sunni Acoli-Squire already knows how tired she feels after work, and when she thinks about the future and about the children she wants to have, she sees her future partner playing a role and flextime as an option.

I believe children, especially during their first five years, require a tremendous amount of attention and care. It's during those years that children seem to develop their personalities and self-esteem. I want to be able to give my children the attention and care they deserve. One of the major drawbacks to women entering the workplace is the concern that children receive less parental care. Yet, I also want a career. Ideally, I'd love to work a flexible schedule—perhaps share a job with another parent where we can work with each other's schedules. I'd like to be able to do a lot of my work from home. I also plan to share a lot of the child rearing responsibilities with my husband.

Striving to fulfill their own definitions of success, women are affecting organizational attitudes and prompting dialogue on balance issues. Women can help organizations bring assumptions to the surface and examine beliefs about balancing the personal and professional sides of life. Women's voices have made a difference, warning us of dangers. Now that there are enough women in the system, the system can be changed.

CHANGING THE SYSTEM

I think it's important to find out how to work within the system. Before you can bring about change, you've got to be accepted. It's hard to make changes from the outside. You have to first be accepted, play by the rules, add value, and then you can start to make the changes, make a difference and have an impact. So you have to establish your credibility and show your skills and the value you add to the environment before you can change it. And throughout the process, how you treat people and the reputation you acquire are very important.

KWOK LAU, Vice President
Apple Computer, Inc.

Since Robert Reich left his position as secretary of labor, some of his writings have been questioned, but the deep truth of one editorial on the dignity of work drew my attention.

Work has always been more than just an economic transaction. It helps define who we are. It confirms our usefulness. What we do on the job—the people with whom we work and the ways in which our bosses, our colleagues, our customers, patients, clients or charges respond to our work—gives meaning and dignity to our lives. Dignity at work is not simply a matter of status or power. Dignity depends in large part, I think, on whether one feels valued. And the sense of being valued at work comes both from appreciation shown by others and from one's own pride in doing a job well, no matter how humble. In this respect, work is a moral act as well as an economic one.[1]

These ideas resonate with the feelings of the women I interviewed. Because they believed in the dignity of women, because they took pride in their work, because they believed that it was important to demonstrate the meaning and the value of their own work as well as the work of other women in their companies, they raised their voices to make change in their organizations. And they also reached out to affect their communities. Helping others, contributing to the well-being of others and the organization—*making a difference*—is part of women's definitions of success. Making a difference is a moral act. And each woman's voice is important because each woman can influence outcomes in some way.

Although it's difficult to transform corporate cultures, it's *not* impossible. Women with a strong sense of self have brought new perspectives to the business world. Ellen Gabriel, a partner in the Boston office of Deloitte & Touche and the national director for the retention and advancement of women, told me she knows her voice has been beneficial for everyone.

> *After I started working with men in senior management on the Women's Initiative, they came back to me and told me how my presence made a big difference. They thanked me for the good points I made and the different dimension I added to the discussions. They were clearly aware I was there and they valued my thoughts and views. I brought not only a woman's perspective, but a younger partner's view.*

Every time a woman's voice is heard, it presents an opportunity for change. Each voice that is heard encourages someone else to speak and someone else to step forward. Sue Manix, the assistant vice president of employee communications, who job shares with Charlotte Schutzman at Bell Atlantic, emphasizes how important each small step forward is because each step opens up more possibilities.

> *I think one of the reasons that Charlotte and I were selected for this assignment was because our current boss, who reports directly to the CEO, thought that he could make a statement by picking us. Not only was he going to pick women, but he was going to pick job-sharing women who have children. His move made a difference and our presence makes a difference. It makes a difference in little ways—for example, at a staff meeting when we're discussing the snow policy and our boss is inclined toward the position of "no work, no pay" or "take a vacation day," we have a totally different perspective. And our perspective is heard. It might not prevail the first time, but it's listened to.*

Working together, women have begun to weave a new corporate tapestry in which they, too, are central figures. The social fabric of companies can be rewoven if each woman consciously decides to stitch her own pattern into the corporate quilt. The stories in this section illustrate how a few women came together in their corporations to make change and advance the position of women in management. As we move from an individual to a collective level, as in the initiatives and programs described in this chapter, possibilities become tangible enough that they start to become real, altering perceptions and behaviors.

WOMEN WORKING ON BEHALF OF WOMEN

In 1988, women were still a minority in the male-dominated engineering environment at Texas Instruments (TI), but a grassroots effort for women, driven by two female managers from corporate services, sprang up after female managers attended an Outward Bound Leadership Training course. The Outward Bound week was the first time so many women had an opportunity to work together, and through their experience the women realized the benefit of joining together to solve problems. Shaunna Sowell said the training course was such a wonderful experience that afterward the women approached management, explaining their desire to form a women's network to address career-related issues. Receiving encouragement, ten women joined together and presented a business plan for a Women's Initiative to the leadership in the division.

> *One of our objectives was to foster initiatives in the other businesses. We had no idea that in 1996 we would have over 20 women and minority initiatives across the company. At that time, as women we thought that we had already made it, though looking back we were all first line supervisors or managers. Yet, relative to many other women in the company, we were doing well and we wanted to make it easier for other women coming up behind us. Now in 1996, so many more doors at all levels have opened for women in this company and many of the people who were actively involved in the initiatives have experienced career growth.*

Working on the initiatives gave the women an opportunity to demonstrate their capabilities outside their core work. They not only had a chance to lead teams, but they also gained visibility talking to people in the community and external leaders in public forums. By 1990, the Corporate Services Women's Initiative at TI began holding forums at corporate headquarters in Dallas, where career paths of successful TI men and women were discussed and compared. The goal was to develop an understanding of the problems and to learn more about people's expectations, feelings, and assumptions. This type of open forum sent a message that the company was willing to talk honestly about women's issues.

The Corporate Services Women's Initiative opened the way for action on the part of other groups. Minority and women's initiatives began popping up in different business groups and locations. The Semiconductor Group started a Women's Initiative in its division. Tegwin Pulley, who was then Semiconductor's worldwide financial and capacity planning manager, joined with ten other women to see if the success of the Corporate Services Women's Initiative could be duplicated. But before the women took any steps, they had to overcome some of their own reservations.

> *We talked about the risks and the possible backlash and decided if we as women weren't willing to work on these issues, who was going to. We were realistic, but we also knew that the leadership of the company wanted women to be full participants in the business. However, we also knew that with all the business pressures that any company has, it was unlikely that the president of the Semiconductor Group was going to be sitting in his office working out a strategy for us. But we thought if we worked out the strategy, he would probably be happy to help us with it. So, following the example of those who had come before us, we created a vision and a mission that we presented to the Semiconductor management team.*

Tegwin's group stressed inclusiveness and set up quality improvement teams to examine career development, work/life balance, community involvement, special programs, and sexual harassment elimination. The team held a forum at which the leadership at Semiconductor took part in a panel discussion and a question and answer session, and this first forum became the model the group continues to use. Tegwin claims the audience learned that the leadership in the company cared about women in the workforce, while the men in the leadership gained greater understanding of women's issues.

> *My feeling has always been that most people have good intentions, but sometimes those good intentions cause other people problems. Once men know what they should be doing differently, and understand the impact of their actions, they have the ability to act differently.*
>
> *As a group, we've been very empowered and we've focused on identifying the barriers in the workforce and recommending solutions. Any initiative in which you try to change a culture, whether it's quality or diversity, takes the same kind of strategy and the same kind of change management steps. When you have a problem with a machine, you don't ask the supervisor in the corner to figure it out, you get the person who is operating the machine to provide suggestions. That's what we did with the initiatives at TI.*

Julie England, another TI female leader, said her expectations about opportunities for women didn't meet the reality she encountered when she entered corporate life—she was disappointed to find so few women in management. Prompted into action, she led the Initiative in TI's Defense Systems and Electronics Group, and dedicated herself to making change in her division.

> *I grew up under the assumption that women could do whatever we wanted to do, just like men. That was a poor assumption. When I got out of college I thought there were women in management, but I found out I was misinformed.*

Demonstrating the power one woman holds, Julie ended up winning TI's "One Person Can Make a Difference" Award. She had taken it upon herself to meet with every vice president in the group and to make presentations about the women's initiatives at the VPs' staff meetings. Taking action and making a stand on issues is never easy. Julie admitted that she felt uncomfortable and was concerned that she might be putting her job on the line. But rather than risking her position with the company, her efforts have helped change the culture. She now conducts workshops on career development and counsels other people, sharing the lessons she has learned. Her determination to turn her assumptions about women's abilities to manage into reality has energized her to continue working on women's issues.

> *In order to remove systemic barriers, companies need to unveil the myths about women in our corporate cultures. There are beliefs and myths that people hold about each other that are unfounded, and corporate cultures can reinforce some of those myths. As women in upper management, we can add value now by correcting those myths, removing barriers, and working strategically with our peers.*
>
> *We must continue to accelerate progress. Companies need to enhance business processes such as promotion and leadership development to accelerate the company's ability to attract, retain, and fully utilize the potential of all employees. Likewise, individuals need to be responsible for their own career development.*

Julie believes individual responsibility is crucial for women, both in taking personal control of their careers and in assuming responsibility for changing corporate cultures.

> *The individual is responsible for sending persistent messages. There were vice presidents and supervisors who were willing to take a risk on me. So I had help getting where I am today. I didn't do it alone. But you have to send the message. And the message must transmit your confidence. You must be willing to speak out even when you're different. It's okay to be different; in fact, difference is valuable.*

Making change is a shared responsibility of both the company and the individual. In the case of the TI and its female executives, the energy invested in change has paid off. Since 1989, TI has significantly increased the number of women with management and leadership responsibilities at the same time that management positions and workforce numbers have fallen as a result of downsizing. By 1992, a woman had joined TI's board and the women involved with starting the initiatives perceive a link between the initiatives and the appointment of that first woman. TI's diversity efforts are spreading to its organizations located in countries around the world where the state of women in management lags far behind that in the United States. Between 1994 and 1995, five women were promoted to vice president, and, in 1996, TI was a Catalyst Award winner, receiving recognition for its inclusive team environment. By breaking down hierarchical structures and creating multilevel, cross-functional teams, TI changed its culture to provide a more level playing field for all its managers.

MINORITY WOMEN SPEAKING UP

At Polaroid, the voices of several women stirred the company from the complacency it had slipped into in the 1980s and helped return it to a commitment to diversity. In the late 1960s and early 1970s, Polaroid was known as a progressive leader in diversity. CEO Edwin Land implemented "1075," a program designed to increase the number of minorities at every level of the company; however, with the passage of time, the energy that originally fueled the program waned, and eventually the focus dropped back to merely complying with affirmative action policies.

In 1988, however, a significant meeting took place. As African-American Joyce Cofield, assistant to the president, tells the story, then-CEO I. MacAllister Booth was meeting with a small group of HR people, including Joyce. The conversation turned to expanding the participation of women and minorities at both the board and officer levels, since for all its early work on diversity, Polaroid still did not have a black or a woman officer. When directly questioned about taking actions to develop candidates, Booth admitted the issue wasn't high on his agenda and the meeting ended up somewhat charged—enough to prompt Booth to look into the matter further. As I sat listening to Joyce's soft voice describe the impact that initial meeting had on her, I could still hear the emotional wallop it carried.

> *I was so emotional at the end of that first meeting that I didn't talk about it. I literally didn't talk about it to people for almost a week and then only when I was pressed to because the CEO sent someone to talk to me. The CEO felt he knew me fairly well—before I went into HR, I was a biochemist, and in that role, I had worked with him on several projects. When he later realized how different his thinking was from mine, as well as the other people who had been in the room, he sent the most senior woman in the organization to talk to me. I had actually started thinking of leaving the company. I just clicked out. I had been in the company about 17 years and I left that meeting thinking that I had put 17 years in and it was no further along than it was the day I started.*

The meeting stimulated Booth to assess whether his thinking was out of step with diversity issues. He had the Affirmative Action Office bring in a consultant to continue the conversations, resulting in a workshop to bring senior blacks, senior women, and corporate leaders together to develop a strategy for tackling diversity. Recognizing that Joyce and the other women had taken some risk in confronting him, he asked Joyce, who at that time was not a senior manager, to participate. Joyce credits Booth for listening to, and acting on, what was said to him, and, since that day in 1988, Joyce claims the culture at Polaroid has changed dramatically in many areas.

> *I'm in this job today because of that first meeting. It changed my life. It really did. I saw that I could be influential if I exerted myself a little and I saw it was possible to make change. The last eight years of my life have been very different in many ways, and much of it goes back to that meeting and being involved in that change process, shaping something to make it look like you want it to look and then moving forward. It reinforced my commitment to being responsible for helping to build the organization.*

Diversity at Polaroid is becoming the norm. Although there are still pockets of white men, particularly at the leadership level, there are many more forums that have a significant mixture of people. It's much more unusual now, Joyce says, to walk into a setting and find a homogeneous group of white males. In addition, Polaroid now has a female group vice president of manufacturing and a female vice president of emerging markets, as well as two black male vice presidents, one of whom is an executive vice president for Asia Pacific.

Polaroid, like many other progressive companies, ended up with a diversity strategy that rests on three fundamental goals: retention of talent—it's expensive and a waste of money to hire and train people and then lose them; competitive advantage based on managers who think like and understand their customers; and solutions through diversity—the complexity that diversity brings provides more options for better solutions. Diversity in management enables companies to relate with greater understanding to multiracial, multiethnic male and female employees and customers. It plays a role in making companies competitive: With diversity as a driver, companies can choose the brightest and best from a broad selection of people, bringing a variety of perspectives to the problem-solving and strategy-forming tables. Diversity also fortifies the organizational system, making it more capable of adapting to the demands of a complex marketplace, because the more adaptable a system is, the more long-lasting it becomes.

SUCCESSION PLANNING: BUILDING FEMALE LEADERSHIP INTO THE SYSTEM

Leading-edge companies recognize that not only must they develop women and minorities as leaders, but they must also provide them with access to leadership positions. Development programs and succession planning are crucial elements in initiatives or change processes. Workshops alone won't create change; the system itself must alter. According to the Glass Ceiling Commission, development programs are more likely to be successful if a systematic process for identifying high-potential candidates at all levels of the organization exists and if career paths for moving from one level to another are clearly defined.[2]

At Motorola, systemic changes have helped advance women and minorities. Roberta (Bobbi) Gutman, Motorola vice president and director of global diversity, claims awareness is a key factor in changing systems. "Once you get it," she told me in her deep, booming voice, "you can move on it." Motorola seems to get it: The company won the Catalyst Award in 1993 for adapting its succession planning system to include the growth and development of women and minorities. The company's succession planning system not only identifies and tracks development, but it provides a mechanism for making sure women and minorities get slotted into the succession lineup. The process provides an easy method for quickly determining whether the company is on track with its diversity efforts and serves as a swift means of assessing the readiness and abilities of particular individuals.

Motorola restructured its High Potential List by adding race and gender to a person's name, title, and salary grade; now, with a glance, the list can be scanned to see how females and minorities are represented. The company also created the Women and Minority Vice Presidential Planning Process, which identifies women and minorities who have the ability to become vice presidents within three years of being named to the list. If a candidate can move to vice president from her present position, her present title, job level, and the amount of time it will take to move are noted. Likewise, if a candidate can't move from her present position, the interim jobs, titles, levels, and amount of time necessary to learn the required skills must be indicated. Thus, the process offers a simple tool for determining whether potential candidates are properly positioned and for charting their career development. People gain visibility and help with development, and they are protected from being set up to fail by being promoted too soon.

In addition, Motorola's Replacement Chart identifies key jobs and the people who are waiting on the bench to fill them. Previously, each job had only two slots: an immediate replacement and a person who would be ready in three to five years. Each job was given an additional slot naming the woman or person of color closest to being qualified for the job. Changing the system enabled the company to identify a variety of people more easily. Once people's names were in front of senior management, the ball started rolling for women and minorities. Four years after these systems were restructured, 25 percent of the people in slot three had moved into slots one or two. The company also instituted the Officer Parity Goal, a plan to name at least three women and three people of color each year to the officer corps. It tracks the functional positions into which people are promoted, making sure that line, as well as staff, jobs are filled. When the plan was first instituted in 1989, only two women and six people of color were vice presidents. By 1996, 37 women and 41 minorities held the title.

GROWING POWER NETWORKS

Women are discovering with great satisfaction the power that is unleashed when they work together. At Hewlett-Packard (HP), two female engineers gave birth to a networking concept in 1986 that has since grown into an annual event that now draws thousands of company women together. With almost 100,000 employees, these two women realized HP was certainly big enough for women to hold their own technical event where they could openly share knowledge, talk about their projects, and develop themselves professionally. The women approached senior management and, on an experimental basis, they were given approval to develop a Technical Women's Conference (TWC). The core conference committee, cochaired by Darlene Solomon, worked at night and on Saturdays for two and a half years to put a high-quality conference together.

The actual idea arose at a national meeting of the Society of Women Engineers (SWE). Two HP women—Nancy Huelsman and Petere Miner—had the initiative to raise some important questions: Why should HP employees need to come to a SWE meeting to meet each other and share ideas? HP is big; why couldn't HP women hold a meeting and create a mechanism by which they could get together and discuss their work?

At the same time, I was representing HP at a set of meetings sponsored by the California State University System. They were interested in the retention and recruitment of women faculty, and HP was interested in the subject from a corporate view. I had written up a report, so my name was visible. Personnel brought me and Nancy together and the two of us started working on the idea. Eventually we formed a core conference committee. We based our model on SWE and our goal for the initiative was to share our knowledge and improve our technical and professional skills. We wanted to do two things: to acknowledge the contribution of women engineers and to provide opportunities for career growth and professional development.

Management's approval indicated that the company was willing to take a chance, but the committee knew the conference had to be first rate.

We couldn't have created the conference without support coming from management and without motivation coming from women at the grassroots level. Timing was a big issue. Should it be held on a Saturday or a weekday? This was 10 years ago and the conference was an experiment: Management was open, but unsure. Therefore, we were closely watched. We had to establish credibility. If we screwed up, there wasn't going to be a second conference. Management was willing to take a chance and we were supported in that sense: we were financed through corporate personnel. Women didn't have to pay to come and their managers didn't have to pay for them. There was, however, an underlying fear by management that if they said yes to us, they would have difficulty saying no to somebody else. So, in order to maintain their support, the quality of the event was crucial. We had to prove it was providing a benefit beyond just enabling women to get together.

The first conference, held in 1988 on a Saturday in the corporate cafeteria, was a sold-out, one-day event attended by 400 people, with 400 turned away during preregistration. By 1995, the conference was held off-site, spanned three days, and was attended by 2,700 women. Over time, TWC's agenda expanded as more tracks were added, and it has now grown into a networking vehicle for all professional HP women. The latest TWC offered three tracks of interest: engineering; sales, marketing, and support; and professional business disciplines such as finance, training, and human resources. The objective of the conference has also expanded: It aims at making sure participants have greater awareness of the achievements of HP women, increased knowledge of opportunities and paths to success, and shared understanding of issues facing technical and professional women.

The women proved that TWC provides a benefit to the company: As well as giving females exposure, it gives them the opportunity to deliver technical papers and discuss their work. Because of confidentiality issues, people working in lab environments often can't discuss their projects at national conferences. But with an internal conference, ideas can be shared openly, enabling HP to discover ways to leverage its knowledge, technologies, and skills. Over the years, the acceptance of TWC papers has become more competitive, raising the bar on the quality of work presented; thus, excellence within the company is fostered at the same time that women showcase their work. TWC helps females gain experience communicating their work. Through the presentation of papers, they gain credibility and visibility, and because the proceedings and papers are published, managers throughout the organization become more aware of the expertise of female engineers and managers. In addition, the TWC planning committee actually operates like a cross-functional team: Women working on it hone their teamwork, organizational, and communication skills. As women meet new people across the organization, their own networks expand.

Because two women raised their voices and management was open enough to listen, Hewlett-Packard now has a vehicle for women to communicate and grow. The quality and reputation of the event has expanded and men as well as women want to attend. People at HP sites around the globe are clamoring for more of this type of networking. The 1998 conference is being designed to accommodate 3,500 people. An ongoing women's network has developed: Regional conferences have sprung up around the country, and an electronic, interactive women's newsletter has been created. TWC stands as a monument to what can be achieved when a few women, who put their heads together to make change, receive support from an enlightened senior management team.

Women's networks inside corporations are growing in power and influence. In findings from a Catalyst survey of Fortune 500 companies, over 70 percent of formal corporate networking groups for women offer advice to senior management, and over 60 percent receive budgetary support from their corporations.[3] Corporate networks support corporate missions, while providing additional connections for women. At Baxter International, corporate women formed Baxter Women INC., a networking group with the mission to promote professional and personal development. The group sponsors events and forums, and circulates a newsletter about women's issues. At Xerox and Procter & Gamble, minority networks offer assistance for ethnic and racial groups. At McDonald's, a Women Operators Network (WON) helps women who operate McDonald's restaurants succeed with their business plans by sharing best practices. McDonald's won the Catalyst Award in 1992 in recognition of the role WON played in assisting female operators of McDonald's franchises. WON, like many of the women's networking groups, is a chartered organization that charges membership dues, but it also receives assistance from the corporation. The network is extremely active: When new women owners join, other operators take them under their wings, showing them the ropes and guiding them through the ins and outs of running a successful business. In addition to WON, the Women's Leadership Network serves as a vehicle for female employees of McDonald's to join together in support of each other. Although the two networks are separate, they share many activities and events as they work toward helping women in the McDonald's family succeed at business.

Monica Boyles, an assistant vice president responsible for McDonald's National Operators Advisory Board, serves as the liaison between the company and WON. Monica's role provides her with vital insight and positions her to make recommendations to senior management in support of women.

I have the opportunity to see first hand what's going on inside the company, looking at individual women microscopically as well as assessing collectively how well we're doing as a group. I pass on to senior management the barriers that seem to be looming and suggest how we can best resolve or remove them.

The benefit of formalized internal networks is the two-way communication channel that gets established. The network provides a vehicle for women to communicate their wants and needs to senior management, while it gives senior management a means of working directly with women to affect change for the good of the organization.

Women are also becoming increasingly adept at creating their own networks. In Boston, for example, there is a "new girls network" made up of savvy professional women in their 40s and 50s who are members of the Massachusetts Women's Forum. These high-powered women supported Cathy Minehan in 1994 when she was being considered for the presidency of the Federal Reserve Bank of Boston and she ended up becoming the first female to hold the position. They also backed Margaret Marshall for a seat on the state's supreme judicial court in 1996. They offered support to Marian Heard, president of United Way of Massachusetts Bay, when she came on the scene in the early 1990s, and to Elaine Ullian, who led the merger of Boston University Medical Center with Boston City Hospital. These women have honed their networking skills and are pushing women into the spotlight in the male-dominated business arena of Boston.[4]

In Iowa, Teresa Wahlert, vice president of public policy for US WEST, has learned the value of belonging to a host of formalized networks. She must work closely with local and state government officials to promote legislation beneficial to her telecommunications company, but because these Midwestern officials have not been used to working with senior corporate women, Teresa has had to learn how to break into their male network.

Women at high levels of business must use different methods for entering communities, and the method you use depends on the community. I have worked in North Dakota and now in Iowa, and there are fewer role models and fewer women in executive positions in business in these areas of the country than in New York or Boston.

The real movers and shakers in these communities still tend to be traditional white males. There really isn't a business network of women to help you. The women of power tend to have lived in the community for a long time, perhaps 30 years or so, and have come up gently and carefully through the ranks—perhaps as community legislators or as school board members. It's very different to enter into a community as a higher level corpo-

rate woman. It has to be handled fairly delicately and you must seek balance between being accepted and not alienating yourself while striving to meet your goals. There are still issues of credibility and questionable areas, which a man wouldn't face, that influence what you can actually get accomplished. So you need to be able to quickly identify the people who can shoot you into the right circles.

One of the ways Teresa has succeeded in identifying and hooking up with the right people is by actively participating in organizations relevant to her work and the community. Looking at her resume, I noted that, over the course of her career, she has belonged to two dozen significant associations and boards and is presently involved in seven state and national organizations.

Women have indeed caught on to the power of networking: Of almost 700 women who responded to the national survey, 71 percent network through professional associations. As well as a means to gain knowledge and support, four out of five women find these networks helpful in providing contacts and links to new jobs, vendors, customers, and suppliers. Within the American Bar Association, for example, there is a relatively new group called Women Rainmakers, who build business by networking in female ways—women invite clients to bring their kids with them to social activities, and rather than schmoozing at the ballpark, they entertain female clients at theaters and art galleries.[5] And as these networks grow, so grows women's leverage in the business arena.

SOCIAL RESPONSIBILITY: THE AWESOME POWER OF CORPORATIONS

The companies that employ the women in this book provide work for over a million and a half people. If each employee has even one other person in her family, that means that *just 23 corporations directly affect the lives of at least three million people.* Multiply that by other corporations in the Fortune 500 and the impact is huge. When suppliers and customers are included in the equation, the effect is even more dramatic. America needs corporate involvement and it needs female leadership actively involved in making a difference in society.

Healthy corporations—companies that are fiscally profitable and responsive to their employees and customers—help to sustain a healthy society. The corporate sector in America has tremendous power and wields enormous influence. The 50 top companies in the Fortune 500 had total revenues in 1994 of $1.8 trillion—that's three times Canada's entire gross domestic product.[6] Over the course of their organizational lives, the top 10 corporations alone have created one-third of a trillion dollars in wealth for their stockholders.[7] Major corporations also collectively contribute billions of dollars a year toward social and political causes. These large companies are a major force, shaping the economic and social systems in America.

Women leaders are supporting and applauding the efforts of their companies in accepting responsibility for social issues and adding value to employees' working lives. These efforts mesh with women's definitions of success—women want to make a difference in their organizations and in society. They want to add value and make life better for others. If corporate America wants to keep its most talented people, Judy Beaubouef, chief legal executive at Barnett Banks, says that work has to provide meaning beyond a paycheck. The corporation, she told me, has to offer something to individuals for the time and personal sacrifice they put into their jobs. Judy feels civic and volunteer involvement gives employees psychological benefits that make coming to work and being part of the company more meaningful.

> *At Barnett, we focus on community outreach programs and we encourage people to become involved. Individual departments work on specific projects like homeless shelters. We are making a big push in education. Our "Take Stock in Children" is a wonderful statewide program in Florida. We are committing millions of dollars to impact education in the state. People are really excited about it. Beyond helping the community, it helps build employee loyalty and commitment.*

Many of the companies in this book are noted for being responsible corporate leaders. The programs supported by their corporate dollars reach out into wide sectors of our society, from Ronald McDonald houses for children across the country, to improved management of schools in Texas, to telecommunication installations in rural schools in Wyoming. Xerox has programs designed to help minority women make it in hard-to-enter areas such as manufacturing. J.C. Penney reaches out to help women running small companies develop their businesses, providing them with support and income through the purchase of services and products.

Recent years have seen a growing community service movement. Companies are investing in community partnerships and employee volunteerism because companies are beginning to understand how directing corporate dollars into these areas provides a long-term positive impact for the company. One of the biggest commitments made by a company occurred in the fall of 1996 when AT&T announced that its 127,000 employees would receive a day off with pay in 1997 to do volunteer work. If everyone participates, the company will be donating one million hours of volunteer time worth $20 million.[8] This type of corporate volunteering boosts employee morale and builds better relationships with the communities in which companies operate. Employees at Xerox and IBM also get social service leaves to do volunteer work. At Xerox, employees are paid for social service leaves for community projects that can last as long as a year. In Marlene O'Toole's group at IBM in Atlanta, 300 employee volunteers worked together on community projects. In addition to feeding the homeless, they built a park and painted a housing complex for the elderly. IBM also acts as a partner in education. Marlene trades places one day a year with a principal at one of the local schools and firmly believes companies need to start targeting their efforts to younger children.

> *I think we need to get in the junior and senior high schools and talk about the careers we have available and the skills that are needed. We especially need to do more at the middle school level and have corporate women talk to 13-year-old teens.*

No longer can we rely on government to stimulate desperately needed improvements in our social systems, particularly our educational system. Corporations, recognizing their own requirements for skilled and knowledgeable workers in the future, understand the significance of supporting and upgrading the education systems in their communities and states. Procter & Gamble, a business pioneer in the financial support of higher education, contributes $12 million annually to education.[9]

At Texas Instruments, one of the key strategies for building a competent workforce in the future is to improve education. Shaunna Sowell, a former teacher, has become the executive partner of a TI team that has adopted a Hispanic elementary school in Dallas. Being the executive partner of this team is not part of Shaunna's core work, but TI supplies her with the resources she needs to meet her commitments to it, enabling her to fit the volunteer time into her schedule. Shaunna told me assisting at the school captured her imagination and presently she devotes two hours a week to mentoring and coaching the school principal and her staff.

In addition to helping improve top-down performance at the school, Shaunna emphasizes the significance of assisting girls in developing their technological skills so they can compete for the best jobs in the future. Without better backgrounds in math and science, she firmly believes girls will miss out.

> *Our future as a country is in technology and I feel very passionate about guiding girls towards technology jobs. We've made so many strides in law and medicine in terms of the percent of women in those jobs today, but in the last 10 years, we've not made the same progress in technology.*
>
> *The big increase in overseas exports is coming from electronic, software and telecommunications sectors. Our future economic well-being resides in these areas. Women account for only 15 percent of engineers in the marketplace. We still don't have enough technical women in the pipeline today because the pipeline has to start in our school systems. We have to start investing in girls in the fifth and sixth grade, because without a solid science background throughout elementary and high school, girls will have eliminated options for themselves when they get to college. Statistics show that up until sixth grade, girls perform as well as, and in some cases better than, boys in math and science. Starting in seventh grade, however, the statistics dive, and we start losing girls.*
>
> *When I speak to young girls I ask who fixes things that break in their home and at least 30% of them indicate that they do. When I tell them the ability to fix things is mechanical engineering, a light dawns and for the first time they get it. Somehow we have to intervene in the fourth, fifth and sixth grades and give girls role models and encouragement and keep them interested in math and science.*
>
> *There are many opportunities in technology in corporate America. Today, about 48 percent of the labor force is made up of women. I would like to think that within the next generation, 48 percent of all technology jobs will be filled by women. This is a great time: It's like standing in the middle of a candy shop deciding what piece of candy to choose. We have a tremendous opportunity to help our girls make the best selection.*

At US WEST, part of Teresa Wahlert's job is working with the vocational education system, where Teresa believes there is still a gap in training younger people to meet future responsibilities.

> *One of my big pushes is to concentrate on the 80 percent of youth that don't go on to college. They feel like second-class citizens and they don't have good careers or good alternatives to think about. And we are not, based on my experience, giving that group of very employable people the skill sets they need to go out and be productive.*

As the federal government pulls further away from supporting the nation's system, the quality of education is further jeopardized. Forward-thinking corporations and female executives are helping communities tackle local educational issues in order to produce a qualified pool of workers in the future.

Collaborations between universities, private foundations, and the business community offer promising concepts. The University of Southern California has implemented an aggressive minority outreach program to prepare minorities for competing in mainstream America. Since Proposition 209 in California seems to be ending affirmative action, new alliances between the public and private sector can help minorities climb corporate ladders without the use of quotas by offering scholarships to promising students.[10]

Known as a corporate leader in the area of education, Motorola starts helping minority women while they are still in college. Bobbi Gutman told me Motorola is trying "to utilize diversity as a competitive weapon"—making conscious efforts to increase its minority female ranks.

> *We want to attract the best and the brightest. We want to show that people will be evaluated on the amount of developed gray matter they have versus the color and kind of skin they are wrapped in. It's a matter of strategic survival. We are over 60 years old and we need to renew ourselves continually, which means we are constantly looking at internal and external factors that impact the way we do our work. We've got to be inclusionary. Studies have shown that different cultures have different ways of identifying and solving problems. If we can corral differences and focus them on solving Motorola's business problems, we will have a far greater range of potential solutions, raising the probability that we will resolve our problems more effectively.*

Motorola developed the Minority Internship Investment Scholarship Program to increase the number of minority female engineers in its recruitment pool. Talented minority students, majoring in engineering or finance, are hired for summer jobs. If the students do well, the company gives them $2,000 to apply to their college tuition, brings them back the following summer, and then offers them permanent positions. Since the program started, 83 percent of the participating students have joined the company. This scholarship program helps motivate minority women to finish school while providing Motorola with new talent.

J.C. Penney has operated a program for minority-owned businesses for 20 years, but several years ago, it recognized that women-owned businesses face different issues than businesses run by men or minorities. Lucy Berroteran, who became the first head of the Minority and Women Owned Business Development Program, said her company recognizes that women need special kinds of assistance in establishing and running their businesses. This program reaches out to regional and local female vendors and suppliers.

> *Our business development programs have been good for the company and good for the community. Sixty percent of the nation's poor are women and children. They are our customers in our communities. Beyond the fact that helping them is the right thing to do, it also makes good business sense. Women employ local people, who hopefully shop in our stores. We should help these women grow their businesses. They turn out products on a dime and produce much quicker for us. They bring us products and services that we can't match anywhere else.*

As we ready ourselves to enter the twenty-first century, companies are realizing that success comes when "soft" as well as "hard" performance measures are valued: Employees, customers, and quality products matter as much as profit margins and return on investment. Smart CEOs are seeing the value of tying the company's needs to the community's needs to benefit both. Social financial management is based on understanding that financial benefits result when closer attention is paid to the social capital of human relationships and to building connections among different groups. There is a link between corporate profits and social change. Studies continue to show the positive correlation between strong financial performance and social actions in communities.[11]

Teresa Elder, an AirTouch Cellular general manager, has discovered how important corporate power can be in making social changes. And, unfortunately, her knowledge comes from personal experience. In the fall of 1995, Teresa and her husband discovered their oldest son has cystic fibrosis. As Teresa says, "It added a whole new dimension to our lives." Teresa went to a Jesuit college and was originally a sociology major, because she thought a sociologist could help change the world, but now she recognizes that her corporate position gives her much more power to influence actions in her community that might help her son.

> *I believe things happen for a reason. In my current position, we've been able to help with fundraising for the disease. We've linked up with other leading people in our area who are working on fundraising and research and we believe our efforts can help find a cure.*
>
> *I guess I'm just an optimistic person and I have to find some reason in everything. It's really hard when your kid has a serious illness to find anything positive, but I think my husband and I are the kind of people who can make an impact and make a big difference. This is what we were called to do. The goal of Jesuit philosophy is to train the leaders of society. And I think that is what I am supposed to do—influence and help society.*
>
> *If I had become a social worker, I would have had a lot less influence and power than I do now. In my position, I have been on the governor's committee to put telecommunications into rural schools in order to make sure that small rural areas that are poor have the same access to education as other places, helping to balance the haves and the have-nots. I was also involved in the rapid deployment of enhanced 911 throughout the whole state, which helps save lives.*
>
> *So I think I've had more influence than if I had stayed in sociology. As a business, we're very much involved.*

At present her son is undergoing therapy, taking his medication, and trying to be a normal little boy who goes to school every day and plays with his friends. Needless to say, having a child with a disease of this magnitude has been devastating. And, understandably, it gave Teresa reason to step back and evaluate what her role as a working mother should be. Even though she faces an enormous challenge, she has decided to keep working.

I questioned whether I should stay at home and spend more time with him. And I had guilt feelings wondering if we would have known earlier if I hadn't been working. You really kind of beat yourself up, even though it's a genetic disorder and there is nothing we could have done. So we have thought it through and talked to a lot of people, and we are glad we have our lives structured the way we have. If there ever was going to be a point where I would say I'm screwing my life up and something has to change, this would be one of those times. And I don't feel that way. I feel like we're doing the right thing. We are going to keep our priorities the way they are.

Teresa went to California during the 1996–1997 school year to participate in the Sloan School of Management fellowship program at Stanford, and her entire family went with her. This opportunity came at the right time, even though Teresa recognized the value of it from the very beginning of her career.

I knew two months after I was hired that I wanted to do it. I met a woman who had just finished the program and when she told me about it, I thought it sounded really neat. At the time I was about 21, and I asked her how I could sign up for it. She kind of chuckled and told me that you don't exactly sign up for it: You have to be at least at a director's level; you have to have worked for ten years; and you have to be selected. And I remember thinking at the time, "Okay, I'll go do that." And then I told every manager I ever worked for that it was a long-term goal.

Meeting her goal and moving to California for the year was beneficial for Teresa's son as well as for her career growth. Living in California was much better for his condition than Colorado's high altitude. And her husband worked out an arrangement with his law firm whereby he continued working with some clients while fund-raising for cystic fibrosis. So, as Teresa says, perhaps, things happen for a reason.

WOMEN'S VOICES: CONFIDENCE IN THE FUTURE

Women have been in the system long enough to begin influencing it and shaping it according to their values. Women now have a collective maturity that strengthens their credibility. There *is* a parallel to what women as individuals feel and where we are as a group. As 45-year-old Cynthia Cannady describes her own process of maturing, she says she has "a presence" and "confidence" that comes with her age.

> *I've been through all sorts of things and I've come to a point where I know what I'm talking about. Even when people and situations are difficult, you can learn from them. As you develop expertise, you gain confidence. If you know how to do something people will respond positively to you because they need you. A reinforcing cycle operates: You know how to do something which is needed, so people respect you for what you can do. In turn, as you feel needed and respected, you become more authoritative. As you gain authority, people begin to defer to you, and you gain even more confidence. As long as you keep learning and don't become arrogant, it's a positive cycle that builds and builds.*

Our desire for relationship and our need to make a difference benefit the systems within which we operate. However, it's up to each of us. We often think that it's not possible for some personal action to be the cause of larger change, but every surprising invention, every once unthinkable achievement, started as an idea in someone's mind. The women in this chapter saw possibilities and had the courage to raise significant questions. They worked within the system long enough to establish their credibility and value. Then they raised their voices to make change. The structure of corporations is finally giving room for women's voices to be heard and space for women managers to lead. By following the examples of these successful female managers, women can work with their companies to ensure that corporate actions reflect the sound of their voices and impact the future in positive ways.

We are entering a new phase in which women are becoming full participants with men in conducting the nation's business. Organizations can be sparked by determined women and enlightened leaders. And as more companies tune in to the benefits provided by women in management and adopt programs in support of all workers and their families, corporate definitions of success will begin to resemble women's definitions of success. Corporations will discover that success has three prongs: achievement of bottom-line goals, a loyal and committed workforce supported by a flexible workplace that allows employees to balance their lives, and future financial prosperity through social commitment to the surrounding community. Armed with that success, corporate America will have evolved to a higher level of operating and we will have advanced further as a society.

When I think of the collective gains made by women in business and of the individual accomplishments of the women in this book—extraordinary, ordinary women—I can't help thinking of Susan B. Anthony's words: "Failure is impossible." Women have found their voices and their own management styles. And they have achieved success on their own terms.

May the road rise to meet you.
May the wind be always at your back.
May the sun shine warm upon your face.
And the rains fall soft upon your fields.
And until we meet again
May the goddesses hold you in the palms of their hands.

A feminine adaptation of an old Irish blessing

APPENDIX A:
EXTRAORDINARY,
ORDINARY WOMEN

This appendix lists the 45 women, their ages, and the positions they held in 1996 when I interviewed them. Several women experienced career moves and promotions during the time I was writing and I was able to incorporate some of those changes into the women's stories. Other more recent changes include some great career achievements. Karen Moreno attained her career goal and in April 1997 was named the president of Gannett Supply Company. Cynthia Danaher was made a vice president at Hewlett-Packard. Cathy Spotts took a lateral move to Allegiance Healthcare Corporation, Baxter's spinoff, positioning herself for a future presidency within the corporate family. Ann Delvin moved up a notch on the career band at GE Plastics and is now a step closer to entering the executive ranks. Florence Williams relocated and is now a product manager at Digital Equipment Corporation. Carol Tuthill moved from her position heading organizational excellence and was given broader HR responsibility; now, all HR in North America reports to her. And Teresa Elder, who finished second in her class at Stanford's Sloan School, was made a vice president of operations at MediaOne.

Name	Age	Title	Company	Race
Acoli-Squire, Sunni	27	Operations Supervisor	Con Edison of New York	AA
Allen, Becky	54	President and CEO	Barnett Private Client Services	C
Andre, Erin	37	Director, Staff & Succession Planning	Pacific Gas & Electric	C

Name	Age	Title	Company	Race
Bailey, Joyce	44	Director of Labor Relations	Gannett Co., Inc.	AA
Beaubouef, Judy	50	Chief Legal Executive	Barnett Banks, Inc.	C
Bell, Diana	44	Operations Manager, Worldwide Remarketing Operations	Hewlett-Packard Co.	AA
Berroteran, Lucy	35	Communication Manager, Finance	J.C. Penney	H
Boyles, Monica	47	Assistant VP, National Operators Advisory Board	McDonald's Corp.	C
Brennan, Jean	42	Director, Staff & Succession Planning	Pacific Gas & Electric	C
Cannady, Cynthia	45	VP, Law, Manufacturing, & Development	Apple Computer, Inc.	AA
Chapman, Sari	35	Technology Manager	Bell Atlantic Federal Systems	C
Cofield, Joyce	50	Assistant to the President, Diversity	Polaroid	AA
Crump, Lynn	39	Regional VP, Operations	McDonald's Corp.	AA
Danaher, Cynthia	37	General Manager, Medical Products Group	Hewlett-Packard Co.	C
Davis, Margo	54	Program Manager, Corporate Education	Hewlett-Packard Co.	C
Delvin, Ann	43	Commercial Leader, Resin Recovery & Sales	GE Plastics, Inc.	C
Dudley, Beth	46	VP, Quality & Regulatory Affairs	Baxter Healthcare Corp.	C
Eidson, Donna	43	Executive Director	Polaroid Foundation	C
Elder, Teresa	34	General Manager	AirTouch Cellular	C
England, Julie	38	VP, Quality, Semiconductor Group	Texas Instruments	C
Fischer, Meredith	43	VP, Communications, Marketing & Future Strategy	Pitney Bowes	C
Gabriel, Ellen	41	Partner	Deloitte & Touche LLP	C
Gaumer, Gail	44	Executive VP	Allegiance Healthcare Corp.	C
Ginn, Ann	39	VP & Branch Manager	Chubb & Son, Inc.	C

Name	Age	Title	Company	
Hains, Kim	31	Senior VP & Director, Work/Life Programs	NationsBank, Inc.	C
Kaplan, Beth	38	Executive VP	Rite Aid Corporation	C
Lau, Kwok	38	VP, Business & Operations, AppleSoft	Apple Computer, Inc.	A
Manix, Sue	38	Assistant VP, Employee Communications	Bell Atlantic Corp.	C
McClam Mitchell, Vela	41	Director of Sales & Marketing, Airlines and Associates	Worldspan	AA
Monroe-Jones, Diann	35	Business Development Manager	Xerox Corporation	AA
Monserrate, Carmen	27	Manufacturing Supervisor	Xerox Corporation	H
Moreno, Karen	40	VP, Purchasing	Gannett Supply Co.	AA
O'Toole, Marlene	50	Regional Manager, Customer Support South	IBM Corporation	C
Rader, Elizabeth (Beth)	44	Director	Deloitte & Touche LLP	C
Santona, Gloria	45	VP, Associate General Counsel & Secretary of the Corporation	McDonald's Corp.	H
Schutzman, Charlotte	37	Assistant VP, Employee Communications	Bell Atlantic Corp.	C
Sinclair-Parker, Jacqueline	31	Senior Project Manager	Xerox Corporation	AA
Solomon, Darlene	36	Manager, Chemical Systems	Hewlett-Packard Co.	C
Sowell, Shaunna	42	VP, Corporate Environmental, Safety, & Industrial Hygiene	Texas Instruments	C
Spotts, Cathy	35	VP & General Manager, I.V. Therapy Group	Baxter Healthcare Corp.	C
Tomlinson, Jan	45	President	Chubb Insurance Co. of Canada	C
Tuthill, Carol	44	VP, Human Resources, Organizational Excellence	Procter & Gamble	C

ne	Age	Title	Company	Race
an Zandt, Connie	37	Director of Planning & Fulfillment	Gannett Co., Inc.	C
Wahlert, Teresa	47	VP, Public Policy for Iowa	US WEST	C
Williams, Florence	32	Plant Quality Assurance Manager	Xerox Corporation	AA

AA = African American; A = Asian; C = Caucasian; H = Hispanic

APPENDIX B:
METHODOLOGY

The main body of this book is derived from interviews I conducted with 45 women who work in major American corporations in a variety of industries and functional areas. The industries include publishing, utilities, computers and office equipment, electronics, travel, insurance, banking, accounting and financial services, scientific photo equipment, telecommunications, health care equipment, retail, food services, and manufacturing. And the functional areas cover customer service, employee communications, engineering, finance, human resources, legal services, marketing communications, manufacturing, operations, purchasing, research and development, sales and marketing, strategic planning, and quality control.

The women range in age from 27 to 54. Of the 45 women, 1 is Asian, 3 are Hispanic, 11 are African Americans, and the balance are Caucasian. These women occupy various rungs on the management ladder. One is in the uppermost executive circle of her corporation as chief legal counsel, two are presidents, two are executive vice presidents, 13 hold the title of vice president, one is a vice president and a general manager, two are group general managers, and one is a partner in a big-six accounting firm. The balance spans upper and middle management layers from assistant vice presidents to directors to managers down to new, young engineering supervisors in management training programs.

As expected, almost all are college graduates; however, there were several surprises: 3 women dropped out of college and 1 dropped out of high school. On the other end of the spectrum, 1 has a Ph.D., 4 are CPAs, 4 are lawyers, 10 have MBAs, and 11 have a variety of other master's degrees.

Women succeeding in corporate America are well compensated. The lowest salary range of less than $50,000 is found among the new supervisors in management training and the top figure for salary and compensation peaks at about $500,000. Forty percent of the women make over $200,000.

The women represent a full range of life experiences. Only 5 are single and have never been married, and these 5 are all minority women; 10 are divorced or separated, one is widowed, and the remaining 29 are married or remarried for the second time. Of the 33 women who have children, 2 married men with children, creating merged families, each consisting of five children; 9 of the women have three children each; 14 have two; and 8 have one. One woman has successfully battled cancer; another has fully recovered from a paralyzing stroke. I interviewed 2 women who had to deal with alcoholic husbands and 2 who have mothers with Alzheimer's disease. One woman lost a child to Down syndrome and congenital heart problems, and another has a child with cystic fibrosis.

Their family backgrounds are also extremely diverse. At one end of the spectrum, one woman was the youngest of 11 in a German-Catholic family and grew up on a Midwestern farm. At the other end, one woman describes her drive to succeed as coming from her desire to provide for her children because she was orphaned when she was less than eight years old. Most, however, talked about living in supportive families and being influenced by both their mothers and fathers.

Prior to publication, numerous people asked me how I chose the women, so I'll share my selection process here. I read about Cynthia Danaher in the *Boston Globe* and about Vela McClam Mitchell in *Working Women* magazine. Ann Delvin sat next to me at a conference and Marlene O'Toole is an old friend of a friend. I read about the work/life programs at Atlantic Bell in an article in *Working Mother* and called Marilyn Mecchia, the director of those programs, who had been quoted in the article. During my phone conversation with her, she told me about Charlotte Schutzman and Sue Manix and their job share and about Sari Chapman's work on telecommuting. Donna Eidson is a personal friend and she in turn gave me Joyce Cofield's name. In my research, I read about the Women's Initiative at Deloitte & Touche LLP and both Ellen Gabriel and Elizabeth (Beth) Rader were mentioned in several articles. I contacted the public relations department and asked for interviews.

APPENDIX C:
KEY FACTORS FOR
SUCCESSFUL WOMEN'S INITIATIVES

Research by the Glass Ceiling Commission indicates that the following factors are necessary for the success of women's initiatives:

- Have support from the CEO.
- Assess existing barriers, preconceptions, and stereotypes within the company through internal research on the organizational culture, the work environment, demographic data, and issues important to employees.
- Assess reasons for turnover, using exit surveys.
- Have leaders commit to retaining and advancing women and demonstrate commitment through development programs, education, training, and information sharing.
- Identify and develop multifaceted, systemic approaches and initiatives for eliminating cultural, structural, and attitudinal barriers.
- Tie initiatives to the organization's business plans.
- Establish goals, track progress, and hold managers accountable for progress.
- Be inclusive of minorities and white males.
- Select, promote, and retain qualified individuals and adopt high-performance workplace practices.
- Initiate work/life and family-friendly practices.
- Benchmark actions of successful companies and specific programs or initiatives.

APPENDIX D:
ELEMENTS OF A
JOB-SHARE PROPOSAL

The following outline is derived from Sue Manix and Charlotte Schutzman's job-share proposal, which they used to create their groundbreaking position at Bell Atlantic.

Introduction

Position Requested
- Full job description attached with responsibilities detailed

Definition of Job Sharing
- Definition as it pertains to the job share

Advantages Job Share Provides to the Company
- Description of skills each individual brings to the job and how those skills are complementary
- Attachment of résumés and performance appraisals
- Description of cost-effectiveness with regard to retention
- Explanation of continuity and coverage factors

Accountability
- Description of who is responsible for what
- Schedule of coverage: who works when
- Communication plans: methods by which the team will communicate
- Compensation factors: how compensation will be determined for each person with regard to salary, bonuses, and raises
- Benefits: benefits for which each person will be eligible

- Trial period: how evaluations will be made
- Duration: how long the agreement is in place and when it will be renewed
- Modifications: how modifications to original plan will be made

NOTES

INTRODUCTION

1. Joann S. Lublin, "Women at the Top Still Are Distant from CEO Jobs," *The Wall Street Journal* (28 February 1996), p. B1.
2. Stuart Silverstein, " 'Glass Ceiling' over Women Still Intact in Workplace," *Los Angeles Times* (18 October 1996), p. A1.
3. "20% of Fortune 500 Firms Have No Women Directors," *The Boston Globe* (10 December 1996), p. C8.
4. Harris Collingwood, "Party of One: Women in the Boardroom," *Working Woman* (February 1996), p. 16.
5. Joseph B. White and Carol Hymowitz, "Broken Glass: Watershed Generation of Women Executives Is Rising to the Top," *The Wall Street Journal* (10 February 1997), p. 1.
6. Federal Glass Ceiling Commission, *Good for Business: Making Full Use of the Nation's Human Capital* (Washington, DC, March 1995), p. 14.
7. U.S. Department of Labor Women's Bureau, *Facts on Working Women* (Washington, DC, May 1995), No. 95-1.
8. Collingwood, p. 16; "20% of Fortune 500 Firms Have No Women Directors," p. C8.
9. Diana Furchtgott-Roth and Christine Stolba, *Women's Figures: The Economic Progress of Women in America* (Arlington, VA: Independent Women's Forum, 1996), p. 7.
10. Joline Godfrey, *Our Wildest Dreams* (New York: HarperBusiness, 1992), p. 38.

CHAPTER ONE

1. Margaret Foegen Karsten, *Management and Gender: Issues and Attitudes* (Westport, CT: Praeger, 1994), p. 12.

2. Alice Kessler-Harris, *Out to Work: A History of Wage Earning Women in the United States* (New York: Oxford University Press, 1982), pp. 300–320.
3. Ibid.
4. Ibid.
5. Betty Lehan Harragan, *Games Mother Never Taught You* (New York: Warner Books, 1977), p. 157.
6. Margaret Hennig and Anne Jardim, *The Managerial Woman* (Garden City, NY: Anchor Press/Doubleday, 1977), p. xii.
7. Caryl Rivers, "Read All about It! (But Don't Believe It.)," *The Boston Globe* (26 May 1996), p. 64; Rosalind C. Barnett and Caryl Rivers, *She Works; He Works: How Two Income Families Are Happier, Healthier, and Better Off* (New York: Harper-Collins, 1996), pp. 24–38.
8. Deborah Tannen, *Talking 9 to 5* (New York: Avon Books, 1994), pp. 21–42.
9. Naomi Wolf, *Fire with Fire* (New York: Fawcett Columbine, 1993), pp. 284–289.
10. Hennig and Jardim, pp. 11–18.

CHAPTER TWO

1. Margaret Hennig and Anne Jardim, *The Managerial Woman* (Garden City, NY: Anchor Press/Doubleday, 1977), p. 14.
2. U.S. Department of Labor, Women's Bureau, *Working Women Count: A Report to the Nation* (Washington, DC, 1994); Susan Baer, "Mothers Fondly Recall the Stay-at-Home Mom," *The Boston Globe* (9 May 1997), p. A3.; Rosalind C. Barnett and Caryl Rivers, *She Works; He Works: How Two Income Families Are Happier, Healthier, and Better Off* (New York: HarperCollins, 1996), pp. 3–8.
3. Ann Cassidy, "Who's Happy? 1000 Moms Reveal Their Secrets for Enjoying Life," *Working Mother* (November 1995), pp. 27–38.
4. Betty Lehan Harragan, *Games Mother Never Taught You* (New York: Warner Books, 1977), p. 147.
5. Hennig and Jardim, p. 201.
6. Jean Baker Miller, *Toward a New Psychology of Women* (Boston: Beacon Press, 1976), pp. 115–124.
7. Naomi Wolf, *Fire with Fire* (New York: Fawcett Columbine, 1993), pp. 243–249.

8. Margaret J. Wheatley, "Quantum Management," *Working Woman* (October 1994), pp. 16–20; Margaret J. Wheatley, *Leadership and the New Science* (San Francisco: Berrett-Koehler, 1992).

9. Joline Godfrey, "Been There, Doing That," *Inc.* (March 1996), pp. 21–22.

10. Interview with Lawrence A. Pfaff, "Study Reveals Gender Differences in Management and Leadership Skills," Kalamazoo, Michigan, Lawrence A. Pfaff and Associates (16 January 1995) and "Latest Study Again Shows Gender Differences in Management and Leadership Skills" (3 September 1996).

11. Interview with Caleb S. Atwood, *The Quality of Management in America: A Report on the E.R.I.C., Inc., National Survey of Leadership Styles and Effectiveness in Managing Diversity,* Caleb S. Atwood and Lynn A. Evans (1994).

12. Diane E. Lewis, "Women Top Men," *The Boston Globe* (19 September 1996), p. C2.

13. Thomas Moore, *Care of the Soul* (New York: HarperPerennial, 1992), pp. 3–21.

14. Maggie Jones, "25 Hottest Careers for Women," *Working Woman* (July 1995), pp. 31–42; Lisa Kalis, "25 Hottest Careers for Women," *Working Woman* (July/August 1996), pp. 37–48; Marilyn Moats Kennedy, Skills Transfer, Career Strategy for the 21st Century," *Executive Female* (September/October 1996), pp. 27–31.

15. Pamela Mendels, "How Women Have Fared," *Working Woman* (October 1995), p. 44.

16. Riane Eisler, *The Chalice and the Blade* (San Francisco: HarperSanFrancisco, 1987), pp. 135–136 and p. 150.

CHAPTER THREE

1. Ann Crittenden, "Up the Corporate Ladder: A Progress Report," *Working Woman* (May 1996), p. 22.

2. Anne Fisher, "Six Ways to Supercharge Your Career," *Fortune* (13 January 1997), pp. 46–48.

3. Margaret A. Jacobs, " 'New Girl' Network Is Becoming a Big Boon for Women Lawyers," *The Wall Street Journal* (3 March 1997), p. 1.

4. Amy Saltzman, "Woman versus Woman: Why Aren't More Female Executives Mentoring Their Junior Counterparts," *U.S. News & World Report* (24 March 1996), pp. 50–53.
5. Margaret Hennig and Anne Jardim, *The Managerial Woman* (Garden City, NY: Anchor Press/Doubleday, 1977), p. 149.
6. Harris Collingwood, "How Better People Management Adds to the Bottom Line," *Working Woman* (March 1996), p. 18.
7. Rosabeth Moss Kanter, *Men and Women of the Corporation* (New York: Basic Books, 1977), p. 25.
8. Betty Lehan Harragan, *Games Mother Never Taught You* (New York: Warner Books, 1977), pp. 75–77.

CHAPTER FOUR

1. Federal Glass Ceiling Commission, *Good for Business: Making Full Use of the Nation's Human Capital* (Washington, DC, March 1995), p. 10.
2. "CEO Briefing: Executive Update" (14 November 1995) taken from *HR Magazine,* November 1995 (America Online: Investors Business Daily, 1995).
3. Federal Glass Ceiling Commission, p. 32.

CHAPTER FIVE

1. *Flexible Work Arrangements Executive Summary* (New York: Catalyst).
2. "Executive Update: CEO Briefing," *Investor's Business Daily,* 14 November 1995 (America Online: Investor's Business Daily, 1995).
3. Melanie Warner, "Working at Home—The Right Way to Be a Star in Your Bunny Slippers," *Fortune* (3 March 1997), pp. 165–166.
4. *Recommitting the Work Force* (Boston: Work/Family Directions, Inc.); Julia Lawlor, "The Bottom Line on Work Family Programs," *Working Woman* (July/August 1996), pp. 52–58.
5. Ann Cassidy, "Who's Happy? 1000 Moms Reveal Their Secrets for Enjoying Life," *Working Mother* (November 1995), pp. 27–38.
6. *Recommitting the Work Force,* p. 18.
7. Helaine Olen, "Getting a Handle on Flextime," *Working Woman* (February 1996), pp. 55–57.

8. Rhona Rapoport and Lotte Bailyn, *Rethinking Life and Work: Toward a Better Future,* (November 1996), pp. 6–7.

CHAPTER SIX

1. Bella English, "Fringe Benefit: Happier Children," *The Boston Globe* (25 August 1996), p. D1, D5; Debra Kent, "The Psychological Payoff," *Working Mother* (December 1994), p. 30.
2. Andrea Gabor, "Married, with Househusband," *Working Woman* (November 1995), pp. 46–50, 96.
3. Diane E. Lewis, "More Men Seeking Family-Career Balance, *The Boston Globe* (3 December 1996), p. D15.
4. Ibid.
5. U.S. Department of Labor Women's Bureau, *Facts on Working Women* (May 1995), No. 95-1; Carolyn Shaw Bell, "Exposing Fallacies of 'Family'," *The Boston Globe* (11 July 1995), p. B6.
6. Harriet Brown, "The Little Day Care Center That Could," *Ms.* (September/October 1995), pp. 62–68.
7. Avis Thomas-Lester, "Choose Day Care with Great Care," *The Washington Post* (30 August 1996), p. F5.
8. "Major Corporations Join Forces to Invest $100 Million for Dependent Care: Estimated 1,000 Projects to be Funded in Largest Private Sector Initiative," American Business Collaboration Press Release (14 September 1995).
9. Diane E. Lewis, "Corporations Tackle Child, Elder Care," *The Boston Globe* (21 February 1997), p. C2.
10. Charles Rodgers, president, Rodgers & Associates, the research and consulting arm of Work/Family Directions, a major provider of consulting advice on corporate work/life programs, interview; Rhona Rapoport and Lotte Bailyn, *Rethinking Life and Work: Toward a Better Future* (November 1996).
11. Juliet F. Brudney, "Study Reveals Benefits of Family Leave Act," *The Boston Globe* (14 May 1996), p. 44.; U.S. Department of Labor Women's Bureau, *A Workable Balance: Report to Congress on Family and Medical Leave Policies* (Washington, DC: May 1996).
12. Harris Collingwood, "Surprise! Men Use Work-Family Benefits, Too," *Working Woman* (February 1996), p. 15.
13. Barbara Vobejda, "Day Care Children at No Loss," *The Boston Globe* (4 April 1997), p. A3.

14. Deloitte & Touche LLP, *Women at Work: Executive Summary*, p. 10.

CHAPTER SEVEN

1. Robert B. Reich, "The Moral Basis of Our Labor," *The Boston Globe* (2 September 1996), p. A19.
2. Federal Glass Ceiling Commission, *Good for Business: Making Full Use of the Nation's Human Capital* (Washington, DC, March 1995).
3. Bronwyn Fryer, "The New Muscle of Corporate Women's Groups," *Working Woman* (June 1994), p. 17.
4. Maria Shao, "Women's Forum: High-Caliber Network Helps Members Shatter Ceilings," *The Boston Globe* (4 October 1996), p. C1
5. Margaret A. Jacobs, " 'New Girl' Network Is Becoming a Big Boon for Women Lawyers," *The Wall Street Journal* (3 March 1997), p. 1.
6. Alan Farnham, "Why the Fortune 50 Club Gets No Respect from Conspiracy Buffs," *Fortune* (15 May 1995), pp. 210–212.
7. Terence P. Pare, "The New Champ of Wealth Creation," *Fortune* (Sept. 18, 1995), pp. 131–132.
8. Jay Mathews, "AT&T to Pay Employees for Volunteering," *The Boston Globe* (17 November 1996); Joann Muller, "Companies Giving Workers a Break," *The Boston Globe* (10 November 1996), p. A1.
9. Procter & Gamble corporate material.
10. Howard P. Greenwald, "How Business Can Preserve the Ideals of Affirmative Action, *The New York Times* (5 January 1997), p. F10.
11. Kathy McCabe, "Era of Social Investing," *The Boston Globe* (3 May 1996), p. 25; Maria Shao, "Profit Whatever the Cost?" *The Boston Globe* (21 April 1996), p. A1; Steven Waddell, " 'Social-Financial' Management," *The Boston Globe* (21 November 1995), p. 39.

SELECTED BIBLIOGRAPHY

Aburdene, Patricia, and John Naisbitt. *Megatrends for Women: From Liberation to Leadership.* New York: Fawcett Columbine, 1992.

Bailyn, Lotte. *Breaking the Mold: Women, Men and Time in the New Corporate World.* New York: Free Press, 1993.

Bancroft, Nancy H. *Feminine Quest for Success: How to Prosper in Business and Be True to Yourself.* San Francisco: Berrett-Koehler, 1995.

Barnett, Rosalind C., and Caryl Rivers. *She Works; He Works: How Two Income Families Are Happier, Healthier, and Better Off.* San Francisco: HarperSanFrancisco, 1996.

Barrentine, Pat, ed. *When the Canary Stops Singing: Women's Perspectives on Transforming Business.* San Francisco: Berrett-Kohler, 1993.

Baruch, Grace, Rosalind Barnett, and Caryl Rivers. *Life Prints: New Patterns of Love and Work for Today's Women.* New York: McGraw-Hill, 1983.

Belenky, Mary Field, Blythe McVicker Clinchy, Nancy Rule Goldberger, and Jill Mattuck Tarule. *Women's Ways of Knowing: The Development of Self, Voice and Mind.* New York: Basic Books/HarperCollins, 1986.

Blalock, Jane, and Dawn-Marie Driscoll. *Gimmies, Bogeys and Business.* New York: MasterMedia Limited, 1996.

Capra, Fritjof. *The Web of Life.* New York: Anchor Books/Doubleday, 1996.

Chappell, Tom. *The Soul of Business. Managing for Profit and the Common Good.* New York: Bantam Books, 1993.

Cohen, Allan R., and David L. Bradford. *Influence without Authority.* New York: John Wiley & Sons, Inc., 1989.

Driscoll, Dawn-Marie, and Carol R. Goldberg. *Members of the Club: The Coming of Age of Executive Women.* New York: The Free Press, 1993.

Drucker, Peter F. *Managing for the Future: The 1990s and Beyond.* New York: Truman Talley Books/Plume, 1992.

Duff, Carolyn S. *When Women Work Together.* Berkeley, CA: Conari Press, 1993.

Eisler, Riane. *The Chalice and the Blade.* San Francisco: Harper-SanFrancisco, 1987.

Faludi, Susan. *Backlash: The Undeclared War against American Women.* New York: Anchor Books/Doubleday, 1991.

Friedan, Betty. *The Second Stage.* New York: Summit Books, 1981.

Friexe, Irene H., et al. *Women and Sex Roles: A Social Psychological Perspective.* New York: W. W. Norton & Co., 1978.

Gilligan, Carol. *In a Different Voice.* Cambridge, MA: Harvard University Press, 1982.

Godfrey, Joline. *Our Wildest Dreams.* New York: HarperBusiness, 1992.

Goleman, Daniel. *Emotional Intelligence.* New York: Bantam Books, 1995.

Gray, John. *Men Are from Mars, Women Are from Venus.* New York: HarperCollins, 1992.

Harragan, Betty Lehan. *Games Mother Never Taught You.* New York: Warner Books, 1977.

Harris, Anita M. *Broken Patterns: Professional Women and the Quest for a New Feminine Identity.* Detroit: Wayne State University Press, 1995.

Helgesen, Sally. *The Female Advantage: Women's Ways of Leadership.* New York: Doubleday/Currency, 1990.

Hennig, Margaret, and Anne Jardim. *The Managerial Woman.* Garden City, NY: Anchor Press/Doubleday, 1977.

Horney, Karen. *Feminine Psychology.* New York: W. W. Norton & Co., 1967.

Jamieson, Kathleen Hall. *Beyond the Double Bind: Women and Leadership.* New York: Oxford University Press, 1995.

Kanter, Rosabeth Moss. *Men and Women of the Corporation.* New York: Basic Books, 1977.

———. *When Giants Learn to Dance.* New York: Simon & Schuster/Touchstone, 1989.

Karsten, Margaret Foegen. *Management and Gender: Issues and Attitudes.* Westport, CT: Praeger, 1994.

Kessler-Harris, Alice. *Out to Work: A History of Wage-Earning Women in the United States.* New York: Oxford University Press, 1982.

Kleiner, Art. *The Age of Heretics.* New York: Doubleday/Currency, 1996.

Kotter John P. *A Force for Change: How Leadership Differs from Management.* New York: The Free Press, 1990.

————. *The New Rules: How to Succeed in Today's Post-Corporate World.* New York: The Free Press, 1995.

Kotter, John P., and James L. Heskett. *Corporate Culture and Performance.* New York: The Free Press, 1992.

Levinson, Daniel J. *The Seasons of a Woman's Life.* New York: Alfred A. Knopf, 1996.

Lougheed, Jacqueline. *Women in Leadership: Ten Year Perspective.* Rochester, MN: Oakland University, 1993.

Lunardini, Christine. *What Every American Should Know about Women's History.* Holbrook, MA: Adams Media Corporation, 1997.

Miller, Jean Baker. *Toward a New Psychology of Women.* Boston: Beacon Press, 1976.

Moore, Thomas. *Care of the Soul.* New York: HarperPerennial, 1992.

Morrison, Ann M., Randall P. White, and Ellen Van Velsor. *Breaking the Glass Ceiling.* Reading, MA: Addison-Wesley Publishing Co., 1992.

Rapoport, Rhona, and Lotte Bailyn. *Rethinking Life and Work: Toward a Better Future.* The Ford Foundation, 1996.

Rosener, Judy B. *America's Competitive Secret: Utilizing Women as a Management Strategy.* New York: Oxford University Press, 1995.

————. "Ways Women Lead." *Harvard Business Review,* November-December 1990, 119–125.

Scheele, Adele. *Career Strategies for the Working Woman.* New York: Simon & Schuster, 1994.

Scheinholtz, Debra F., ed. *Cracking the Glass Ceiling: Strategies for Success.* New York: Catalyst, 1994.

Schwartz, Felice N. *Breaking with Tradition: Women and Work, the New Facts of Life.* New York: Warner Books, 1992.

————. "Women as a Business Imperative." *Harvard Business Review,* March-April 1993, 106–113.

Siress, Ruth Herrman. *Working Woman's Communications Survival Guide.* Englewood Cliffs, NJ: Prentice Hall, 1994.

Sommers, Christina Hoff. *Who Stole Feminism?* New York: Simon & Schuster/Touchstone, 1994.

Stephens, Autumn. *Wild Women.* Berkeley, CA: Conari Press, 1992.

Swiss, Deborah J. *Women Breaking through: Overcoming the Final 10 Obstacles at Work.* Princeton, NJ: Peterson's/Pacesetter Books, 1996.

Swiss, Deborah J., and Judith P. Walker. *Women and the Work/Family Dilemma.* New York: John Wiley & Sons, Inc., 1993.

Tannen, Deborah. *Talking from 9 to 5.* New York: Avon Books, 1994.

———. *That's Not What I Meant!* New York: Ballantine Books, 1986.

———. *You Just Don't Understand: Women and Men in Conversation.* New York: Ballantine Books, 1990.

Waterman, Robert H., Jr. *What America Does Right: Lessons from Today's Most Admired Corporate Role Models.* New York: Plume, 1995.

Wheatley, Margaret J. *Leadership and the New Science.* San Francisco: Berrett-Koehler Publishers, Inc., 1992.

Wolf, Naomi. *Fire with Fire.* New York: Fawcett Columbine, 1993.

Wylie, Janet C. *Chances & Choices: How Women Can Succeed in Today's Knowledge-Based Business.* Vienna, VA: EBW Press, 1996.

INDEX

255

ABOUT THE AUTHOR

Virginia (Ginny) O'Brien has held positions as the director of communication for organizations in the small business and nonprofit sectors, and has worked as a communication consultant and freelance writer and editor. Most recently she has been involved with a research group at MIT that is developing "learning histories," documents that serve as tools for transferring learning in organizations.

She is the author of *The Fast Forward MBA in Business* (New York: John Wiley & Sons, 1996) and a contributing author to *Winning in the New Europe: Taking Advantage of the Single Market*, edited by Liam Fahey (Englewood Cliffs, N.J.: Prentice Hall, 1992). She holds a bachelor of arts degree in psychology and a master of science from Boston University's College of Communication.